No-One's Dad's a Plumber

Musical Truth Volume 4

Mark Devlin

Musical Truth Volume 4
Mark Devlin

Paperback Edition First Published in Great Britain in 2025
Hardback Edition First Published in Great Britain in 2025
eBook Edition First Published in Great Britain in 2025

Copyright © Mark Devlin 2025

Mark Devlin has asserted his rights under 'the Copyright Designs and Patents Act 1988' to be identified as the author of this work.
All rights reserved.

No part of this document may be reproduced or transmitted in any form or by any means, electronic, mechanical, photocopying, recording, or otherwise, without prior written permission of the Author.

Disclaimer

All reasonable efforts have been made to contact the copyright holders and that anyone who believes their copyright to be infringed is welcome to contact the author.

The views and opinions expressed in this book are entirely those of the author and do not necessarily reflect the opinions, policy or position of aSys Publishing.

Paperback ISBN: 978-1-913438-89-0

Hardback ISBN: 978-1-913438-90-6

aSys Publishing
http://www.asys-publishing.co.uk

ABOUT THE AUTHOR

Mark Devlin is a UK-based club and radio DJ, music journalist and author.

In 2010 he underwent what he refers to as a conscious awakening, bringing a new awareness of what's really going on in this world. His special area of interest has been how this ties into the mainstream music industry, and the way in which A-list artists have been used to manipulate and mind-control the masses in line with a much larger agenda.

He now presents public talks on these subjects, as well as appearing on radio, and producing two regular podcast series.

In early 2016 he published his comprehensive book, '*Musical Truth.*' Its follow-up, Volume 2, appeared in early 2018, with Volume 3 in late 2021 and Volume 4 in 2025. His allegorical novel, '*The Cause & The Cure*' appeared in 2019, with its sequel, '*The Gift & The Curse*' in 2023.

To e-mail: markdevlin2022@protonmail.com

www.djmarkdevlin.com

FOREWORD

*"I don't know how you were diverted.
You were perverted too.
I don't know how you were inverted.
No-one alerted you."*

George Harrison: 'While My Guitar Gently Weeps'

Although this book *could* be considered the fourth in the '*Musical Truth*' series, I'd been quite clear following the previous tome that I intended to cap the main series as a trilogy. If I hadn't, there was the danger that I'd be churning these out for the rest of my days, clocking up more and more volume numbers for however long I end up being around.

Having said that, what was also clear was that the story was very far from over. And it never will be in a subject area as colossal as that of the controlled, corporate music industry and the *real* reasons for it being in place.

With every passing year more and more information breaks surface, some after being kept under wraps for decades ... and the stories need telling. The shocking (though only for those who had not been paying attention!) revelations from the P Diddy scandal have reminded us of that.

'*Plumber*,' then, is intended to reinforce many of the points unveiled in the earlier three books, and will bring the most dividends if read only after its predecessors.

I had originally intended for it to follow in the style of the '*Sound Bites*' section in '*Volume 3*' - a compendium of short, standalone stories. But, as I assembled the information I had, the clear patterns started to form - "elite" family backgrounds; social-engineering agendas; MK-ULTRA-style mind-control; SRA; sonic manipulation; occult symbolism, etc. And so the data started arranging itself into the familiar long-form chapters.

Many have been kind enough to tell me that I possess the skill of being able to aggregate huge amounts of disparate information, to compartmentalise it logically, and to present it in easily-digestible form, and that's what has been involved here. I make no claim to be breaking new ground throughout, since much of what is contained has been previously disclosed ... but never together in a single, convenient one-stop-shop.

The title reflects the observation which has been so apparent since having my eyes opened by the research of the late David McGowan in his 2014 book '*Weird Scenes Inside The Canyon*' - that no matter how much any musician or other public figure might appear to be your 'friend," we never *really* know who these individuals are.

And thorough studies of their family backgrounds rarely throw up the kind of results one might have expected to find before discovering that this world - and the groups and individuals who control it - is *very* different from the one that mainstream society works so hard to convince us it is.

Those with leaky sinks will not find the solution to their problems between the covers of this book!

Mark Devlin
2025

(If any reader would like a handy pdf document e-mailed containing all the URL links listed at the end of each chapter, just drop an e-mail to markdevlin2022@protonmail.com to request.)

*

This book is dedicated to the memory of my beloved mother, Patricia Ann Devlin, 1942-2025.

*

Big thanks to Robbie Allen (robbieallenartist.com) for another phenomenal cover design, to Nicola Mackin of aSys Publishing (asys-publishing.co.uk) for the usual assistance, and to Daniela 'Razor Eye' Voglino for the proofreading.

Contents

ABOUT THE AUTHOR...iii

FOREWORD iv

CHAPTER 1: WHO'S YOUR DADDY?... 1

Rock stars' dads... Builders? Dockers? Plumbers?? In rather short supply, I'm afraid. Generals, Admirals and Politicians on the other hand? No problem!

CHAPTER 2: THE SPOOKS' PLAYGROUND 21

The links to military intelligence operations just keep on coming, further justifying the title the 'Military Entertainment Complex' to accurately describe music, movies and TV.

CHAPTER 3: BEWILDERING BEATLES BONDINGS............ 51

Further revelations linking the most influential music group of all time with occult teachings and esoteric elements.

CHAPTER 4: HOW MANY PAULS DOES IT TAKE TO CHANGE A LIGHTBULB?................................... 65

Is contemporary "Paul" really the original "Paul"? And was the "Paul" considered to be the original "Paul" really a replacement "Paul"? If your mind's not yet been turned to scrambled eggs, give it 'til the end of the chapter.

CHAPTER 5: MARK, JOHN, TODD AND GOD 79

Revisiting the Lennon assassination, Mark Chapman's obvious links to MK-ULTRA, and Todd Rundgren's place in the unsavoury mix.

CHAPTER 6: ALL IS MIND **93**

As previously surmised—and it's not as if there's any shortage of evidence—music and entertainment and the presence of mind-control go hand-in-hand. Programming is applied to many, if not all most household-name artists to ensure they stay "on-script," performing on-cue and pushing many an agenda in the process.

CHAPTER 7: SEX AS A WEAPON **113**

Ritual abuse goes hand in hand with music and entertainment. It should never have been this way, but the evidence speaks for itself.

CHAPTER 8: THE PRICE OF FAME **133**

When comments are made about music "speaking to the soul" and "lifting the spirits," it pays to be cautious as to which souls and spirits we might be talking about.

CHAPTER 9: WHAT'S THE AGENDA, KENNETH? **159**

A Lifetime Actor's work is never done.

CHAPTER 10: THE SICKNESS BENEATH THE SURFACE.. 188

The eventual arrest and jailing of Sean 'P Diddy" Combs in 2024 brought the sordid nature of the entertainment business kicking and screaming into mainstream consciousness.

CHAPTER 11: THE DEPARTED **205**

The music industry has a fairly high casualty rate when it comes to its famous artists. You may have noticed.

CHAPTER 12: I PREDICT A SYMBOL **230**

The occult symbolism and Predictive Programming elements of popular culture show no signs of abating. Indeed, they're getting ramped up all the more.

CHAPTER 13: SONICS — FROM DEMONIC TO HAR-
          MONIC.. 244
CHAPTER 14: THE GATEKEEPERS: CARL COX 251
CHAPTER 15: THE GATEKEEPERS: PETE TONG 268
CHAPTER 16: THE GATEKEEPERS: NORMAN COOK/
          FATBOY SLIM 284
CHAPTER 17: THE GATEKEEPERS: JUDGE JULES 296
CHAPTER 18: THE GATEKEEPERS: PAUL OAKENFOLD .. 314
CHAPTER 19: THE GATEKEEPERS: JAMES HAMILTON ... 327
AFTERWORD 338
INDEX 341

CHAPTER 1

WHO'S YOUR DADDY?

Rock stars' dads...Builders? Dockers? Plumbers?? In rather short supply, I'm afraid. Generals, Admirals and Politicians on the other hand? No problem!

> *"Extraordinary claims require extraordinary evidence."*
> Dr. Carl Sagan

> *"Looking back it's so bizarre, it runs in the family. All the things we are."*
> Level 42: 'Running In The Family'

British singer-songwriter **Sam Fender** probably didn't realise how on-the-money he was when, in an interview for the '*NME*' in February 2025, he bemoaned the contemporary music industry for being "rigged" and containing "90 per cent kids who are privately educated."

He wasn't wrong. Though his comments about feeling guilty while those from his working-class neighbourhood struggled "on the bones of their arse" suggested that he felt success is earned largely through simply having enough money in the bank. As we will continue to discover, it's rather more complicated than that.

Either way, I guess a sensible place to start would be in taking the lead from this book's title. You might want to make sure you're sitting down for this one as I share my surprise as discovering that the father of **Mark E. Smith**, singer and founding member of post-punk band **The Fall** was...a plumber! Well, knock me down with a spanner.

This all goes to assert Smith's working-class roots, though the military connections that we find with more dubious families are still there in that Smith Sr. reportedly applied for army duty as soon as he could, having had an ancestor who fought at the battle of Rorke's Drift during the Anglo-Zulu war as depicted in the 1964 Michael Caine-starring movie '*Zulu*.'

Furthermore, Smith claims to have been present at the the fabled **Sex Pistols**' gig at Manchester's Lesser Free Trade Hall in June 1976, inspiring him to form his own band. Given that the founders of **Joy Division** and the **Buzzcocks** make the same claim it's a wonder there was room for any punters. Call me suspicious, but this mythical event seems to have served as something of a cover story for where all these bands really came from.

Either way, a reader of my work nailed it when he wrote in to say:

> *"The Fall were on Miles Copeland's Step Forward records for a while, but there was no danger of them ever hitting the big time, not with a plumber for a Dad."*

(Irony seems to be hitting yet again when it comes to the CIA-connected Copeland family name — at least if you remove the 'e' from the middle!)

But either way, I won't hold it against Smith (who died of health complications aged 60 in 2018) if it means we really have found our first genuine plumber. Other bands which we have been invited to think of as coming from "organic" working-class sources would, it seems, have rather more skeletons in their cupboards.

A group which seems to share some characteristics with The Fall, (out of Salford, "anti-establishment image,") is the **Happy Mondays**. Brothers **Shaun** and **Paul Ryder** boast 'postman' as their father's profession, (before he became the band's manager,) which is quite something in these circles! The most colourful member of the group, however, was always the highly animated dancer and maracas player Mark Berry, better known as **Bez**.

No postmen here, as his father was a Chief Inspector in a police anti-terrorism squad. Rather ironic then, that Bez became one of the most recognisable figures within 'E'/ ecstasy culture during the UK's burgeoning Acid House scene. In *'Volume 2'* I questioned at length whether the avalanche of Es which conveniently coincided with the changes in the music of the late 1980s could have come through Establishment channels, as the CIA-procured LSD in the 60s counter-culture did.

In his auto-biography, '*Buzzin': The Nine Lives of a Happy Monday,*' Bez himself writes:

> "*The first time I encountered E was in 1987. In my new flat in Fallowfield we had probably the first proper E parties in the country. This was before it took off on a national scale or even in Manchester.*
>
> "*... They called that summer the 'Second Summer of Love,' but to be honest we'd had ours the previous year. We made more money out of the initial ecstasy explosion than we'd ever seen. We had money coming out of our ears.*"

This raises the intriguing question of whether the likes of Bez, along with many of the key DJs helping to push the new culture of those times, could have been doing so without full knowledge of his role, having been somewhat duped himself. In more recent times he has demonstrated a knowledge of "conspiracy" issues and ways in which the world operates that never seem to make the '*BBC Evening News,*' further writing in '*Buzzin*':

> "*I came to understand that we're getting poisoned daily. I learned that modern diseases like Alzheimers, diabetes and dementia were all man-made creations, almost masterminded to make people ill and keep them scared and under control.*
>
> "*In a book about 1960s counter-culture I read about how the U.S. Government had a load of cultural agents like Timothy Leary effectively playing into the hands of a mind-control agenda concocted by the CIA. It kind of ruined the idea that you're doing anything radical or anti-establishment by taking drugs.*"

We might wonder then, how many other enthusiastic pushers of new cultural trends and movements — particularly those who come from "Establishment" families — are in full knowledge of what it is they are a part of, versus them being, to use a rather unflattering term, "useful idiots."

When it comes to more "connected" families it's long been clear that the offspring of many of these are groomed from childhood for some kind of future career in the public spotlight, where they can be put to use in positions of cultural influence. But equally, it seems the *exact* role they will eventually undertake may not be known right from the start, and that a Plan B may get adopted before they finally emerge in the field for which they become best-known.

We might consider Ricky Gervais as an example of this dynamic. Long before he made a name for himself as a comedian on BBC TV shows like '*The Office*' and '*Extras*,' he was a singer in a New Romantic/New Wave band named **Seona Dancing**. The young Gervais clearly modelled himself on his hero **David Bowie**, so must have been made up when Bowie agreed to make a guest appearance decades later, lampooning Gervais' character in '*Extras*.'

Gervais is descended from a French aristocratic family. It's worth considering whether he could have been allotted career handlers, therefore, and if their plan was originally for him to have made it big as a pop star. He clearly didn't, most people having never heard of Seona Dancing, so was it discovered along the way that he had a natural talent for comedy, and was his role therefore re-drawn?

And history could have been written so differently in 1962 when **Pete Best** was axed as original drummer for the Beatles and the role very nearly went to **Lewis Collins**, (any relation to Phil?) rather than to **Ringo Starr**. Prior to becoming an actor Collins was a budding musician. His father, Bill, was a Jazz dance band leader and bought Lewis his first drum kit. Hailing from The Wirral, he and a group of school friends formed a band named the **Renegades** at the start of the Merseybeat music scene in Liverpool in the late 1950s. Legend has it that it was '**Mike McCartney**,' said to be 'Paul's brother, who suggested him for the Beatles gig.

Was the career plan similarly switched, for whatever reason, with him also? Collins' background is a fitting one considering his TV role as secret service agent Bodie in '*The Professionals*' and as an SAS operative in the movie '*Who Dares Wins*.' A black belt in Karate and Jujitsu, he joined a paratrooper unit in 1979, and passed the initial selection process for joining the SAS (Special Air Service) for real the following year, before it was ruled that his celebrity status made him a security risk. He also auditioned to succeed Roger Moore in the role of James Bond, but was rejected on the grounds that he had appeared "too aggressive."

Ever sharp and vigilant on such matters, Dom Waterson of the hugely recommended '*Sheep Farm Studios*' podcast on such matters, commented in this regard:

> "*Sometimes I have to stand back in awe and accept how consistently this system works. The micro-detail is astonishing on a scale which beggars belief, which I suppose is exactly the point. Few can fathom how it works, or that once they set the generational plan in motion, some kind of magnetic, genetic parasitical energy attracts certain psychotic 'entities' together, making for a self-managing system, possibly like biological AI. This is why it <u>looks</u> organic and haphazard, but as we all know it's anything but.*"

This certainly goes some way towards explaining how phenomena like "synchro-mysticism," or "meaningful coincidences" work. What if this reality in which we find ourselves really is a kind of virtual reality simulation, to use these analogies which we can wrap our heads around more readily now that we have the comparable technology? I feel we can too often make the mistake of considering the "elite" controllers to be 5D chess master-like in their planning, with the minutiae of every agenda they unleash under impeccable control.

Is it more likely that they have merely come to comprehend the "rules of engagement" of this realm, and that the "computer coding" which makes it up can cause certain events to occur, or individuals to connect in a way which can seem "miraculous," but in fact is anything but; it's merely the self-regulating AI arranging itself *exactly* the way it was programmed to do by whatever architect(s) somehow set it into place?

Anyway, that's a whole separate book in itself, and I fully intend to research and write it in a couple of titles' time!

Meanwhile...ever since the late author and researcher Dave McGowan published his landmark book '*Weird Scenes Inside The Canyon*' in 2014, thus setting myself and many other researchers on the trail of investigating the key family links of notable celebrities, there seems to have been a concerted effort by the mainstream media to downplay links such as the ones outlined here. You know, as if there's really nothing unusual at all about **Madonna**, **Celine Dion**, Ellen Degeneres and **Lady Gaga** all being cousins, and all being linked by blood in turn to George Bush, Dick Cheney, Barack Obama, Tom Hanks, Brad Pitt, Justin Trudeau, Justin Bieber, etc, etc.

I've even had comments made at many of my public talks like: "Pah! We all have links like this if you go back far enough." But is that true? Really? I can go back several generations on my mother's side and find only peasant types, and I suspect this will be the case for the overwhelming majority of "regular" folk all the way back to Adam.

You might think this would be the case for artists like **Eminem**, who have peddled an image of themselves as poor, white trash. Perhaps there's a clue in his real name being given as Marshall Mathers III. (The III is important, it seems.) Then we discover that his 33rd(!) great-grandfather was the ninth-century Welsh King, Rhodri Mawr (the Great.) (was there an "Unimpressive" one as well then?) How many others on his trailer park can make *that* kind of claim??

This idea that there's nothing notable about finding a queen or a duke or a famous general in your family line has been reinforced for years by the BBC (what else?!) TV programme (the clue's in the word) *'Who Do You Think You Are?'* in which famous people are "stunned" to discover, with the aid of professional genealogists, that they had ancestors of this nature. I remember actor Danny Dyer being "stunned" to be told he was descended from one of the English kings and from the statesman and lawyer Thomas Cromwell. Quite the "coincidence" that whoever they have on always *just happens* to have forebears of this status. I guess the show wouldn't be so interesting if they were told their ancestors had been sewer workers or turnip pickers.

Occasionally, such stories get "revealed" in the mainstream press. "Investigative journalism" can be judged to be a lost art in such institutions, however, through none of the "reporters" involved ever suggesting that any nepotism had been involved, much less feeling inspired to dig further into *why* the fame game is so unfairly rigged towards those of certain bloodlines, and against everybody else.

And so it was that in August 2024, **Janet Jackson** revealed on Zoe Ball's BBC (is there a trend emerging here?) Radio 2 breakfast show that she's cousins with **Stevie Wonder**, Samuel L Jackson and **Tracy Chapman**. The Stevie link comes from her mother's line, she said.

The very same '*Times*' page covering the Janet claim, meanwhile, also covered the story that **Miley Cyrus** and **Dolly Parton** *just happened* to be distant cousins. As are, reportedly, **Britney Spears** and Marilyn Monroe, (also related to Madonna, George Bush, etc . . . see above!) I guess we're supposed to think that all of them *just happened* to find fame and success under their own steam, and that the family factor had absolutely nothing to do with it.

A fair while back, in 2008, '*One India News*' informed us, out of the blue, that:

> "Argentinian-born British musician and songwriter **Chris de Burgh** has traced his family tree back to Robert the Bruce, the King of the Scots. His maternal grandfather, Sir Eric de Burgh, was a British Army officer who served as Chief of the General Staff in India during World War II."

Given his Establishment connections, perhaps it might bring rewards (as there aren't any to be had by listening to his music,) to consider the real inspiration behind his biggest hit, '*The Lady In Red*.' Though the cover story is that he wrote it for his wife after being stunned by her beauty when seeing her in an alluring red dress, in occult circles a "lady in red" can refer to the "scarlet woman," a goddess within Aleister Crowley's system of Thelema, as well as the "whore of Babylon" of the Bible, a symbol of the "anti-christ."

As previously reported, we have always been asked to believe that Madonna's was a genuine rages-to-riches story; that she arrived from Michigan to New York City, unknown and penniless, and worked her way up through grit, determination, and sleeping with the right people. When music mogul Seymour Stein, the founder of Sire Records, died in 2023, his obituaries were used to reinforce this "Cinderella fairy story" about how she had got famous, the UK's '*Daily Mail*' stating:

> "His most lucrative discovery happened in the early 1980s, when he heard the demo tape of a little known singer-dancer from the downtown New York club scene, Madonna.

> "Stein was hospitalised with a heart infection, but was so eager to meet that he had her brought to his room. In his book, he recalled signing her for $15k from his hospital bed as he awaited open-heart surgery in New York's Lenox Hill Hospital in mid-1982."

Next you'll be telling me that the Beatles were just four regular working-class lads from Liverpool who wrote a few catchy songs, punted a few demo tapes around, and *just happened* to become the most successful and influential band in music history. Aren't pure, random chance and serendipity wonderful things, folks?

In more fun with cousins, clock-wearing Public Enemy hype-man **Flavor Flav** revealed to '*The Source*' magazine in 2023 that he's related to three members of the **Wu-Tang Clan**. Their obvious talent notwithstanding, (there's still something of a hip-hop purist deep down within me,) I guess this would explain why both groups became as hugely influential as they did. Flavor, real name William Jonathan Drayton Jr., said:

> "In the Wu-Tang Clan, I have three blood family members that a lot don't even know. **RZA**, **GZA**, and **ODB**. ODB was my cousin."

Two of the most recognisable graduates of the Laurel Canyon set, as highlighted in Dave McGowan's book, are **Jim Morrison**, frontman of the **Doors**, and **Frank Zappa** of the group **Mothers of Invention**. Both had fathers with high-ranking military roles... as did pretty much every other musician who would come to shape the "counter-culture" rock scene of late-1960s California.

When this many all fit the same profile it's only common sense to deduce that the whole "movement" was a military-grade operation. But in the cases of Zappa and Morrison, some early parading of these assets on television occurred prior to their "rebellious rock icon" makeovers being applied.

Morrison appeared as a clean-cut, collegiate student in a commercial for Florida State University in 1964. A year later he had grown out his hair, ditched the college blazer, and joined his Doors bandmates to become 'The Lizard King'/ "Mr. Mojo Risin'" of rock mythos. We're left wondering if, in 1964, Jim's handlers still didn't quite know in what way he would be inserted into culture, *or* that they had already decided he was to be used to sell that generation's sex, drugs and rock 'n' roll revolution, and the University ad served as a useful warm-up gig.

(Morrison was far from The Doors' only military-grade member. Just as connected was keyboard player **Ray Manzarek**. Though we are told he attempted to enlist in the Army Signal Corps as a camera operator, he was instead assigned to the highly selective Army Security Agency as a prospective intelligence analyst just prior to his musical career fortuitously taking off.

Ray was posted to the Japanese island of Okinawa, and later Laos. A fellow recruit named Britt Leach who was on the island with him, has written of how Ray somehow escaped having to be clean-shaven and short-haired, as per military requirements, but was able to sport long flowing locks and an impressive handlebar moustache — a look far more fitting for a rock star. Ray also escaped having to sign a security clearance document, reasoning that he had Polish ancestry, that Poland at the time was a communist country, and that signing the paper might limit his opportunities to visit Poland in the future. Ah, fair enough then. Upon his return to the states Ray enrolled in UCLA's graduate film program in 1962, where he "serendipitously" met an unknown undergraduate film student named Jim Morrison.

Neither does Doors guitarist **Robby Krieger**'s background disappoint. According to his obituary his father, Stuart Krieger, stated that he graduated in aeronautical engineering, (see also the dad of Rolling Stone **Brian Jones** mentioned below,) then "helped out the war effort" by designing fighter planes, (you know, like you do,) before going on to work with Northrop Grumman, an aerospace and defence technology contractor which boasted the U.S. Department of Defense as one of its clients. Not a ballcock in sight there.)

Morrison's family dynamic was not a million miles from that of **Bob Marley**, funnily enough. Bob's (Caucasian) old man, Norval Sinclair Marley, was an officer in the British Navy. While I do suspect Jim Morrison's "death" in 1971 as part of the fabled 27 Club to have been faked, however, I consider Bob's eventual death on 11th May 1981 to have been for real. In my view, all the research shows that Bob was a *genuine* political activist, and had made an enemy of the all-powerful CIA, and so had to be got rid of. (See more on both the Morrison and Marley stories in '*Musical Truth Volume 1.*')

So in Marley, we at least have what *appears* to be one musician who *really* did rebel against his father's value system and tread his own path. Too bad that most, if not all of the prominent musicians to ever have done so have met with an early grave.

Perhaps a childhood **Phil Collins** being drafted in as an extra in the Beatles' movie '*A Hard Day's Night*' in 1964 constituted the same "grooming" dynamic? It would be years before he would become the drummer for prog-rock pioneers **Genesis** in 1970, (a role which, reportedly, almost went to **Roger Taylor** of **Queen**.)

A bit of childhood acting experience is never going to be wasted in the case of someone who, it has already been decided, is going to be famous, even if it's not yet been decided exactly how. A few years later he had joined the rest of Genesis as they graduated out of the exclusive Charterhouse School in Godalming, Surrey under the tutelage of fellow alumni Jonathan King . . . later exposed as having been a prodigious paedophile. There's a lot of it around, it turns out. Especially at the BBC.

On considering Phil's family name, my suspicious mind goes to John Todd Collins, the "illuminati" insider who was raised within one of the key bloodline families as a witch, put to use within the American music industry, and whose later testimonies as a whistleblower were discussed in '*MT1.*' Could Phil be of this same important Collins bloodline? Makes you wonder. It does me, anyway.

Matt Sergiou of the '*Occult Beatles*' and '*Conspiromedia*' blog sites, another walking encyclopedia, informs us that for a time a young Collins holed himself up in the very same hotel in Russell Square, Bloomsbury, London where Jimmy Savile kept a room. This appears to have been the Aaland Hotel. Collins reveals this himself in a 2014 video. Also staying there, he says, was **Taylor Stratton Smith** of Collins' previous band **The Freehold**, and **Jimi Hendrix**'s roadie. Collins says that his band's singer's aunt owned the hotel which he described as "quite an interesting place" and "a real high-energy place." All of this makes it sound like a London equivalent of New York's Hotel Chelsea, the goings-on at which I covered at length in '*MT2.*'

Savile worked for many years out of the BBC's Broadcasting House, right opposite which is an address in All Souls Place (the irony,) once occupied by the notorious English occultist, and hero to incalculable numbers of rock stars through the decades... Aleister Crowley. Again, this causes me to ask the question; is it even *possible* that this amount of "synchronistic" overlaps and connections could be the result of impeccable human planning, or can such "clustering" only occur on this scale as a result of the way this illusory reality is really structured at its core?

Back to the Canyon, and for his part, Zappa appeared on an edition of the '*Steve Allen Show*' in 1963, clean-cut and lacking his trademark moustache, with the novelty act of playing bicycles as musical instruments. By this point he was already an accomplished musician and had provided the score for the Tim Carey movie '*The World's Worst Sinner.*' Within a couple of years he too would have grown out his hair, becoming "ringmaster" to the other influential bands in Laurel Canyon, and embarked on his apparently "anti-establishment' rhetoric and satire through his musical output.

From the same year comes an early TV appearance from a 17-year-old, pre-fame **David Bowie**, still known then as "Davy Jones." He appeared on an episode of the BBC's '*Tonight*' programme as one of the representatives of, wait for it... The Society for the Prevention of Cruelty to Long-Haired Men (!) This sequence seems have served simply as a means of ushering the future Bowie into the public's consciousness. Host Cliff Michelmore asks the lads if they're simply trying to mimic the **Rolling Stones**, which they deny.

Despite his denials the young Bowie looks very similar to another Jones, Stones founder Brian. In a piece of footage from the same era a very posh-sounding Jones, (his father is listed as having been an aeronautical engineer who, given that the family came out of Cheltenham, may have been attached to that town's Government Communications Head Quarters,) comments that being a rock star had not satisfied him either artistically or personally, and that he had never really intended to become one. Which does rather beg the question — well, why did you then? Was this a decision which was out of his hands?

In '*Musical Truth Volume 2*' I revealed some of the unlikely links between serial killers and punk musicians. It doesn't stop there, it turns out. Though frequent claims have been made that **Taylor Swift** is the illegitimate daughter of Zeena La Vey, daughter of Anton La Vey, the founder of the Church of Satan, there is no verifiable evidence to show this to be the case, (though certainly something of a physical resemblance.)

What we *can* know for sure, however, is that Taylor is a ninth cousin of the psychopathic murderous cannibal Jeffrey Dahmer. ('Guess who's coming for dinner' takes on a whole different meaning within that particular bloodline.) They share a common ancestor, Nathaniel Warren. The French royal, Charlemagne, from whom all but one of the American presidents so far are descended, is Taylor's 39th great grandfather. Perhaps we're getting close to the *real* reason she has been promoted and paraded so much over all other competition in the "pop princess" field.

One of Nathaniel's descendants was Richard Warren who was a passenger on the Mayflower, and his own descendants include the likes of U.S. presidents Franklin D Roosevelt and Ulysses S Grant, founding father Joseph Warren, writer (and CIA spy) Ernest Hemingway, another serial killer in the form of John Wayne Gacy, and . . . **Elvis Presley**.

Meanwhile, in a loose Beatles connection, Prudence Farrow, the sister of '*Rosemary's Baby*' actress Mia Farrow, and the inspiration for the Beatles song '*Dear Prudence*,' dated American real estate heir turned serial killer Robert Durst for around three years.

Anyone for a few more? As film critic Barry Norman used to say, (or was that just his '*Spitting Image*' puppet?) "and why not?"

No-One's Dad's a Plumber

Becoming Beyonce

Frank Vroegop with Beyoncé Knowles during the shoot of a film for the L'Oréal brand

Date: 13 July 2004, 19:08:12

Source: Own work

Author: Vavox Project

I well recall the unleashing of the group **Destiny's Child** upon the "urban" music scene in early 1998, as I got to meet and interview the group, then just teenagers, ensconced as I was in my Galaxy Radio show back in those times. I never gave much thought to the naming of the group, (as I didn't to a great many things,) but it's clear now that the name was giving us a subtle clue, and that it was always about them being used as a vehicle through which to make Beyoncé famous, so that she could then break out and become the most high-profile R&B singer in the world for a good couple of decades, and to get paired off with Jay-Z, (whom many suspect of being her mind-control handler) in the process.

Beyoncé's destiny did indeed seem to have been cemented by way of her bloodline. Credit goes again to the masterful work of Dom from Sheep Farm. (I don't know how he turns these things up but he always does. I guess it comes down to no longer having any kind of life worth speaking of once you discover all this stuff.)

Dom's research shows Beyoncé to be descended from a long line of European royals and nobles, including King Richard I of England. This is the case all the way up to one Agnez Buyince, born in Louisiana in 1909. It seems Beyoncé's distinctive first name was actually derived from the original family name, (not that this takes away from 'Beyoncé' being an anagram of 'boy once'!)

Agnez's daughter is Celestine Ann Knowles-Beyince, Beyoncé's biological mother. As is so often the case with celebrities, the bloodline stuff comes from the mother's side, the fathers in such cases being relegated to little more than sperm donors.

Somewhere in the above tangled mess I seem to recall Aleister Crowley's name cropping up. It generally does. One of his descendants turns out to be one Alex Crowley, OBE (go figure.) His Linked In résumé reads like a PR-friendly word-salad with talk of "helping clients change the minds of policy makers" and "raising awareness of important issues." In between crowing about having helped Boris Johnson achieve two election victories, however, we find an almost throwaway reference to his clients in the world of film-making including… Ministry of Sound, the pioneering nightclub in London.

I've long suspected the 'Ministry' tag as giving us a knowing hint that this was an Establishment/ government-sponsored operation all along. No such names come about by accident. Given that Aleister reportedly became an asset of the British government during World War 2 with, allegedly, James Bond creator Ian Fleming installed as his handler, perhaps we shouldn't be too surprised. Aleister (really an Edward) himself organised a 'Rite of Eleusis' in London in 1910, where participants took peyote, danced to bongoes and listened to Crowley declaiming his magickal poetry. This sounds like a very early version of a rave.

The American punk rock band The Strokes, like so many others, is marketed as having an "edgy" image. How to reconcile that then, with the fact that two of its members, Julian Casablancas and Albert Hammond, Jr., attended the ultra-elite Institut Le Rosey private boarding school in Switzerland before returning to New York to set up the group. This school is clearly not one that accepts any old riff-raff, its alumni over the centuries including members of the Rothschild, Rockefeller, Borghese and Du Pont families, and several royals and nobles of various nations as well as... **Sean Lennon**.

How about actor Jack Black, who has also been a musician, performing with the group **Tenacious D**? His mother, Judith Love Cohen, was an aerospace engineer, credited with having worked on the ground station for the Hubble Space Telescope, as well as the Apollo Space Program, through which she is said to have "rescued" the Apollo 13 "astronauts" from their disastrous mission. In short, major fakery and deception at the expense of the public, and yet another musician/entertainer to have come out of a highly-connected military-grade family.

A friend wrote to ponder whether the art world operates in the same way as the music world, in selecting chosen ones and elevating their work above that of all other contenders — invariably for the pushing of society-affecting agendas. He cites Francis Bacon (1909-1992) as an example, opining that his paintings were ugly and poorly-executed, yet didn't stop him becoming lauded as one of the greatest artists of his time. *Not* through popular opinion, but at the hands of what Edward Bernays referred to as "men we have never heard of."

Bacon was a descendant of his namesake, the equally lauded statesman and philosopher of the 16th century. Sure enough, in Bacon Junior's background we find the same military family connections as with so many well-promoted musicians. Wikipedia informs us:

> "*His father, army Captain Anthony Edward Mortimer Bacon... was a veteran of the Boer War, a racehorse trainer, and grandson of Major-General Anthony Bacon, who claimed descent from Sir Nicholas Bacon, elder half-brother of The 1st Viscount St Albans, (better*

known to history as Sir Francis Bacon), the Elizabethan statesman, philosopher and essayist."

The Cinderella Fairy Story rears its head again here, too. As my correspondent friend wrote:

"And they build this legend about these people being stone broke, and suddenly their genius becomes recognised and they get rich. Even when Bacon wasn't selling many paintings, he was living in decent accommodation in the heart of London. And to cover for the fact he was able to drink in the Colony Club (the most expensive drinking house in Soho) all day long, we're told that the owner thought he was really interesting, and she gave him £10 a week just to come in and drink, and bring his friends. Sometimes, they struggle to cover their tracks.

Bacon came from one of the wealthiest families in Ireland. Also, he was regularly raped as a child by the stable manager. His father regularly beat him too."

We could throw so many other examples from the art world into the mix (Banksy?) and get these same types of connections. So the long and short of it, in my opinion and in response to the original question, is a resounding "yes!"

I should have known I was tempting fate by making the comment, on a few occasions, that the Soulful House genre seemed about the only contemporary one not to exhibit any potentially dodgy characteristics among its key content creators. Aside from some regrettable pictures of producers **Masters at Work** and the **Basement Boys**' **DJ Karizma** and **DJ Spen** striking the same tired "one eye" pose in promo pictures, I got alerted to the fact that the father of DJ/ producer **Sean McCabe** is a senior Royal Air Force officer. Is nothing sacred?

Still, regardless of that, there's no way the Jazz-Funk style purveyed by the veteran group **Incognito** could be embroiled in this whole mess, right? Well, you say that, but... frontman Jean-Paul Maunick, better known as '**Bluey**,' turns out to be the cousin of Kobita Jugnauth (née Ramdanee,) the wife of Pravind Jugnauth, the leader of the Militant

Socialist Movement (MSM) and Prime Minister of the nation of Mauritius. Good reason why they would call themselves 'Incognito,' perhaps.

*

I feel that the advent of famous people's elite ancestral links making it into the mainstream media has been *purposely* ramped up in recent times as a direct result of the type of research that so many of us are now doing into such links. Whereas in decades previous these connections were kept under wraps, the availability of internet research means they are now relatively easy to find, so attempts are underway to devalue reveals of the type McGowan originally presented. And, if I may humbly suggest, the work of researchers like the Sheep Farm boys, Matt Sergiou, myself and so many others who delve head-first into these rabbit holes.

This, I think, we can consider to be a very positive thing. The fact that so much effort and resource is being ploughed into these exercises suggests that there is genuine concern about the degree to which this information is getting out and so much dot-connecting is getting done. Just *imagine* the overtime bill at Tavistock every time a new episode of '*Sheep Farm*' drops.

Resources:

NME: 'Sam Fender describes music industry as "rigged" and "90 per cent kids who are privately educated":

- https://www.nme.com/news/music/sam-fender-describes-music-industry-as-rigged-and-90-per-cent-kids-who-are-privately-educated-3840554

Irish Times: Musician, poet and satirist, Mark E Smith was driving force of The Fall

- https://www.irishtimes.com/life-and-style/people/musican-poet-and-satirist-mark-e-smith-was-driving-force-of-the-fall-1.3368245

Hit The Floor Magazine: Interview with Bez of the Happy Mondays:

- https://www.youtube.com/watch?v=My0okX4rvyk

Miles Copeland interview: mentions Step Forward Records and The Fall:

- https://pleasekillme.com/miles-copeland/

https://www.irishtimes.com/life-and-style/people/musican-poet-and-satirist-mark-e-smith-was-driving-force-of-the-fall-1.3368245

Frank Zappa plays bicycle on The Steve Allen Show:

- https://youtu.be/QF0PYQ8IOL4?si=Eqm5AzDQ21c91tbh

Jim Morrison in "Florida State University: Toward a Greater University" (1964):

- https://www.youtube.com/watch?v=7u5P0fyWLyc

David Bowie • BBC Tonight Programme • 1964:

- https://www.youtube.com/watch?v=5W38suFC0Ow

Brian Jones Rare Interview:

- https://www.youtube.com/watch?v=JcNXmkyYjDw Phil Collins in The Beatles' movie 'A Hard Day's Night' (1964):
- https://www.youtube.com/watch?v=gx-gzHFO_oU

Wikipedia: Ray Manzarek:

- https://en.wikipedia.org/wiki/Ray_Manzarek

Tommy Mars, keyboard player in Zappa's band being interviewed re brain implants and UFOs:

- https://www.youtube.com/watch?v=KiIUfqDcMBs

Young Ricky Gervais performs in 1980s band Seona Dancing:

- https://www.youtube.com/watch?v=OfOmaf00kkg

Janet Jackson reveals Stevie Wonder, Tracy Chapman & Samuel L Jackson are her cousins:

- https://www.latimes.com/entertainment-arts/music/story/2024-08-14/janet-jackson-stevie-wonder-tracy-chapman-samuel-l-jackson-cousins

Los Angeles Times: Miley Cyrus and Dolly Parton aren't just like family — they are blood relatives:

- https://www.latimes.com/entertainment-arts/music/story/2024-09-25/miley-cyrus-dolly-parton-cousins-godmother

Britney Spears and Marilyn Monroe are related:

- https://www.instagram.com/thatillusivelife/p/C1pBISKI1ar/?img_index=1

Wikipedia; Kobita Jugnauth, cousin of 'Bluey' from Incognito:

- https://en.wikipedia.org/wiki/%C3%89douard_Maunick

The Source: Flavor Flav Says He is Related to Members of Wu-Tang Clan:

- https://thesource.com/2023/09/28/flavor-flav-wu-tang/

Alex Crowley OBE (descendent of Aleister Crowley):

- https://uk.linkedin.com/in/alex-crowley

Crowley's Children:

- https://www.philosophyforlife.org/blog/crowleys-children

PHIL COLLINS UNFILTERED: TELLS THE FULL STORY OF HIS CAREER TO 1980. A REVEALING 2 HR INTERVIEW:

- https://youtu.be/LEbk8e__JlA?feature=sharedjg

One India: Chris De Burgh's Scottish Roots Revealed:

- https://www.oneindia.com/2008/03/24/chris-de-burghs-scottish-roots-revealed-1206356760.html

Sheep Farm Studios Podcasts:

- https://www.sheepfarm.co.uk/

Rise Above Live:

- https://www.youtube.com/@riseabovelive

Matt Sergiou's Occult Beatles Wordpress archive:

- https://theoccultbeatles.wordpress.com/

Matt Sergiou's Conspiromedia Facebook page:

- https://www.facebook.com/conspiromedia/

CHAPTER 2

THE SPOOKS' PLAYGROUND

The links to military intelligence operations just keep on coming, further justifying the title the 'Military Entertainment Complex' to accurately describe music, movies and TV.

> *"Beware of pretty faces that you find,*
> *A pretty face can hide an evil mind.*
> *Oh, be careful what you say,*
> *Or you will give yourself away."*
>   Johnny Rivers: 'Secret Agent Man'

> *"But you can reach the top of your profession,*
> *If you become the leader of the land.*
> *For murder is the sport of the elected,*
> *And you don't need to lift a finger of your hand."*
>   The Police: 'Murder By Numbers'

As we delve further into where so many of the household names that have been served up to us, inviting us to like and be influenced by them come from, we find yet more unlikely background stories, further indicating that the rags-to-riches fables of such people *just happening* to make it to the top entirely on their own, amounts to nothing more than PR spin.

It doesn't get more blatant that the story surrounding the electronic dance music producer **Moby**, for example, real name Richard Melville Hall. In 2017 Moby claimed via social media postings that he had "insider information" from "friends who work in DC" about Donald Trump and alleged Russian interference in his first presidential election campaign. Moby claimed he had been asked to DJ at Trump's inauguration party but had declined, being no fan of him and his policies. Moby expanded on this in an interview with WFPK's Kyle Meredith.

> "So they passed on some information to me and they said, like, 'look, you have more of a social media following than any of us do. Can you please post some of these things just in a way that... sort of puts it out there?'"

Later, he did deny being directly connected to the CIA, commenting:

> "Ha, no, the CIA didn't ask me to post about Trump and Russia, as much fun as that would be. But, for what it's worth, I do have friends at other intelligence agencies who have told me that... Trump is a dirty foreign agent, and one way or another the depths of his campaigns, collusion (and treason) will be revealed."

Whichever way you cut it then, this indicates that Moby is rather more than simply a dance music producer/ film score composer, reinforcing the notion that his rise to prominence in that field was an orchestrated, rather than organic one.

An artist from an earlier era who reportedly admitted to similar ties was 1950s rockabilly pioneer **Gene Vincent**. In an article posted on his '*Conspiro Media*' website, Matt Sergiou told of an informal chat he was having with a former member of a prominent 1960s band who, he says, toured with the likes of the **Beatles**, the **Rolling Stones** and the **Beach Boys**. By the time he met him he had become the manager of a nightclub where Matt used to DJ in the 1990s. Matt writes that, during the conversation, out of nowhere, the guy piped up:

> "Gene Vincent was backing us. I mean, he was like God to us, you know, like one of the inventors of rock 'n' roll. We were top of the bill— Gene Vincent backing us. He was pretty gone by then and he had a gun, and he said to me, 'oh, this whole rock 'n' roll thing is just a farce really.' He said, 'I'm actually working for the CIA. This rock 'n' roll thing is a front so I can travel all over the world... he was kinda crazy, really."

The phrase "it's always the ones you least suspect" seems to ring true with some of these names. Fast forward a few decades, and step over to a different genre, and we find the case of **Pras Michel**, a member of the 90s hip-hop collective the **Fugees**.

In April 2023 he was found guilty of conspiracy and of acting as an unregistered agent of a foreign government. Choosing to testify at his own trial, he had stood accused of funneling funds from a fugitive Malaysian businessman, Jho Low, through donors to Barack Obama's 2012 campaign, trying to impede an investigation into Low's money laundering scam, and trying to persuade the Trump Administration to extradite a Chinese dissident. During the testimony he told the court that he has met and shared information with the FBI voluntarily.

Pras was found guilty of ten criminal counts that year, which saw him potentially facing up to 20 years in prison.

Jho Low's name became connected to other celebrities, too. In 2024 the '*Malay Mail*' and '*Straits Times*' reported on a lawsuit filed by 1Malaysia Development Bhd (1MDB) against Malaysia's former treasury secretary-general and a former 1MDB chief executive.

Contained in the details presented by Richard Templeman, a financial fraud investigator, was the accusation that US$2.4m (S$3.1m) had been funnelled out of 1MDB's coffers and into bank accounts owned by **Kanye West**'s former wife Kim Kardashian and producer and singer **Pharrell Williams** back in 2011. The transaction was said to have been facilitated by Low's shell company Good Star Ltd.

Templeman contested that the the billions flowing through Good Star were moved to a Suntrust Bank account under the name of Talamasca Inc. Transactions between August and November of 2011 were notated as "part payment for music production" and "Letter of Agreement DD 3 NOV 2011 Red Spring Investments And Talamasca/Pharrell Williams."

This is far from the only accusations of high-level crime which had been directed at Kardashian in particular. Much more may well come out as the P. Diddy trial, and all that will follow in its wake, continues. More on that later.

Spies with Spliffs

Sometimes it's looking beyond the most prominent members of a band—usually the lead singer—that offers the intriguing military links. It was certainly the case with the **Police**, where drummer **Stewart Copeland** brought the connection to the CIA.

It's also the case in **R.E.M.**, with bassist **Mike Mills** admitting in a 2024 interview with Rick Beato that his father was a marine who "flew fixed-wing and rotary aircraft for the Marines." He was also a Jazz musician, Mills reveals, a factor commonly associated with military men.

R.E.M.'s singer **Michael Stipe** has commented that his own father "flew helicopters in Vietnam," and a connection between R.E.M. and the Copelands comes from drummer **Bill Berry**. In the late '70s he worked at Paragon Booking Agency in Macon, Georgia alongside **Ian Copeland**, Stewart's brother and son of career CIA operative Miles Axe (what's in a name?) Copeland. Paragon's offices were next door to the apartment block in which both Bill Berry and Mike Mills lived. Berry and Copeland both left Paragon in 1979, the latter going on to form Frontier Booking International, (F.B.I — it's not like they don't give us the clues!)

Was this entire band put together as a military-grade outfit? We can be thrown off-track when groups put out such hauntingly touching songs as '*Everybody Hurts*' which, judging by comments left under its video on YouTube, has prevented countless people from committing suicide through making them realise that so many others are going through their struggles too.

But still, military operations are not generally known for their desire to uplift and inspire all of humanity, so we can logically deduce that there must be another reason for so many bands coming out of this field.

The comments made by **Eugene Robinson**, vocalist with the experimental rock band **Oxbow**, are worth repeating here. As I reported in '*Volume 3*,' when interviewed by thequietus.com in 2018 he stated:

> "*My first introduction to Nina Simone was via my father who had been a Jazz bassist who was working for U.S. Air Force intelligence. He was a bass-playing spy, essentially. He spoke four languages and the Air Force made him form a Jazz trio so they could tour Eastern Bloc countries at a time when nobody would expect three black guys to be speaking any other languages than English.*"

How many other travelling performers would have been undertaking similar missions over the decades but who *haven't* admitted to it in interviews?

A similar scenario emerges from the world of acting. The '*Daily Mail*' reported in 2023 that Chaim Topol, the star of the film '*Fiddler on the Roof*,' was secretly an Israeli Mossad intelligence agent, who used his position as an award-winning actor to spy on Israel's Arab enemies. This was only revealed following his death, mind, his family mentioning in an interview for Israeli newspaper '*Haaretz*' that Topol had used his London home as a base to welcome Mossad spies from Israel, with whom he plotted to use his VIP status to gain entry to sensitive locations.

Olivia Newton-John. All-singing, all-dancing, all-spooking.

Date: 11 August 2017

Source: Olivia Newton-John - I Honestly Love You - Festival de Viña del Mar 2017 HD 1080P

Author: FESTIVALDEVINACHILE

A better example than **Olivia Newton-John** of a singer/ actress with high-grade military family credentials is hard to find. Though often considered Australian owing to her family relocating to Melbourne when she was six, she was British-born.

Her father, a Welshman named Brinley "Bryn" Newton-John, was an officer for MI5, worked on the Enigma project out of Bletchley Park during World War 2, and was involved in taking German defector Rudolf Hess into custody. After the war he became headmaster of the Cambridgeshire High School for Boys.

Olivia's mother, Irene, was the daughter of Max Born, who became a physicist at Gottingen University, and was reportedly terminated from his position by Adolf Hitler due to his being Jewish. He went on to become one of the pioneers in the field of quantum mechanics, winning a Nobel Prize in 1954. Through her great-grandfather's wife we are told Olivia is related to Protestant theologian Martin Luther.

Olivia became an actress best known for her role as Sandy in '*Grease,*' (keeping things cosy her sister, Rona, was married for a time to Jeff Conaway, the actor who played Kenickie in the movie,) and a pop star with hits such as '*Physical*' and '*Xanadu*' and duets with **Cliff Richard**, of whom she was a close personal friend. Well, what else is the daughter of an MI5 agent going to do for a career, right?

Oh, and her third cousin is comedian, author and former BBC actor Ben Elton. But don't worry, it's just a coincidence.

Anyone up for another example of the same dynamic in action? OK, how about the story of **Phil Manzanera**, guitarist with **Roxy Music** and later the bands **801** and **Quiet Sun**?

Born Philip Geoffrey Targett-Adams, he took his professional name from that of his mother, a Colombian. His father, an Englishman named Duncan Targett-Adams, worked for BOAC (British Overseas Airways Corporation — a forerunner to British Airways,) his work seeing the family move around different parts of the Americas, including Hawaii (as noted elsewhere, a hotbed of military and CIA activity,) Venezuela, Colombia and Cuba, during the Batista regime.

In his autobiography, '*Revolución to Roxy,*' Manzanera admitted that his old man had had connections with "local spooks" and, whichever country they would find themselves temporarily based in, there would often be some kind of political revolution. As a 2024 interview article with the '*Daily Express*' puts it:

> "In his book, Manzanera recounts spending the following New Year's Eve 'crouched on the bathroom floor, (my head) pressed down by my shrieking mother, and (my heart) pounding. Bullets were flying all over the place, lighting up the darkness outside, and a gun battle was taking place (in) our back garden... It was terrifying.'
>
> "But if a knack for being in the wrong place at the wrong time seemed like just bad luck at the time, later revelations caused Manzanera to wonder whether it really was just coincidence. His father had also been in Argentina when President Juan Perón was ousted, and in Paraguay when rebel forces had fought against President Higinio Morinigo.
>
> "A local newspaper at the time even commented: "Targett-Adams... is an old hand at South American revolutions.""

(Could there be yet further irony in the first part of his name, considering the stories?)

Manzanera says that his suspicions regarding his father's *real* job were raised by the Graham Greene novel '*Our Man In Havana*,' which centres on a British ex-pat living in Cuba who is recruited by an MI6 handler to become a spy for the British government. Greene turns out to have written the story at the time the family were living in the city, and just yards from Phil's father's office. The British Ambassador lived opposite their house. The movie version of '*Our Man In Havana*' was filmed just weeks after the family were evacuated from Cuba amidst the revolution.

In the '*Express*' interview he adds:

> "Of course, in real life MI6 would never ever reveal whether or not these things took place. When the Spanish version of my book came out, I was at the Hay Festival in Cartagena, Colombia. I'm giving my talk and I'm rabbiting on about MI6 and my father's possible spying activities for the British secret intelligence services, and then I look down and see that, sitting in the audience in front of me, is the British Ambassador. "So I joke and say that I probably shouldn't really be talking about this, and then I look over at the British Ambassador

and I can see him looking very serious, shaking his head slowly and frowning at me!"

All of this suggests that Manzanera is either very skilled at diversion … or that he genuinely had no idea until later in life what his father was up to.

And if that's the case with *his* story, perhaps it's the same with other musicians and famous people who may have assumed that they achieved fame and fortune off their own backs — or down to a generous dose of good luck — but who may have *actually* had their influential roles facilitated for them by their family circumstances, *without* their full awareness.

Manzanera was a friend of **David Gilmour** prior to them joining Roxy Music and **Pink Floyd** respectively. A 2024 '*Forbes*' article got into bloodline territory when it revealed of Phil:

> "His aunt told him that his real grandfather was an Italian opera singer from the early 20th century. Even more surprising, Manzanera learned he is a descendant of the 17th-century Jewish pirate Moses Cohen Enriques.
>
> "… 'So I'm reading this stuff,' Manzanera says of Enriques. 'This guy attacked a Spanish galleon. He goes off to Brazil, buys an island, and is hanging out there. And then the Portuguese decide to invade and take Brazil. So he has to get the hell out of there. And he ends up in Jamaica as the right-hand man of the most famous British pirate, Captain Morgan. It was very exciting to discover this'."

Why is this starting to sound like an episode of '*Sheep Farm*'?

Keeping it in the (extended) family, it turns out that **Syd Barrett**, the troubled original singer and songwriter for **Pink Floyd**, is a distant cousin of **Richard Thompson** of **Fairport Convention**, the group which has curated the Cropredy Music Festival in North Oxfordshire since 1976. Thompson himself, whose father was a police detective working at Scotland Yard, revealed this connection in an interview with '*Uncut*' magazine to promote his memoir '*Beeswing*':

> *"Syd Barrett wasn't a great musician in the orthodox sense. But he had a good instinct for the possibilities of music. I recently learned that Syd's father's great-grandmother was a cousin of Elizabeth Garrett-Anderson, Britain's first female doctor, who was my mother's great-great aunt. Syd and I were in fact, distant cousins."*

Adding fuel to the idea that Syd, rather than overdosing on LSD recreationally, was in fact the unfortunate victim of mind-control experimentation gone wrong, were comments made by Floyd's now-deceased keyboardist **Richard Wright** in a 1996 interview:

> *"Would it have always happened, or was it because of a huge overdose of acid? Who knows? I suspect it was a bit of both. All I know is one week he was fine, and a week later he turned up again and was completely different. It's just a terrible tragedy."*

Syd's father had been a pathologist with connections to Cambridge University. His Floyd colleagues sent Syd for evaluation by Dr. Ronnie Laing, a key figure in the 60s counter-culture of London credited with having spearheaded "the anti-psychiatry movement" from which, we might reasonably conclude, he was a Gatekeeper for those times.

Syd's rapid descent into mental illness is reminiscent of the story of **Peter Green** and **Danny Kirwan** of **Fleetwood Mac**. This stems from an incident at the time of the Spring Equinox in 1970 when the band were performing in Munich, Germany.

According to manager Clifford Davis, Kirwan and Green were met at the airport by characters that no-one else seemed to know, and led away. They ended up in some kind of rural hippie commune where they were given LSD. Reportedly, the commune was run by members of the German political activist group Amon Düül. Involved in the group was German actress and model Ursula "Uschi" Obermaier. She and group member Rainer Langhans were described by the media for a time as "Germany's John & Yoko," as they became adopted as poster children for that nation's radical left. Obermaier certainly got around; **Mick Jagger**, **Keith Richards** and **Jimi Hendrix** are listed among her lovers.

Neither guitarist was the same again. Green left the band due to his failing mental health. He was eventually diagnosed with schizophrenia, and spent long periods in psychiatric hospitals undergoing electro-convulsive therapy, (MK-ULTRA) during the mid-'70s. Kirwan was fired from the band in 1972.

Peel the Onion

In '*Volume 2*,' I mentioned briefly the case of John Peel, stalwart of BBC Radio 1 and always promoted as a champion of independent, envelope-pushing music. Peel, whose real name was John Robert Parker Ravenscroft, came from a public school background, (at Shrewsbury School, attended at the same time by '*Monty Python*' performer Michael Palin,) which was always at odds with the working-class 'man of the people' persona with which he presented himself.

Ravenscroft was drafted into the Royal Artillery in the 1950s. Many young men who didn't want to be in the military and could afford it, could buy themselves out for £50; future folk singer **Ralph McTell** was one who did this, yet Ravenscroft, who would surely have been able to afford it, didn't.

After leaving the army he went to live in America for seven years, taking on his first radio jobs at the WRR and KLIF stations in Dallas, before stints in Oklahoma and California. Recordings exist of his shows from this time, on which he speaks with a plummy public school accent; evidently, he had worked on this by the time he joined BBC Radio 1 at its inception in 1967, having affected a light Merseyside accent. Reportedly, BBC bosses insisted on his inclusion in the presenters' roster.

We might also consider why he chose the last name of Peel to replace his original Ravenscroft. Sir Robert Peel founded the English police force: a clue??

We get another case of "right place at the right time" when we are told that, not only did Peel converse with President John F. Kennedy and his running mate Lyndon B. Johnson during their 1960 election campaign, (at a time when he was working as an insurance salesman,) and shake the hand of future president Richard Nixon, but that Peel and a friend, Bob Cook, blagged their way past a police cordon at Dealey Plaza following Kennedy's assassination on 22nd November 1963 by claiming they worked for the '*Liverpool Echo*,' despite showing no ID to this effect. Cook claimed he was a photographer, despite not having a camera. These revelations come from the 2005 book '*Margrave of the Marshes*,' written by Peel before his death in 2004 and finished by his wife, Sheila.

The book goes on to say that later that day, Peel and Cook went to downtown Dallas and persuaded a police officer to give them access to the station which was holding Lee Harvey Oswald. Again, their claim of being journalists was reportedly accepted. The pair sat close to Jack Ruby, (Jacob Rubinstein, who would go on to assassinate Oswald,) as Oswald was paraded in front of the members of the press. (Peel wasn't the only name from the music world to have witnessed the JFK affair; another was a young Marvin Lee Aday, better known as **Meat Loaf**. Having grown up in Dallas, he had seen the President at Love Field airport, and later went with a friend to Parkland Hospital where he witnessed JFK's wife Jackie, covered in blood, getting out of a car.)

Ravenscroft and Cook sure seem to have 'lucked out'... or is there an alternative explanation that makes a lot more sense? Is it possible that Peel was working for some kind of intel agency himself, hence how he was able to get past the police? Could these connections have been forged during his time in the military, and could this have secured his decades-long career with the BBC, a broadcasting arm of British Military Intelligence? Could his role there have involved promoting bands and genres of music that the Establishment had decided that, for whatever reason, they wanted to be made popular?

Either way, despite the image of himself as a 'rebellious' outsider, Peel seems to have fitted right in at the institution. He ran a '*Schoolgirl of the Year*' competition on his radio show, and once posed in '*St. Trinian's*'-style uniform, with stockings and suspenders, to promote it. As noted elsewhere, he married Sheila when she was 15. Of his time in Texas he spoke of having had sex with "an awful lot" of underage girls, one as young as 13.

Engineers Prefer Blondes

Just as Peel's brushes with presidents were most unlikely for a cotton trader/ insurance salesman/ radio DJ, so we find a fortuitous reference in the official biography of **Blondie** singer **Debbie Harry** to her bagging a secretarial job at the BBC's New York offices when she moved there in the 1960s.

Harry had been born Angela Trimble in Miami before being adopted by a New Jersey couple who renamed her Deborah Ann Harry. In 2017, Debbie revealed that she had discovered Scottish ancestry on the part of her birth mother, who was a pianist. Her maiden name, she told the '*Scottish Sun*' newspaper, had been Mackenzie. The Mackenzies are one of the principal clans (bloodlines) of Scotland. Her father had been a singer.

An alternative theory has gained popularity in conspiracy circles, however. Several on-line articles have noted that Debbie used to daydream that Marilyn Monroe was her mother, and that she eventually dyed her hair its trademark blonde in homage, becoming known as "the Marilyn Monroe of Punk Rock."

Well, according to some accounts, she may well *be* the illegitimate daughter of Marilyn, from the days when the actress was still known as Norma Jeane Baker. This question was asked of Harry directly in an interview with Andrew Marr for the UK's '*TV AM*' in 2007, to which she responded:

> "*That sort of became a misquote and it sort of grew in importance, Marilyn being who she was. It was sort of like an homage or some kind of tribute to her blonde-ness, you know.*"

Later, in a 2012 interview for '*Vice,*' Harry commented:

> "*I felt related to her spiritually. I never thought that she was my birth mother.*"

There are certainly parallels between Norma/ Marilyn and Angela/ Debbie's lives, plus, arguably, a physical resemblance. Norma Jeane herself was adopted after her birth mother suffered a nervous breakdown, and was placed into foster care. She never knew her father.

Once she had re-invented herself with the Marilyn persona, taking on the "blonde bombshell" image, she became the prototype for a derivative of MK-ULTRA known as Beta Sex Kitten programming. This effectively involved the preparation, through mind-control, of sex slaves to be gifted to the rich and powerful, sometimes for blackmail purposes. Marilyn was a "presidential model," reportedly being shared by both John and Robert Kennedy.

During her time in New York, one of Debbie's jobs would be as a Playboy Bunny at one of Hugh Hefner's Playboy clubs. The rabbit ears that the "Bunnies" would wear have been identified as a motif related to MK-ULTRA-style programming, and many Bunnies are said to have been pimped out as sex slaves.

Marilyn is not officially acknowledged as having had any children, but to have suffered many miscarriages. Claims persist that she secretly had an illegitimate child when she was 19, however, though these were never substantiated. Norma/ Marilyn was born in 1926 so would have been 19 in 1945, the year Debbie Harry was born.

Raising the Dead

What connection should there be between the **Grateful Dead**, icons for the psychedelic-laden counter-cultural scene of the 1960s and beyond, and the Tavistock Institute in London, arguably the world's leading social-engineering think-tank? Well, there *should* be no connection whatsoever, *if* "the Dead" *really were* a bunch of stoner musicians who put together a band in California which *just happened* to become popular by pure random chance.

In this regard, a character named Alan Trist becomes of interest. In a radio interview with David Gans on the station KPFA in June 1990, Gans asked Trist how he first came to be involved with "the Dead" as their music publisher. Trist replied:

> "*I happened to spend a year in California in 1960-'61, from England, in between leaving school and going to Cambridge University. That's where I met those freaks, and some eight, nine years later, I came back to California and hooked up with them again.*"

Following the trail back to England, therefore, we find that Alan's father, the psychologist Eric Lansdown Trist, was one of the founding members of the Tavistock Institute for Social Research in London. Eric had studied at Yale University, and returned to the U.S. from England to take up a professor role at the University of California, Los Angeles (UCLA.)

Given that the '60s counter-culture/ Flower Power scene has been shown to have been, to a very large extent, a massive social-engineering psy-op with huge involvement by the CIA, (in direct breach of their charter to *not* conduct operations on American soil,) a vigilant researcher should be suspicious of such a direct link between one of the bands most responsible for pushing the drug-based culture of the time, and an institution concerned with observing and monitoring collective social situations.

(The book that Alan was promoting in the interview was a novel based on ancient mythology and folklore, and he revealed that "the grateful dead man" was a way-shower who helped a "hero" on his journey or quest. This would appear to be a collective role that the band took on during its heyday, but we might be suspicious of exactly *where* its fans were being led, Pied Piper-like, given Tavistock's dubious history.)

Having perfected the fine art of mind-control through unseen "behavioural modification," there's no way the Tavistock conspirators would have *not* wanted to export their methods to the American market. Master propagandist Edward Bernays, alongside associate Walter Lipmann, played a big role in getting Tavistock tactics up and running in the United States, and operations which have employed their methods have included Stanford Research Institute, the Esalen Institute, the Rand Corporation, (satirised in Stanley Kubrick's '*Dr. Strangelove*' movie as "the Bland Corporation,") Massachusetts Institute of Technology, the Hudson Institute, and many others. The first three are headquartered in California, a state which has been in the crosshairs of nefarious culture-influencers more than any other.

The official narrative has it that Britain was led in its musical tastes and styles by American trends, the classic example being the "British Invasion" bands of the 1960s effectively taking American Rhythm & Blues, giving it a slight British twist, then exporting it back to Americans dressed up as something new.

At least in the early days, though, Britain was capable of coming up with its own styles. It is said that in the pre-radio days of the early

1900s at least one person in every household played an instrument. The so-called "Tea Room Bands" of the 1920s and '30s played sophisticated live music and were well known all over the world, some decades before **Bill Haley**, **Elvis Presley** and the Rock 'n' Roll explosion in the U.S.

A none-too-subtle clue as to where the Tavistock Clinic, (closely related to the "institute") was aiming to take society, came from comments made by the military psychiatrist and brigadier general John Rawlings-Rees, (born on the "anti-Christmas" date of 25th June, appropriately,) who authored the book *'The Shaping of Psychiatry by War.'* According to Daniel Estulin, who wrote the highly informative book *'Tavistock Institute: Social-Engineering the Masses,'* he used:

> *"Methods of political control based upon driving the majority of the human population towards psychosis."*

And, that his methods were aimed at creating:

> *"A world full of unwitting neurotics; a population in need of psychiatric treatment that is also unable to see that it is mentally ill."*

Doesn't that go such a long way to explaining why human society is the way it is in these times? And all by design from mind-manipulators who invariably pass themselves off as "philanthropists," and "humanitarians." It's funny. I don't ever remember signing a contract to say I agreed to having my thoughts, perceptions and entire worldview shaped and moulded for me by people I don't know. You?

From the point of view of the manipulators, there's not much point in cultivating certain social trends and conditions if you don't have in place an effective way of monitoring them. A project which appeared to constitute just that was what was referred to as the Mass Observation "social research project" which officially ran from 1937 to the mid-1960s, being revived again in 1981 at the University of Sussex. Officially, the instigators were three former Cambridge University students.

Wikipedia tells us:

> *"Run on a shoestring budget with money from their own pockets and the occasional philanthropic contribution or book advance, the project relied primarily on its network of volunteer correspondents."*

The free festival community largely spearheaded by early music/ traveller festivals on the Isle of Wight and at Stonehenge and Windsor in the early 1970s would appear to have further informed research of this nature. Some who attended such events have contacted me to say they always felt as if the participants' activities were being surveilled and recorded. The same suspicions have been raised by attendees of early Acid House "raves" in the UK. Perhaps the same was going on there?

Closely related to Tavistock is the Frankfurt School in Germany. This is where the doctrines of Cultural Marxism were perfected. The modern expression of this ideology is "woke"-ism, permeating from the earlier "political correctness." It is a "Leftist" mindset designed to achieve what the former KGB whistleblower Yuri Bezmenov described in the 1980s as "cultural subversion."

It is far easier to wage war on a population through stealth, he observed, than through open warfare. Send soldiers and tanks into the streets and a populace will be in no doubt that they are at war, and will be inclined to fight back. Achieve the same destruction of nations in slow, incremental steps through manipulating cultural attitudes, and they will not be *aware* that they are at war, or that any defensive action needs to be taken.

The founders and key members of the Frankfurt School were Jurgen Harbernas, Max Horkheimer, Herbert Marcuse and Theodor Adorno. Another common conspiracy trope related to the Beatles suggests that the academic Adorno was actually responsible for writing the music and/or lyrics to many of the songs attributed to Lennon and McCartney.

This idea was popularised by the former British military intelligence officer John Coleman in his landmark book '*Conspirators' Hierarchy: The Story of the Committee of 300.*' Unfortunately Coleman didn't provide any citations for his claim so it's difficult, if not impossible to verify. This is perhaps understandable, however, if we consider that Coleman was revealing highly classified information which would not have appeared in publicly-available documents.

Perhaps we should also note that Adorno died in August 1969, right around the time that the whole Beatles operation was winding down. Adorno, a "high-brow" intellectual, was known for his contempt towards the pop culture of the '60s, declaring it decadent and vacuous.

(Intriguingly — certainly from the point of view of this reality being some kind of coded "matrix" — both Adorno and the aforementioned Eric Trist were born on September 11th. Jimmy Savile was born on Samhain/ Halloween. **Shane MacGowan**, best known for the **Pogues**' classic Christmas record, was born on Christmas Day. George Michael, best known for the lyric "last Christmas I gave you my heart" died on Christmas Day of reported heart failure. George's sister Melanie, at odds of 1/365, herself died on Christmas Day three years later in 2019. George's Sony label-mate Michael Jackson died on George's birthday, 25th June, in 2009, similar to how **Chester Bennington** died on his musician friend **Chris Cornell**'s birthday. I do hope you're paying attention — there'll be questions later.)

In the four-part '*The Second Summer of Love*' podcast that I recorded in 2023, we turned our attention towards the UK's Acid House/ Rave phenomenon of the late 1980s, and during our discussion, Dom Waterson homed in on many of the provable links back to the world of the military from prominent British and American record labels.

> "*The repercussions of the 1929 crash, (orchestrated and backed by J.P. Morgan, who was in turn backed by the Rothschilds,) led to huge losses in the recording industry. In March 1931 J.P. Morgan, as a major shareholder, steered Columbia Graphophone Co., (along with Odeon Records and Parlophone which it had owned since 1926,) into a merger with the Gramophone Company (HMV,) to form a company called Electric and Musical Industries Ltd., better known as EMI.*
>
> "*So, via JP Morgan Bank, the Rothschilds did get hold of the Beatles, as they funded J.P. Morgan.*"

It was a similar story with labels such as Decca, Parlophone and RCA, all of which had their roots in military operations. The latter, Radio Corporation of America, came directly out of the U.S. Navy, and initially employed many of the sonic manipulation techniques that had been developed for military deployment.

So the music industry can be described *literally* as a military-grade operation. Mass mind-control by covert means, dressed up as "harmless" fun and entertainment, has always been the name of the game.

Who Indeed?

The **Beatles** and the **Rolling Stones** aren't the only British bands whose names come up when discussing Tavistock and its involvement in popular music. Another is the **Who**, (is this another name clue in that we don't *really* know *who* these people are?)

In 2016, Jan Irvin and Joseph Atwill put out an episode of their now-defunct '*Unspun*' podcast examining aspects of the band and their songs. Jan has been scornful of rock music and what he sees as its obvious links to intel agencies, reserving particular contempt for the CIA and their aims of degrading the morals of the "baby boomer" generation, through the "sex, drugs and rock 'n' roll" lifestyle.

The pair discussed the cultural and psychological impact of the Who's music, concluding that it promotes themes of identity loss, psychosis, and societal disintegration. Whilst difficult, if not impossible to prove, Irvin suspected that the group would have had connections to Tavistock and therefore, by default, to British "military intelligence" (an oxymoron.)

Atwill focussed on the sentiments behind the song '*My Generation*:'

> "First of all, it identifies the people that he's singing to as a separate generation. Because, a teenage generation as an element of isolation was really not that common a phenomenon... They talk about, you know, that the prior generation is basically evil. They say, 'things they do look awful cold, I hope I die before I get old'."

Though **Roger Daltrey** was the frontman, the band always seemed to be driven by guitarist **Pete Townshend**, (a similar dynamic to that of **Freddie Mercury** and **Brian May** in **Queen**, and **Simon Le Bon** and **Nick Rhodes** in **Duran Duran**.)

No-One's Dad's a Plumber

Pete Townshend. Who, what, when, where ... and why?
https://commons.wikimedia.org/wiki/File:Pete_Townshend_-_Phyllis_Keating.jpg
Description: Pete Townshend in 2008.
Date 2008
Source https://www.flickr.com/photos/flipkeat/2982239847/
Author Phyllis Keating

We get tenuous military links from Townshend's parents, since his father Cliff, an alto saxophonist, and his mother Betty, a singer, both performed in the entertainment division of the Royal Air Force during World War 2. Cliff had attended London's Latymer Upper School, one of the most prestigious in England, and known as a breeding ground for "Establishment" types. He was expelled before he could complete his schooling there, however.

Many aspects of Pete's activities and behaviours mark him out as a potential MK-ULTRA subject. Even his 2012 auto-biography, '*Who I Am*,' tells of his maternal grandmother denying him food and holding his head underwater at the age of six, and of how, five years later, he was sexually abused by two leaders on a Sea Scouts trip. He commented:

> *"I suffered from a deep sexual shame ... Why should a victim of child abuse feel any shame at all?"*

He is said to have channelled this trauma into his art, expressed profoundly in the rock opera *'Tommy,'* later made into a film directed by Ken Russell, and its accompanying soundtrack.

The song *'Cousin Kevin'* sees the protagonist being abused by his sadistic cousin, (played by singer **Paul Nicholas**, whose father was a lawyer to Sean Connery and the **Beatles**,) then molested by his Uncle Ernie (played in the film by Who drummer **Keith Moon**) in *'Fiddle About.'* The character of Tommy is founded upon dissociation through trauma after he witnesses his father, an army captain, kill his wife's new lover in front of him. (Townshend's own mother reportedly had many affairs while his father was touring with his band.)

This manifests itself in the form of his psychosomatic deaf, dumb and blindness. The soundtrack also includes the song *'Smash The Mirror,'* symbolising the fracturing of a traumatised mind. When his mother pushes him through the mirror, Tommy regains his senses.

Townshend said he had gained inspiration for the *'Tommy'* story from the work of the Indian spiritual teacher Meher Baba. In 2017 Townshend said he was still so traumatised by his childhood memories that he would no longer perform songs from the album.

'Tommy' wasn't the only Who-related project to explore themes of mental illness. There was more in the 1973 album *'Quadrophenia,'* (an amalgamation of the words "quadraphonic" and "schizophrenia" according to the sleeve notes,) and its 1979 film treatment directed by Frank Roddam.

This chronicled the "Mod" scene of the '60s for which the band were considered flag-bearers. The Mods were one of the earliest youth sub-cultures to emerge complete with their own fashion, consumer durables and drugs — specifically speed. Beneath the narrative's depiction of the fights that Mods and Rockers would arrange in seaside towns on Bank Holidays, however, we see Phil Daniels' character, (a surrogate Townshend figure, presumably,) being told by his father that he's "dissociating." He ends up rejecting the Mod movement when he discovers his "hero", Ace Face, is a fraud. Ace Face is portrayed by CIA-manufactured band frontman **Sting**! '*Quadrophenia*' also starred **Toyah Willcox** in an early role helping her to find fame. Daniels went on to voice **Blur**'s '*Parklife.*' Roddam directed Sting again in '*The Bride*' in 1985.

Back to the military links, a young Townshend is said to have been turned on to American Jazz, Soul and R&B, as well as marijuana, by Tom Wright and Campbell "Cam" McLester, both sons of officers stationed at the U.S. airbase in West Ruislip, just outside London. This location had a secret "intelligence" component. Tom Wright became the Who's American tour manager in the late '60s, and indeed, the group held the honour of being the only British act selected to perform at both the Monterey and Woodstock music festivals, doing their bit to help push 60s hippie culture alongside their American counterparts.

Where trauma-based mind-control is found, paedophilia is rarely far from the surface. Townshend found himself embroiled in controversy in 2003 during the Metropolitan Police's Operation Ore investigation into child pornography. He admitted that he had used his credit card to access a website containing images of child sexual abuse. He claimed this was for research purposes, as he was intending to reveal the financial trail of child abuse from Russian orphanages to British banks. As no incriminating evidence was found on his computer he received a caution, but was not charged.

Townshend told '*The Times*' newspaper:

> *"It's a product of success. I had experienced something creepy as a child, so you imagine, what if I was a girl of nine or ten and my uncle had raped me every week? I felt I had an understanding, and I could help. What I did was insane."*

Though there's little of note in Roger Daltrey's background, Who bassist **John Entwistle** was a Freemason. Townshend expressed his apparent surprise at discovering this only after Entwistle's death at the age of 57 of a heart attack, apparently induced by a cocaine overdose. Prior to his music career Entwistle had worked as a tax officer for the Inland Revenue.

Keith Moon checked out much earlier, at the age of 32, fulfilling the familiar tenet of at least one member of every majorly successful British band dying at an untimely age. (There are very few exceptions to this rule — feel free to research it!) Moon succumbed to an overdose of pharmaceutical meds in 1978 in the same flat that **'Mama' Cass Elliott** of the **Mamas & The Papas** had died in four years earlier, aged 34. The flat, in London's Mayfair district, was owned by singer **Harry Nilsson**, who had commented that he thought it was cursed following Elliott's passing.

Moon's own residence, Tara in Chertsey, Surrey held similar fascination. Its roof peaked in five pyramids — a favoured design element of those "in the club," it seems. It had previously been owned by Peter Collison, the director of the Michael Caine-starring *'The Italian Job,'* and would go on to be owned by **Kevin Godley** of **10CC** and **Vince Clarke** of **Depeche Mode/ Yazoo/ Erasure**.

Two other names which figure in the Who's early story are Kit Lambert and Chris Stamp, (brother of the actor Terence Stamp.) As aspiring young record producers and managers, they are said to have been attracted to the group when they were still known as the **High Numbers**, and wished to free them from their contract with their manager Helmut Gorden.

They reportedly took his contract to David Jacobs, a music attorney who represented Brian Epstein and the **Beatles**, (and who, just like Epstein, died young in suspicious circumstances.) Despite being broke, and with little industry experience, the pair took on the group's management. They later formed their own label, Track Records, signing up the likes of **John Lennon & Yoko Ono**, **Jimi Hendrix**, **Arthur Brown** and **Thunderclap Newman**. Prior to this, still only in his early 20s, Lambert had worked as an assistant director on some very well-known films, including *'The Guns of Navarone,'* *'The L-Shaped Room'* and the James Bond film *'From Russia With Love.'* Quite a lucky break for a fresh-faced unknown.

Lambert's grandfather had been an official war artist for the Australian government at Gallipoli during World War 1. His father, Constant Lambert, was connected to Anthony Powell, a military intelligence officer-turned-novelist with probable ties to Tavistock. Powell was clearly born for the role, his family descending from an ancient line of Welsh kings.

Was Kit, therefore, through this association, specifically groomed to take on management of the Who, so they could fulfill the military-grade social-engineering requirements of the time? The band's Townshend-penned '*Won't Get Fooled Again*' is all about the dynamic of culture-creation, indicating that he knew a thing or two about how it gets done, with lines like:

> *"There's nothing in the street,*
> *Looks any different to me,*
> *And the slogans are effaced, by-the-bye.*
> *And the parting on the left,*
> *Is now parting on the right,*
> *And the beards have all grown longer overnight."*

Kit himself was another who died young, at the age of 41, of a hemorrhage after falling down a flight of stairs. He had earlier been beaten up by a drug dealer, according to Townshend, over an unpaid debt.

In the interests of completism, might I throw another Townshend-helmed endeavour into the mix?

In 1969, Pete teamed up with Kit Lambert to form a side project named **Thunderclap Newman**. This combined the musical talents of **John "Speedy" Keen**, **Jimmy McCulloch**, (who later played guitar in **Wings**,) and **Andy Newman**, who had the nickname "Thunderclap." Townshend played bass guitar on their album and singles, some of which he recorded and produced at his Twickenham home studio, using the alias **Bijou Drains**.

We are told that Newman earned his "Thunderclap" moniker through his aggressive piano-playing style — amply demonstrated on the group's signature hit single '*Something In The Air*.' The song is ostensibly a call-to-arms for social revolution, a common theme for the Who.

Yet there was an intelligence project hatched by the British Air Ministry towards the end of World War 2 with the codename Operation Thunderclap. This proposed the mass aerial bombing of several cities in Germany, bringing mass casualties. The plan was scrapped, though a variant led to the smaller-scale bombing of Dresden and other locations.

Is it possible, in further links with expressions of the military, that this song was harking back to that operation — particularly considering its title, and some of the lyrics?:

> *"Call out the instigators,*
> *Because there's something in the air."*
> *"Lock up the streets and houses,*
> *Because there's something in the air."*
> *"Hand out the arms and ammo,*
> *We're gonna blast our way through here."*

All Bases Covered

The evidence shows that there is a bespoke psy-op specially designed to lure in every societal demographic. The controllers have recognised that music tastes are wide and varied, as are the age ranges, cultures, income brackets, politics, sexuality, family status and social standing of all they wish to control. All bases have been covered, therefore. If one music genre doesn't drive you towards certain behaviours and mindstates, then the next just might.

One blatant element of this approach can be seen in the rap and hip-hop field. The material passed off as belonging to this genre in contemporary times is beyond description, so low has it sunk into satanism, depravity, degraded morality and moronic, low-IQ stupidity, the obligatory Auto-tune treatment making all these idiots sound like demonically-possessed gibbering robots. So much so that I can't even bear to wallow in this garbage for research purposes, and I'm happy to leave that job to others who can!

I'm more concerned with the output of what are considered to be hip-hop's golden years, from the mid-80s to the mid-90s. In '*Volume 1*' I covered the letter which had allegedly been written to the music press in the early 2000s by a record company insider, who stated that, in the early 1990s, he and several other record label personnel were summoned to a meeting at a private residence in LA, where an individual who identified himself as a representative of America's private prison industry outlined a plan for his business to collaborate with theirs.

The record labels' input, he said, would be to deliberately and systematically dumb-down the lyrics of the rap records they would release, instructing artists to write songs which glorified criminal lifestyles — slinging crack, drive-by shootings, pimping out women, etc.

Indicating the contempt that the Establishment has towards societal consumers, he stated that impressionable fans — young black males for the most part — would try to emulate the lifestyles of their heroes on the records, thus supplying an endless stream of new inmates for the privately-owned prisons, and netting a fortune in government money which, the representative said, his industry would then share with the labels. Few of the artists were *real* gangsters, of course, meaning they would remain free as birds to continue spreading their nihilistic messages and getting paid in the process.

Though it has been impossible to authenticate the letter, what it contained goes a long way to explaining why the genre *did* head in that general direction from the early 1990s onward.

Decades later, in 2024, **Ice Cube**, (real name O'Shea Jackson Sr.,) who had been one of the principal members of **NWA**, (Niggaz Wit' Attitudes,) confirmed in an interview with host Bill Maloney that this was indeed the case. He would have been in a position to know, given that NWA was one of the main acts associated with the "gangsta rap" genre, their tracks '*Fuck Tha Police,*' '*Gangsta Gangsta*' and '*Straight Outta Compton*' cited as examples of the group's glorification of ghetto life and criminality.

Cube observed:

> "*The same people who own the labels own the prisons ... the records that come out are really geared to push people towards the prison industry.*"

Maloney asked:

> "*But didn't they make you write those lyrics?*"

To which Cube replied:

> *"It's not about making somebody write the lyrics. It's about being there as guard-rails to make sure certain songs make it through and certain songs don't. Some records are made by committee, meaning record company guys sit around and tell the artist, 'this is hot, say that. Do this. We're gonna have this guy write the lyrics. We're gonna have that.'*
>
> *"You have, you know, the record company pushing the narrative. Some social-engineering going on here, to make sure those prisons stay full."*

Some months later, in an interview on the Patrick Bet-David podcast, former industry executive **Damon Dash** confirmed that Cube's comments were accurate. He too would have been in a position to know, given that he was the co-founder of Roc-A-Fella Records alongside **Jay-Z**, (with whom he later fell out,) and was dating singer **Aaliyah** at the time of her death by plane crash in 2001.

And now, on to some happy music industry news … oh … wait … *

Resources:

All Religions Are One article on music industry — an impeccably-researched article which covers much of the same ground that these volumes have, but also adds some further nuggets into the mix:

- https://allreligionsareone.org/the%20Music%20Industry.html

Pitchfork: Moby Says CIA Agents Asked Him to Spread the Word About Trump and Russia:

- https://pitchfork.com/news/moby-says-cia-agents-asked-him-to-spread-the-word-about-trump-and-russia/

Moby interview with Kyle Meredith on WFPK:

- https://www.youtube.com/watch?v=SHI6LfICx6k&embeds_referring_euri=https%3A%2F%2Fmixmag.net%2F&embeds_referring_origin=https%3A%2F%2Fmixmag.net%2F&source_ve_path=MjM4NTE

The Star Report: Pras Michel Of The Fugees accused of being a Federal Informant:

- https://www.youtube.com/watch?v=6IzjzNxV7XY

Fugees Rapper Pras ADMITS To Being FEDERAL INFORMANT, Facing 22 Years In PRISON For $100M Fraud:

- https://www.youtube.com/watch?v=E4PqhXaBszw

Mike Mills: The Story Of R.E.M.:

- https://www.youtube.com/watch?v=VRfhX-XAIiY

Mike Mills and Bill Berry: Historic Macon Music Registry

- https://www.hmdb.org/m.asp?m=186842

Tommy Mars on why Zappa was the greatest composer of the 20th century:

- https://www.youtube.com/watch?v=KiIUfqDcMBs

Mental Floss: 10 Facts About Blondie's Debbie Harry:

- https://www.mentalfloss.com/article/597936/blondie-debbie-harry-facts

DEBBIE HARRY on MARILYN MONROE — Diva on Diva:

- https://www.youtube.com/watch?v=hVi5vvT5wHs

Roxy Music's Phil Manzanera Guests on Gary Kemp and Guy Pratt's 'Rockonteurs' podcast:

- https://player.fm/series/rockonteurs-with-gary-kemp-and-guy-pratt/s7e3-phil-manzanera

Phil Manzanera Details His Musical Adventures And Family Roots In 'Revolución To Roxy':

- https://www.forbes.com/sites/davidchiu/2024/04/12/phil-manzanera-details-his-musical-adventures-and-family-roots-in-revolucin-to-roxy/

Daily Express: Was my air line executive father really Our Man In Havana?:

- https://www.pressreader.com/uk/daily-express/20240420/282364044728939?srsltid=AfmBOoq47fDJwXeCrApHpY_nBDLzvIDxxec3UgDUDRt6f02MVkkL1bSb

The Guardian: Even hippies need a toilet door: The story of "Uschi" Obermaier:

- https://www.theguardian.com/music/2007/nov/16/popandrock5

The Grateful Dead: 1990 Radio Interview with Alan Trist:

- https://www.dead.net/features/gd-radio-hour/grateful-dead-hour-no-386?fbclid=IwAR0AqmNQkPUehc_aviALjL-0V9uMl_qEws61vp9GKlOdUb3sVMBmy0SMfwgA

Daily Mail: Israeli actor Chaim Topol lived a double life as a Mossad agent using his VIP status to gain entry to sensitive sites on daring missions around the world, his family reveals after his death aged 87:

- https://www.dailymail.co.uk/news/article-11974059/Israeli-Fiddler-Roof-star-Chaim-Topol-lived-double-life-Mossad-agent-family-reveals.html

The Guardian: They got rhythm: the interwar British dance bands who pointed towards pop:

- https://www.theguardian.com/music/2022/may/04/they-got-rhythm-the-interwar-british-dance-bands-who-pointed-towards-pop

John Peel in Dallas, 1963:

- https://www.youtube.com/watch?v=0aHDJy0R8nQ

'Unspun' podcast, no. 44: The Who — Who are you?:

- https://www.last.fm/ru/music/Jan+Irvin/_/UnSpun+044+%E2%80%93+%E2%80%9CThe+Who:+Who+Are+You%3F%E2%80%9D

The Guardian: Pete Townshend book describes 'insane' attempt to expose internet child abuse:

- https://www.theguardian.com/music/2012/sep/28/pete-townshend-internet-child-abuse-images

The Guardian: Pete Townshend: 'Who Am I' book review:

www.theguardian.com/books/2012/nov/04/pete-townshend-who-am-review

Billboard: The Who's 'Tommy': 50 Years Ago, Pete Townshend Turned Childhood Trauma Into a Classic:

- https://www.billboard.com/music/rock/the-who-tommy-album-8512828/

Pete Townshend reveals he is too traumatised to perform The Who's 'Tommy' again because of childhood memories of sexual abuse:

- https://www.dailymail.co.uk/news/article-7462189/Pete-Townshend-says-traumatised-perform-certain-songs-childhood-sexual-abuse.html

Third Airforce South Ruislip Secrets:

- https://www.ruislip.co.uk/secrests-from-usaf-south-ruislip

Pretend You're In A War: The Who And The Sixties by Mark Blake:

- https://pdfcoffee.com/pretend-youx27re-in-a-war-the-who-and-the-sixties-pdf-free.html

Ice Cube Admits 90's Gangster Rap was a Government Psy-op:

- https://www.youtube.com/watch?v=Zsrupdk3lsI

"100% True" — Roc-A-Fella Founder Dame Dash CONFIRMS Hip Hop Is A CIA Psyop:

- https://www.youtube.com/watch?v=0TbmoIGcVF0

Straits Times: 1MDB trial: Staggering US$2.4m went into Kim Kardashian and Pharrell Williams's bank accounts:

- https://www.straitstimes.com/asia/se-asia/1mdb-trial-staggering-us24m-went-into-kim-kardashian-and-pharrell-williams-s-bank-accounts

Malay Mail: US$2.4m 1MDB money routed into Kim Kardashian, Pharrell Williams' bank accounts, Irwan-Arul Kanda trial told:

- https://www.malaymail.com/news/malaysia/2024/09/09/us24m-1mdb-money-routed-into-kim-kardashian-pharrell-williams-bank-accounts-irwan-arul-kanda-trial-told/149831

CHAPTER 3

BEWILDERING BEATLES BONDINGS

Further revelations linking the most influential music group of all time with occult teachings and esoteric elements.

> *"Turn off your mind, relax and float downstream,*
> *It is not dying,*
> *It is not dying.*
> *Lay down all thoughts, surrender to the void,*
> *It is shining,*
> *It is shining."*
>
> The Beatles: 'Tomorrow Never Knows'

As has become the tradition, no book in this series is complete without a free-fall deep dive into conspiratorial and occult aspects of the **Beatles** and the McCartney "situation." This band is the gift (or possibly curse?) that keeps on giving to researchers within this genre.

The machine behind the "Fab Four" mythos works overtime to keep this group's legendary flame burning, barely a week going by without some new story emerging, or a movie, documentary, box set, album re-issue or photo exhibition. It's as if the group's legacy is so important to their controllers, and so much resource has been expended upon them, that new generations far too young to remember the group's music, or any of the members' solo output, are nevertheless having the Beatles religion thrust upon them from all directions.

As well as fulfilling the social engineers' agendas, of course, this dynamic also ensures there's never any shortage of new information for a suspicious researcher (me) with which to seek the *real* reasons for this group having been elevated to a mythical status way beyond that of any of their competitors. *Why* this group in particular, their great music notwithstanding? What *is* it about the Beatles?

Little Drummer Boys

Where to start with this one then? Well, let's see. I mentioned in the earlier chapter that actor Lewis Collins was in line to replace Beatles drummer **Pete Best** in 1962 before the role went to **Ringo Starr**, at that time the drummer for **Rory Storm & the Hurricanes.** One reason given for that choice was that Pete was a good looking young lad, and the Beatles' controllers wanted the girls to be looking at John, Paul and George rather than the drummer. So Pete was swapped out for Ringo and, problem solved!

A more plausible reason, however, is that Pete became the unfortunate victim of an embarrassing affair where his mother, Mona, became impregnated by Neil Aspinall, a close associate of the Beatles who, like roadie Mal Evans, ran with them throughout their career. The result was that Mona gave birth to a son, named Vincent, or "Roag."

A question arises here: why was Neil not axed from the Beatles inner circle and Pete kept on? This implies that Neil was a more important asset to the group than Pete. Some kind of a handler, perhaps? Indeed, Neil went on to head up the group's Apple Corps record label. He was also, rumour has it (though it's never been proven) the "IAmAPhoney" blogger/ YouTube poster who was majorly responsible for the "Paul Is Dead" McCartney replacement theory gathering so much momentum. (We'll get to that.) Interestingly, Aspinall died in 2008, at which time the IAmAPhoney output fizzled out.

Back to Pete and Mona Best, anyway. Mona was the owner of a property in the West Derby suburbs of Liverpool and used a huge win on the horses to finance a venue, the Casbah Coffee Club, which operated out of the basement. It was here that the Beatles, during their transition from the **Quarrymen** and the **Silver Beatles**, played some of their earliest gigs before landing at the more celebrated Cavern Club in the city centre. A young John Lennon painted the ceiling with an array of occult symbols, from moons and stars to Aztec-inspired artwork, demonstrating that he had knowledge of such things from early on.

In 2024, it was reported that the building which housed the Casbah, as well as having been Pete and Roag's home, had been converted into "luxury" AirBnB apartments, with rooms named after Lennon,

McCartney, Harrison, Best and original bassist **Stuart Sutcliffe**, (but no Ringo.) Pete and Roag curated the transition.

Prior to all this, however, a 2002 book published by Roag titled '*The Beatles: The True Beginnings,*' told us that Mona, having been born in Delhi in 1924, had been raised in colonial India. Her father, Thomas Shaw, had headed out there following a Cambridge University education to pursue a military career, (surely not?!) ending up a major in the British Army. While stationed in India, the book reveals, Thomas had fought off competition to win the affections of the "Belle of the South" as she was apparently known, one Mary Shelverton. They married and had four children, of whom Mona was the youngest.

The worlds of music and the military meet yet again in the rest of her India back story. We are told that it was at a big band concert where a 15-year-old Mona first realised she had strong musical leanings. The bandleader invited her on stage to sing with him, which she did, nervously at first, but going on to bring the house down as she grew in confidence. Her musical passions having been ignited, she was ideally poised to usher her son Pete into the music business upon her return to England.

And so, to summarise, the early drummer in what would go on to become the most famous band in the world came from a military family upbringing. Neither the first nor the last time that we will encounter this dynamic.

Family Affairs

Few would disagree that the relationship between Mona and Neil Aspinall which led to the birth of Roag was a rather strange one. Far more solid and exemplary were the marriages of Paul and Linda and John and Yoko, right? . . . Right??

Well . . . perhaps not. Paul and Linda's relationship has always been peddled as having been built on love and happiness, made all the more tragic by Linda's untimely passing from cancer in 1998. But, as we have discovered, the Beatles mythos has been hugely embellished to spin a certain narrative, so why should we expect it to be any different when it comes to the personal affairs of the individual members?

John's relationship with Yoko was always a... strange one to say the least. Yoko is descended on her mother's side from a one-time emperor of Japan, while her father headed up a prominent banking dynasty. When he relocated the family to the United States he settled in the town of Scarsdale in Westchester County, New York.

At this time there was a young woman growing up there named Linda Eastman — or to give her the original family name... Epstein. Her father, Leopold Vail Epstein, who became an entertainment lawyer and was involved in the legal dissolution of the Beatles, was of Belarusian-Jewish stock, and changed his name to sound more all-American. Linda, of course, went on to marry Paul McCartney, (well, one of them.) Epstein would appear to be a fairly common Ashkenzai-Jewish last name, possibly originating from the German town of Eppstein, in Hesse, and I've not uncovered anything to link Linda's father to Brian or Jeffrey Epstein.

But, this notwithstanding, what — really — are the chances of two young women who would go on to marry the two most celebrated singer-songwriters of the 20th century, and the frontmen of the most successful pop group of all time, *just happening* to grow up in the same town if down simply to random chance and "coincidence"?

To my mind it rather suggests that there's something about Scarsdale; that it's used to groom and cultivate future celebrities. Indeed, many famous people grew up in this small town which few Americans have ever heard of, including Liza Minelli and '*Stranger Things*' actor Noah Schnapp. Interestingly, Scarsdale's Wikipedia page used to list the household names who hailed from the town, but this information has since been deleted. The town cropped up in the narrative of the 2018 documentary '*Three Identical Strangers*' which told of how three brothers were placed into three families — one working class, one middle class and one upper class — as part of a social experiment. The brother who got the upper class home was raised in... Scarsdale, NY!

Lennon, 17 at the time, lost his mother Julia in July 1958 when she was struck and killed by a car driven by an off-duty police constable, Eric Clague. He was acquitted of all charges and given a short suspension before leaving the force. I wonder if the system would have been so lenient towards any of of us if we had done the same?

No-One's Dad's a Plumber

Not surprisingly, the death of his mother had a traumatising effect on the young John, who is said to have turned to drinking and fighting. It inspired him to write the solo songs '*Mother*' and '*My Mummy's Dead,*' both reportedly as a result of the "Primal Scream" therapy he had undergone under its treatment's inventor Arthur Janov, as well as one credited to "the Beatles," '*Julia*' from 1968's '*The White Album.*' On this song's composition, Lennon remarked in one of his '*Playboy*' interviews that it was:

> "Sort of a combination of Yoko and my mother blended into one."

This, perhaps, gives us a clue as to Yoko's principal role in John's life — as an older surrogate mother figure. Indeed, Lennon used to frequently refer to her as "mother."

There are startling parallels with Paul McCartney in this regard, since Paul also lost his mother when he was a teenager; mother Mary (inspiration for the line in the song '*Let It Be,*' as well as for the naming of his eldest daughter . . . if we for a moment imagine there only to have been one Paul!,) died on Halloween of 1956 of complications from breast cancer.

Their shared grief is said to have created a strong bond between the two young men, and they found solace in Yoko and Linda respectively. Both weddings took place within days of each other in 1969, and, "synchronistically," both Paul and John's fathers died within days of each other in 1976.

There is another, perhaps more disturbing parallel between them, though. Both publicly admitted to having felt a sexual attraction towards their mothers when teens.

On a leaked tape conversation which got referenced in Philip Norman's book '*John Lennon: The Life,*' John is heard talking of a time when, aged around 14, he put his hand on his mother's breast as she was lying on a bed and wondered if he should "do anything else."

In the 1997 book '*Paul McCartney: Many Years From Now,*' meanwhile, written by the co-curator of London's Indica art gallery, Barry Miles, Paul is quoted as saying:

> "At night there was one moment when she would pass our bedroom door in underwear, which was the only time I would ever see that, and I used to get sexually aroused. Just a funny little bit. I mean, it never went beyond that, but I was quite proud of it. I thought, 'That's pretty good.' It's not everyone's mum that's got the power to arouse."

Paul and Linda's relationship was often touted as "Britain's happiest marriage." It lasted for almost 30 years until, in a parallel with Paul's mother, (though was it a different 'Paul"?!) Linda died of breast cancer. However, comments from Peter Cox, a literary agent who had worked with Linda and who became a key witness in the later divorce between Paul and his second wife Heather Mills, cast their marriage in a different light. In 2006 the '*Daily Mail*' reported him as saying:

> "There were moments when Linda would feel deeply unhappy and depressed about her marriage. Every marriage has its ups and downs, of course. In her low moments, the idea of leaving him did cross her mind, but she immediately rejected it. Her family was the most important thing in her life and there was no way she'd give them up. At the low points, she did feel trapped."

The '*Mail*' article adds:

> "Although he found Paul charming and charismatic, Mr. Cox claimed the star had 'a darker side' and could be very controlling. Linda often had to dance attendance upon him. He bossed her around'."

The article further quotes Cox as saying:

> "I didn't warm to Paul. There was an awful coldness about him. His eyes were deader than any I had ever seen."

All of which is consistent, of course, with the idea that this was not the real 'Paul' but rather 'Billy Shears,' the individual who has been playing the public role of "McCartney" for decades, and who is indeed said to exhibit a darker side, calculatedly masked by the friendly thumbs-up public persona. But we'll come back to that...

Just four regular lads from Liverpool. Could have been anyone.
https://picryl.com/media/beatles-ad-1965-just-the-beatles-restored-14c15b

In the Club

It becomes clear, when doing the research for long enough, that Masonic family ties are often the key to great influence in society. On-line photographs exist of Lennon and McCartney (both of them!) performing known Masonic handshakes, both with each other and with others. There are also publicity pictures showing the pair exhibiting the "hidden hand" sign by placing their right arms inside their jackets, Napoleon-style — another indicator of secret-society affiliation.

Perhaps we have some clues elsewhere, too. Before becoming the Beatles they were known as the Quarrymen, this name being a euphemism for a stonecutter... or mason. The group's famous greatest hits albums from the early 1980s were issued with blue and red sleeves respectively, these being the colours associated with lodges within the Scottish and York Rites of Freemasonry.

One of the best summing-ups I've come across of how Freemasonry's control over all aspects of Organised Society works came from the GoodLion.TV network in its show '*Order Out Of Chaos: Freemasonry Exposed*.' It stated:

> *"Freemasonry takes from the Babylonian Kaballah, an esoteric religion infused in black magic. Sadly, Freemasonry has a dominant presence in politics, religion, and even law enforcement. The elites use secret societies to filter their members and make sure those who take the oath fall in line. Occult rituals mark the pace since initiation, and they get worse from there. Freemasons swear an oath to protect their brothers, even if that means covering up for crimes."*

The group released a compilation in 1988 titled '*Past Masters,*' a term associated with the Order. It contains 33 tracks across its two volumes, 33 being the number of (official) degrees within the Scottish Rite.

Solar worship figures heavily in Masonic teachings, with '*Good Day Sunshine*' and '*Here Comes The Sun*' being two of the group's most popular songs. McCartney formed Wings after the Beatles, with both names evoking Aleister Crowley's book of poetry '*The Winged Beetle.*' The scarab beetle depicted on the cover was an important symbol in ancient Egyptian mythology, whose teachings heavily inspired those of freemasonry, and which also encompassed sun worship. The creature is thought to have inspired the naming of the Beatles.

Lennon's father Alfred/ Freddie, though a merchant seaman by trade, was an aspiring musician himself, and released a handful of songs. One, '*That's My Life,*' was released with a black-and-white checkerboard sleeve design, a common motif within Freemasonic traditions. Was Freddie a mason?

The promotional blurb for Richard Edmunds' book '*Inside The Beatles Family Tree*' speaks of "John's links to British royalty and his descent from famous medieval kings, warriors, poets and saints." A 2022 article on the nation.cymru website proudly proclaims that Lennon had Welsh ancestry on his mother's side, and that he was a descendant of the 14th century Welsh military leader Owain Glyndwr.

This has been fleshed by further research conducted by ever-vigilant Dom Waterson, (no longer the heart and soul of social occasions,) who has discovered that Lennon is also linked through his mother Julia, (maiden name Stanley,) to the Fleetwood bloodline. Thomas Fleetwood, MP, was 'Master of the Mint' under King Henry VIII.

This name also has me wondering whether **Mick Fleetwood** of **Fleetwood Mac** could be in the mix somewhere. Well, would it really be surprising? Particularly as Mick's father, John Joseph Kells Fleetwood (RAF DSO), was a Wing Commander stationed in Egypt in the years leading up to the Suez crisis, and in Norway where he received a NATO appointment. The town of Fleetwood in Lancashire was named after this brood.

Thomas E. Uharriett, the author/ encoder of '*The Memoirs of Billy Shears*' books, which purport to be the tell-all autobiographies of the McCartney replacement, (reported to hail from Scotland hence "Paul"s connection to the Mull of Kintyre,) confesses to being a freemason in these tomes. When walking on to a Jonathan Ross BBC TV chat show, "McCartney" very deliberately flashed a "triangle of manifestation" symbol as he sat down. On the David Letterman U.S. chat show of 2009 where they joked about the replacement trope, McCartney put his index finger to his lips, a gesture which within Freemasonry denotes the telling of no secrets.

It dumbfounds me that vigilant researchers are *still* able to spot new symbolic elements encoded into Stanley Kubrick's films, particularly '*The Shining*', even after all these decades. Might there still be secrets lurking in the most analysed of all Beatles album sleeves too, that of the Peter Blake-designed '*Sgt. Pepper's Lonely Hearts Club Band*'?

As if the array of Beatles "heroes" wasn't tantalising enough, a mirror-image representation of the sleeve, where the two sides are blended together to form a pyramid, offers up even more deeply encoded elements. Subjected to this treatment, we find two representations of Aleister Crowley atop the pyramid. In keeping with Crowley's "sex magick" teachings, meanwhile, the "anchor" design at the foot of the flower bed becomes a blatant phallic symbol, and similar to the stylised way in which Crowley would sign the A of his name.

It has also been noted that actresses Diana Dors and Shirley Temple are positioned on either side of the sleeve, perhaps representing the "doors" to the 'temple' in more imagery straight out of Masonic traditions. The sleeve appears to have been cryptically encoded with cyphers — in much the same way Uharriett's '*Memoirs*' books clearly are — many of which are only now being successfully decoded decades on.

60-Something

Further links between Crowleyism and the '*Sgt. Pepper*' album have come from Mike Williams/ Sage of Quay, who has probably done more work than anyone into occult and esoteric aspects of the Beatles, and in particular, what he is convinced was the death and replacement of Paul McCartney in 1966.

Mike's 4.5-hour video presentation of 2020, '*Did The Beatles Write All Their Own Music?*' uses the band's own official sources as evidence to prove that the boys cannot possibly have written and recorded all the songs on their '*Rubber Soul*' album during the short period at the end of 1965 when they are said to have done so. Assistance in songwriting and recording *has* to have taken place, and if this is the case for a short period in that year, is it not likely that this dynamic was in place for the entirety of their career?

Particularly if John Coleman is correct with the assertions in his '*Conspirators' Hierarchy*' book that the group's sole purpose was to socially-engineer the masses in line with much larger agendas for changing the cultural landscape of the '60s, their sudden switch from clean-cut boy band to long-haired psychedelia-pushers standing as just a fraction of the evidence.

Mike writes:

> "*The Beatles were a huge lever to help move things along and grease the skids to where we are today. The Beatles were all about Crowleyism. The Sgt. Pepper multi-coloured outfits represented the Pied Piper, (pied means multi-coloured). They were in place to lead us into the Aquarian Conspiracy, which was the brainchild of Tavistock's Willis Harman, social scientist. The Pied Piper, of course, is another version (story) of Pan, and Crowley was also a card-carrying member of the Cult of Pan.*"

We're back here to the question of whether non-human forces, representing the very structure of this realm, are in fact responsible for bringing these elements together in the form of computer-type coding?

As further evidence I would point readers towards the mind-melting compendium of "synchronistic" connections between the Beatles and the movie *'Rosemary's Baby,'* via its director Roman Polanski, his wife Sharon Tate, and the 1960s cult leader Charles Manson.

In the 1998 book *'Sleeping Where I Fall: A Chronicle,'* actor Peter Coyote, who was highly involved in the hippie and counter-cultural movements of the '60s, tells of an "envoy" of Hell's Angels sent at the behest of the (CIA-controlled) **Grateful Dead** to meet John Lennon in London. Lennon is said to have sat fascinated as they told him about an enigmatic figure over in California named Charles Manson, so it seems Manson was known to the Beatles before any of the Tate/ LaBianca/ *'Helter Skelter'* business.

There are too many other links to list here without going way off-course, and I documented many in *'Musical Truth Volume 3,'* but some additionals have since come to light owing to the almost superhuman analysis of American researcher Richard Balducci. As he points out:

> *"The satanic movie 'Rosemary's Baby' ends at the exact spot of John Lennon's death, with the camera slowly flying up and away like a departing soul leaving its body! This scene was shot 13 years before John Lennon's murder outside of the Dakota Building (called 'the Branford' in the movie.)*
>
> *"'Rosemary's Baby' was released by Paramount Pictures on June 12th 1968, exactly 13 days before 'anti-Christmas' and 'Global Beatles Day,' the same day that Baby Satan Jr. is born in the movie!"*

Ringo is the Beatle who rarely gets mentioned when it comes to studies of this nature. His real name, Richard Starkey, is interesting in itself in a "synchromystic" kind of way. Starkey = star key = key to the stars? For some reason he opted to trade this in for Ringo Starr. Again we have the "star" idea, but why Ringo? Some have suggested that a "ringed star" could be a depiction of Saturn, an entity revered by the occult controllers of Organised Society.

Again, I would question whether it's even *possible* that all this could be down to intricate planning, or rather, if these correlations can *only* be explained by some other force being involved.

Back to Balducci:

> *"The Beatles recorded the album version of their first hit 'Love Me Do' on September 11th 1962, and the period from this date to the cremation of Beatle John Winston Ono Lennon spans exactly 6,666 days.*
>
> *"Bruce Kelly who designed the Strawberry Fields memorial to commemorate John Lennon, was born on the date of his subject's eventual death — December 8th — in 1948."*

I can add another one to the mix here — though there will be many more. '*Love Me Do*' was released in Britain on 5th October 1962. This *just happens* to be the very date that the first James Bond movie, '*Dr. No,*' was released in UK cinemas. So two very British institutions which, it might be argued, have both been used for propaganda and social-engineering, (see my public talk '*Mind-control in James Bond Movies,*') were unleashed on the very same day.

"Coincidence"?

And the Beat Goes On

If John Coleman was correct in that the Beatles were a creation of Tavistock, then their usefulness appeared to be still getting deployed over 60 years after their creation. In 2023 it was announced that Artificial Intelligence technology had been used to create what McCartney described as "the final" Beatles record. This was based around a cassette recording that Lennon had made in 1978 at his home in the Dakota, singing the outline of a song he had written, '*Now And Then.*' AI was used to "clean up" Lennon's rudimental vocal so that McCartney could add his own, creating the impression that they had recorded together.

The result stood as a topical reminder of how artificial intelligence was now being routinely employed in music-making, with entire songs by that point being written without any human input. Regardless of whether or not the general public would have chosen for this to have become their future reality, the Beatles — of course — played their small part in the society-changing process.

Resources:

BBC News: Let It Airbnb . . . rooms to rent at early Beatles venue:

- https://www.bbc.co.uk/news/articles/cewlyyjnp1yo

The Beatles: The True Beginnings by Roag Best:

- https://www.amazon.co.uk/Beatles-True-Beginnings-Roag-Best/dp/1901680657

Death of Julia Stanley; Effect on John Lennon:

- https://en.wikipedia.org/wiki/Julia_Lennon#Effect_on_John

David Sheff: The Playboy Interviews: John Lennon & Yoko Ono:

- https://archive.org/details/playboyinterview00lenn_0

John Lennon & Paul McCartney both had "mother issues."

- https://www.tumblr.com/quacka-quacka/655786863607644160/john-and-pauls-mother-issues

John Lennon talks of being sexually aroused by his mother:

- https://www.youtube.com/watch?app=desktop&v=-SvITEN92i8&feature=emb_title

Daily Mail:

McCartney marriage tapes exclusive: 'Linda wanted to leave Macca':

- https://www.dailymail.co.uk/tvshowbiz/article-413217/McCartney-marriage-tapes-exclusive--Linda-wanted-leave-Macca.html

Richard A. Edmunds: Inside The Beatles Family Tree:

- https://www.richedmunds.co.uk/inside-the-beatles-family-tree

Sage of Quay/ Mike Williams — Did The Beatles Write All Their Own Music? (Apr 2020):

- https://www.youtube.com/watch?v=ccEhmQ0M4FY

Sage of Quay/ Mike Williams — The Beatles 1960-1963: Organic or Engineered? (Apr 2022):

- https://www.bitchute.com/video/io6w4OfDkuT9/

Three Identical Strangers/ Scarsdale:

- https://nypost.com/2018/06/23/these-triplets-were-separated-at-birth-for-a-twisted-psych-study/

Good Lion Films/ TV:

- https://www.goodlion.tv/

Going Underground: Paul McCartney, The Beatles and the UK Counterculture:

- https://www.youtube.com/watch?v=iDrv8ngD4zI

CHAPTER 4

HOW MANY PAULS DOES IT TAKE TO CHANGE A LIGHTBULB?

Is contemporary "Paul" really the original "Paul"? And was the "Paul" considered to be the original "Paul" really a replacement "Paul"? If your mind's not yet been turned to scrambled eggs, give it 'til the end of the chapter.

> *"While they were crying out, 'beware,'*
> *Your flowers and long hair,*
> *While you and Sergeant Pepper saw the writing on the wall."*
> Terry Knight: 'Saint Paul'

I've joked at many of my public talks that I'm going to introduce a Paul McCartney drinking game. Where every time I mention his name, the audience takes a swig of their liquor of choice. By the end of the evening they'll all be in a hopeless mess on the floor.

The quip does illustrate the degree to which the controllers of this individual — whoever he may be, (we'll come to that) — really are rinsing every last drop of potential out of him, both in terms of income generation, and the subtle pushing of ideas helpful to their overall agendas of complete human control.

As late as 2025, by which point even the *real* Paul would have been into his 80s, "McCartney" was still slogging it out on the international tour circuit. The McCartney legacy — not to mention that of the Beatles — is the gift that keeps on giving for the industry's true handlers.

My research suggests that there are different grades when it comes to music's main assets. Some are required to fulfill their role for only a short period — think Jim Morrison — but then are allowed to retire their public personas through faking their deaths — only possible with the full complicity of the military intelligence services which work in cahoots with the entertainment industry.

Some are granted the same "privilege" but have to put in much longer tenures before earning their release—think **Elvis Presley** or **David Bowie**. Some, it seems, outlive their usefulness and literally become worth more dead than alive—or become publicly outspoken to the point that they become a thorn in the side of the Establishment and earn themselves a dispatching of a different nature—think **John Lennon**, **Bob Marley**, **Jimi Hendrix**, **Janis Joplin**, **Kurt Cobain**, **Chris Cornell**, **Chester Bennington**, **George Michael**. (The jury's still out on **Michael Jackson** and **Prince**!)

Then others—presumably the most valued assets of all—are allotted a different fate—to put in a lifetime of service to the business until they drop. This is the realm of the 'Sirs'—**Sir Elton John**, **Sir Rod Stewart**, **Sir Tom Jones**, **Sir Cliff Richard**, **Sir Mick Jagger**, **Sir Ringo Starr**... and **Sir Paul McCartney**.

When Two Become One?

As many readers will be aware through the sterling work of researchers like Mike Williams, Richard Balducci and others—and as documented at great length in '*Musical Truth Volume 1*'—a great deal of circumstantial and documentary evidence exists—not to mention cryptic clues which seem to have been deliberately placed in Beatles album sleeves, lyrics, backmasked messages and promotional photos—to suggest that the real, biological James Paul McCartney was replaced in 1966 by an individual named William Shepherd, known as Billy Shears, and that Shepherd has been playing the public role of "Paul McCartney" to this day.

The full version of the conspiracy has it that the real Paul died in a car crash on 11th September of 1966 (9/11/66), which may or may not have been "accidental" depending on who's telling the story. Since '*Volume 1*' I've been contacted by a couple of people claiming they distinctly remember a news bulletin being broadcast at that time stating that Paul McCartney of the Beatles had been involved in a car crash. One remembers the story advising that he had been injured, while the other remembers it as stating that he had died.

Both remained on tenterhooks for further bulletins, but none came, which is a strange thing for news of such magnitude... *unless* the first bulletin had been unintentionally leaked and a cover-up operation was quickly put in place. It puts me in mind of Jane Standley on BBC TV News announcing on September 11th 2001 that World Trade Center Building 7 had collapsed some 20-odd minutes before it actually did, and *that* bulletin never being repeated, (and Standley promptly disappearing from our TV screens!)

Additionally, a well-known British record producer told me that he clearly recalls hearing the McCartney news, just the once, back in 1966. We can assume that no public recordings of any such bulletins are in existence, or they surely would have surfaced by now.

Further afield, meanwhile, many viewers of '*The Monkees*' TV sitcom on NBC in America have spoken of remembering a newsflash going out during the airing of the debut episode, '*Royal Flush,*' on 12th September 1966, reporting that Beatle Paul McCartney had been involved in a terrible accident. A further update was promised after the show at 11pm, but never came.

Many viewers have reportedly written sworn testimonies as to what they heard. The phenomenon appears nowhere in the "official" Beatles record. If really just provable nonsense, why would the band's controllers not have gone public to denounce such absurd claims? I attended an event hosted by the Beatles' official biographer, Mark Lewisohn, to mark the 50th anniversary of the '*Abbey Road*' album in 2019. His presentation gave no mention of the McCartney death rumours which emerged in the wake of the album's launch in '69, so I took the opportunity to ask him why. He scoffed, commenting, "you don't believe that old nonsense, do you?" Again, if nonsense, where's the harm in presenting it as such?

(Incidentally, the creators of the **Monkees**' show, Bob Rafelson and Bert Schneider, are said to have been inspired by the antics of the Beatles in their first two films to create an American version of the band.)

Knight Falls

A candidate whose name has cropped up frequently in McCartney research of recent years is Charles Maxwell Knight (OBE), a so-called "super spy" in the employ of British military intelligence. He is taken as having been an inspiration for 'M', James Bond's boss in the Ian Fleming stories, as is Rear Admiral John Henry Godfrey, under whom Fleming had served in naval intelligence during World War 2.

Knight's biography tells us, perhaps inevitably, that he conducted operations from his flat in Dolphin Square, Pimlico. This location was linked to revelations of a paedophile ring centred around the British "corridors of power," and linked to many prominent MPs including 'Lord' Leon Brittan, Margaret Thatcher's Home Secretary.

(A scoot off down a tangent if I may be permitted. It would be remiss of me when mentioning Leon Brittan *not* to point out that Brittan is a bloodline cousin of DJ/ producer Mark Ronson, as well as a second cousin once removed of another MP, Sir (naturally) Malcolm Rifkind. Now you know how Ronson shot to fame so rapidly when he did.)

Joan Miller, a woman recruited by Maxwell as one of his many spies, wrote that, despite his frequent tirades berating homosexuals, he was probably gay himself, and that he was "neurotic, anti-Semitic and obsessed with the occult." Sounds like just the man for the job.

Researcher Richard Balducci is convinced that Knight was in fact the man charged with dispatching biological James Paul McCartney in the aftermath of the mythical car crash in 1966, and that he did so by means of a hammer blow to the head. This, Balducci maintains, was the inspiration for the bizarre *'Maxwell's Silver Hammer'* track on the *'Abbey Road'* album with its lyric "Bang! Bang! Maxwell's silver hammer came down upon his head." The song's lyrics are credited to "Paul McCartney"/ Billy Shears (take your pick,) while the other Beatles are on record as having hated it.

The hammer is said to have been of the Blue Bird brand, which is thought by some to have been referenced on McCartney's later song *'Blue Bird.'*

Balducci maintains that there are "synchronistic" British "intelligence" clues all over the replacement "McCartney"'s work, most notably on the cover for the '*Band On The Run*' album, the third from his group **Wings**. The cover shows a ragtag group of household names posing as if caught in a searchlight whilst trying to escape. Among them are Christopher Lee, who turns out to be a little more than a mere film actor.

Balducci writes:

> "Ian Fleming was inspired to create super spy James Bond, 007, after listening to his step-cousin Christopher Lee's clandestine British military intelligence operations adventures. Lee's connections are why he is shown on the 'Band On The Run' cover. Christopher Lee worked with, and is here representing, Charles Maxwell Knight, the British "super spy", "M", who murdered Beatle James Paul McCartney with "Maxwell's Silver Hammer.
>
> James Coburn, who played "super spy" Derek Flint in the James Bond spoofs, is in the "as above, so below" pose, with his right hand pointing at "Band" and his left hand linking the surrogate "M", Christopher Lee, with the death of the band the Beatles, and is why the surviving band mates are "on the run"."

On the subject of Wings covers, a limited-edition collage poster was given away with copies of the '*London Town*' album. On it, written across a picture of a bare-chested "Paul"/ Billy, posing with Linda, is the word "substitute." At first glance it appears to have been written in biro, but on further inspection it turns out to be part of the print. According to some, the Who song '*Substitute*' with its line "I'm a substitute for another guy, I look pretty tall but my heels are high," was about the replacement of McCartney. The line "I can see right through your plastic mac" follows. (Mac = McCartney??)

Whatever the truth of the crash/ death rumours, there can be no rational denying that there have indeed been at least two individuals playing the role of "McCartney" through the decades. Critical analysis of photographs and video footage gives us all we need to arrive at that conclusion. *If* present-day "McCartney" really is Shepherd/ Shears, I wonder if he would have been made aware, all those decades ago, that he would be living out the charade literally until he would draw his last breath, as appears to be the case?

Swap Shop?

In the last book I offered my theory that the shorter, rounder-faced, slightly chubbier "Paul," (the left-hander) that we see in pre-1966 photographs and footage, and the one with the prominently arched right eyebrow, may well be the "replacement." I arrived at this idea after considering much earlier, pre-fame pictures of "Paul" where he looks distinctly like a younger version of the one we have today. Some have claimed that these early pictures have been digitally manipulated, but some exist in print form as well as on-line.

This idea was expanded upon by a friend, who commented:

> *"As a musician I would personally find it impossible to even attempt to play a guitar left-handed, and bearing in mind how relatively few left-handers there are it would make it a nightmare to create a replacement.*
>
> *"I'm thinking that, logically, Billy was always meant to be a Beatle from the start, but somehow couldn't take up the role at the appointed time, so they put in a stop-gap filler until he was ready. So rather than Billy emulating Paul, was it Paul holding the fort for Billy?"*

This, then, would mean that the stop-gap Paul was retired off, presumably in 1966 as per "Paul Is Dead" lore, and sent back into obscurity. The more sinister take, meanwhile, would suggest that he was sacrificed as part of some kind of ritual. It's always been impossible to prove this due to the lack of verifiable evidence.

What we do have is a world of symbolic, cryptic clues scattered across record sleeves, photographs and songs. So we are left to decide as to whether these clues constituted part of some dark occult belief system, or whether it was a cynically cultivated hoax devised to send researchers off down the garden path for decades to come, (it worked!) and to generate maximum income through increased record sales.

Brimful of Ashers

Another correspondent offered a similar take on the two concurrent Pauls scenario, this one bringing McCartney's long-term girlfriend of the 1960s, the actress Jane Asher, into the picture:

> *"I rather like the idea of there having been two of them right from the start and their being used as interchangeable parts. Why do I say this? Not for any sentimental reasons, but because that would explain a very big question I've always had about how Jane Asher could have been able to do those pics with the new Paul so soon after the crushing blow that the death of the real Paul must have been to her.*
>
> *"How could a grief-stricken broken-hearted young woman do those playful poses like the famous one of them turning to look behind them into the camera? All very explainable as a lark if she had <u>her</u> Paul very much still alive and tucked away somewhere safe for her."*

This person then speculates as to whether — if this theory is correct — Jane's father, Dr. Richard Asher, could have been offed as a result of his having this knowledge? Dr. Asher was involved in the study of deep sleep hypnosis techniques, and according to many, McCartney, (one of them anyway!) was being used as a test subject during the time he was lodging at the Asher family home in Wimpole Street, London, W1, which also doubled as Dr. Asher's clinic. Dr. Asher's body was discovered in the basement of the home in April 1969, a short while after Paul had married Linda following the break-up of his relationship with Jane. The official verdict was "suicide," (what else?) though there are many reasons to suspect foul play.

> *"They weren't worried that he would spill the beans about Paul being dead, because that could be simply laughed away as it has been for years as just another crazy 'conspiracy theory.'*
>
> *"No, they were worried that Dad would reveal that the real Paul was still <u>alive</u>, and that just wouldn't do for these slime buckets!"*

Incidentally, the Ashers — at least Jane and her brother Peter — become interesting candidates for the Dom Waterson ancestral research treatment. Given his findings, (with, as is so often the case, all of the interesting links coming from her mother's side,) it perhaps becomes clearer to understand why Jane and Paul ended up a couple.

The research shows that, through her mother Margaret Augusta Eliot, Jane is distantly descended from King Henry VII, with the lineage passing through the Churchill and Spencer families (as in Winston and Diana.) Well, the controllers weren't going to let Paul get paired off with any old riff-raff, were they? Plus, there was the tantalising bonus of Dr. Asher's work which could be put to good use, and seemingly was.

And the pertinent ancestral connections don't end there. Dom takes up the mantle:

> *"The Ashers via the Eliot line are bloodline-related, no question, to the ancient Viscount Dillons of Costello-Gallen in the County of Mayo, a Peerage of Ireland, created in 1622.*
>
> *We can take the family back to Sir Henry de Leon, who married the daughter of Sir John de Courcy. His wife was Affreca de Courcy, daughter of Godred Olafsson, King of the Isles, a member of the Crovan dynasty.*
>
> *"Look where the Crovan dynasty ruled — the Scottish area of Kintyre!"*
>
> *"If I were a betting man I would say Macca is bloodline-related to these ancient royal families, and Asher was some kind of ancient Royal match-up that possibly didn't work out. Now, that is what I call Matrix coding. What it means I haven't a fucking clue, but it cannot be brushed off as mere coincidence!"*

Perhaps we should consider, therefore, that if the Paul/ Jane relationship didn't work out, Paul, (or "Billy" by this point?) was instead paired up with Linda Eastman due to her Epstein family bloodline? (And, if these relationships were arranged, could the process also have been getting replicated when, in 2024, it was announced that Paul/ Billy's grandson Arthur, son of his eldest daughter Mary, was dating Phoebe, the daughter of Bill and Melinda Gates, providing an ostensible connection between two families long known for pushing "elite" agendas helpfully along their way.)

Further curiosity comes from Jane and Peter's first cousin Diana, too, who passed away in 2024. Matt Sergiou, another impeccable Beatles researcher, revealed in episode 10 of our *'Magical Mystery Talk'* podcast that Diana was credited with having been a co-founder of the Best Friends animal sanctuary. Despite its worthy-sounding title, this organisation turns out to have morphed from the Process Church of the Final Judgement. I mentioned the Process in *'Musical Truth Volume 1'* as having been an offshoot of Scientology founded by Mary and Robert McLean, who renamed themselves "DeGrimston."

The Process played a big part in the 1960s counter-culture scene in San Francisco, where it counted among its associates Sirhan Sirhan, the Palestinian accused of shooting Senator Robert Kennedy, (and ticking all the boxes for having been another MK-ULTRA 'Manchurian Candidate,') Charles Manson, and "Son of Sam" serial killer David Berkowitz. Nice crowd. (*'Weird Scenes Inside The Canyon'* author Dave McGowan had earlier penned a book titled *'Programmed To Kill'* in which he connected the high-profile serial killers of the past several decades back to CIA mind-control experimentation. Hard to believe, I know.)

It was in London that the Process Church began, however. It published a regular magazine, *'The Process,'* with Jimmy Savile gracing the cover of one edition, (in which he spoke of "rising from the darkness and leaping about causing mayhem left and right" late at night, and "Paul McCartney" and Jane Asher being interviewed for another. It also broadcast a regular show, which Diana Asher hosted.

Back to Dr. Richard Asher who, as well as being a senior physician at the Central Middlesex Hospital, had written a 1956 paper titled *'Respectable Hypnosis,'* and was reportedly interested in the study of what happens to the human mind when in deep sleep states. The writer and proprietor of Beacon Films, Redwel Trabant, suggested in a 2014 article that Asher had used "McCartney" as a test subject in some of his experiments, and that this may explain where one of the Beatles' most famous songs came from. Dr. Asher quit his hospital post suddenly in 1964. Was this to focus more on his mind-control experimentation at his home clinic?

McCartney has always maintained that he woke up one morning in Wimpole Street with the melody to '*Yesterday*' in his head, and rushed to his piano to avoid forgetting it. He was, apparently, concerned that he may have plagiarised someone else's work. As he put it at the time:

> *"For about a month I went round to people in the music business and asked them whether they had ever heard it before. Eventually it became like handing something in to the police. I thought if no one claimed it after a few weeks then I could have it."*

In 2006, however, a songwriter and music producer named Lilli Greco claimed on an Italian television show that the melody of '*Yesterday*' was in fact lifted from a Neapolitan aria named '*Piccere' Che Vene a Dicere,*' dating back to 1895. You can hear Greco performing the song in the video linked to in the Resources section at the end. Though Greco claimed this situation most likely arose from McCartney's fondness for Neapolitan songs, would a more likely candidate for having an encylopaedic knowledge of world music not be Jane Asher's mother, Margaret Eliot, given her credentials as an honorary member of the Royal Academy of Music, and as a music teacher to, among other students, Sir George Martin?

Here, a tantalising possibility emerges. Supposing the Ashers were working together on Richard's hypnosis experiments, possibly as a British variant on the CIA's MK-ULTRA. If Richard had wanted to test whether a piece of music could be subliminally implanted into a subject's mind as they slept, might Margaret not have suggested using a composition with which, as a student of world music, she would have been familiar? And would "Paul" not have been the ideal guinea-pig, given that he was already a household-name pop star and, conveniently, was living and sleeping right under the Ashers' roof?

(Equally intriguingly, how about this to truly put the mind into the mincer? Following "Paul"s solo performance of '*Yesterday*' on the '*Ed Sullivan Show*' in 1965, Lennon came off the back of it with the comment: "Thank you Paul. That was just like him!" This was the year *before*, according to P.I.D. lore, the real Paul died and was replaced!)

It's a very small world when it comes to the Ashers and the Beatles, it seems. Jane's boyfriend Paul was, of course, managed by Brian

Epstein, who had a business partner named Nicky Byrne who handled the American side of the Beatles' merchandising, Seltaeb, (see Chapter 19 for more.) One of the partners in this venture was a Lord Peregrine Eliot, not only a descendant of the celebrated T.S. Eliot but... you can see where I'm going with this, can't you?... a relative of Margaret Asher *nee* Eliot!

Things didn't end happily for Richard and Margaret's marriage, however, when Richard went missing for several days in 1969. Reportedly, the family searched the house high and low, but he was nowhere to be found. They then discovered him dead in the basement, (where they presumably didn't think to look before,) on 2nd May. The very basement where "Paul" had reportedly composed a handful of the Beatles' most celebrated songs. Verdict? "Suicide." I bet you saw that one coming. He was 57. The '*Express*' newspaper reported that "two bottles" were found near his body, but didn't say what they may have contained. 1st May is "May Day" or Beltane in the ancient Pagan calendar, and this time of year was/ is associated with human sacrifice. Just saying.

"Paul" had quit dating Jane the previous year when, according to reports, she had caught him in bed with Linda Eastman. Paul and Linda got married on 12th March '69, six weeks before Dr. Asher's "suicide." Had he outlived his usefulness, his work having been completed? Was he considered a liability considering he must have had knowledge of there being two "Paul"s with Jane having stepped out with both of them?

Could part of his work have involved "programming" a replacement Paul? If his death was to silence him, it certainly prevented Jane and her brother Peter from speaking out about anything they may have known. While Peter has remained in the music industry, (as one half of the group **Peter & Gordon** for whom "McCartney" is credited with having written their hit song '*A World Without Love*,') Jane has written novels and baked cakes.

Dr. Asher's "suicide" occurred during an unfortunate spate of deaths within Beatles circles. Brian Epstein had "accidentally overdosed" in August 1967 aged just 32. He had gone to great lengths to conceal his homosexuality at a time when this was still a criminal offence in Britain. Homosexuality was finally legalised on 27th July, one month before Brian died.

Brian's lawyer, David Jacobs, died of "suicide" less than a year later. Then, in July 1970, it was the turn of the paediatric psychiatrist Dr. Emanuel Miller to get tired of living.

Miller had worked with Richard Asher, according to unsubstantiated claims, on Tavistock-sponsored mind-control research, and was the father of political satirist Sir Jonathan Miller (CBE.) Jonathan studied medicine at Cambridge University under Richard Asher. In 1966 he directed a TV adaptation of Lewis Carroll's '*Alice In Wonderland,*' (a known trigger in MK-ULTRA-style programming.) Jane had earlier starred as a child actress in a presentation of '*Alice,*' and in 1985, played Alice's mother in the film '*Dreamchild,*' directed by Dennis Potter and Gavin Millar.

Do you Want to Know A Secret?

When discussing on a TV chat show the writing of the track '*How Do You Sleep,*' acknowledged as a swipe against "McCartney" at a time when the relationship between the pair was at an all-time low, John Lennon was asked if Paul was his best friend, to which he replied, "he was. I don't know about now."

Speculation can be applied to such comments, and interpreted as veiled clues by those who wish to find them. Accusations of "confirmation bias" will come from those who do *not* wish to acknowledge a replacement.

The truth of the matter is that anyone who wasn't personally involved in the Beatles' inner circle cannot know for sure whether the real Paul died. We can theorise all we want, but verifiable evidence is thin on the ground, and possible cryptic clues are all we are left to work with.

Again, what we *can* know, simply from using our eyes, is that *at least* two different men have been publicly presented as "Paul McCartney." We start from there.

Resources:

'Billy Shears' admits many times to not being Paul McCartney:

- https://www.facebook.com/watch/?v=679936344325857

Charles Maxwell Knight:

- https://en.wikipedia.org/wiki/Maxwell_Knight

Beacon Films Blogspot: Beatles Conspiracy/ MK Beatles:

- http://beaconfilms2011.blogspot.com/2014/04/mk-beatles.html

Beatles' Yesterday a cover of old Neapolitan song, producer claims :

- http://beatlenews.blogspot.com/2006/07/beatles-yesterday-cover-of-old.html

From 1 minute, 45 seconds: Lilli Greco performs *'Piccere' Che Vene a Dicere,*' possible inspiration for 'Yesterday':

- https://www.youtube.com/watch?v=mer8BBuDMyU

Discussion on the strange death of Dr. Richard Asher:

- https://invanddis.proboards.com/thread/7819/strange-murder-richard-asher?fbclid=IwAR0iNzUnspUXHvF5qe2I9y-F3eXXDwQFIjJvLJ-1hNZmey4ux1IGVLIQm36g

Paul McCartney vs Billy Shears — voice comparison — Yesterday 1965 vs 1973. Very different voices:

- https://www.youtube.com/watch?v=9vUBDhiN3ac

A Hard Day's Doubles — How many Pauls does it take to make a movie?:

- https://www.youtube.com/watch?v=mvrVxpSSVDE

GIVE MY REGARDS TO WIMPOLE STREET — WHERE PAUL MCCARTNEY LIVED WITH THE ASHERS:

- https://beatlesinlondon.com/wimpole/

Mike Williams/ Sage of Quay McCartney/ "Paul Is Dead" channel:

- https://www.bitchute.com/channel/mK8GIZDrL8lV

The Real Deal. Jim Fetzer with Richard Balducci: More on the Assassination of Paul McCartney:

- https://www.bitchute.com/video/w9MqqvmOdUvH/

Who Buried Paul Blog: What Is Ten Miles North on the Dewsbury Road?:

- https://whoburiedpaul.blogspot.com/2012/09/what-is-ten-miles-north-on-dewsbury-road.html

CHAPTER 5

MARK, JOHN, TODD AND GOD

Revisiting the Lennon assassination, Mark Chapman's obvious links to MK-ULTRA, and Todd Rundgren's place in the unsavoury mix.

"No shit, Sherlock,
The gun is loaded and primed.
No shit, Sherlock,
I've had enough of your lies."
                Julian Cope: 'Don't Call Me Mark Chapman'

It's interesting how fate — or *was* it just that? — saw to it that "the political Beatle" and "the spiritual Beatle," **John** and **George** respectively, would be taken out suddenly and violently at relatively young ages, whereas **"Paul"** and **Ringo**, both of whom went on to become 'Sirs' and to push many a social-engineering agenda — not least the Co(n)vid scam — are alive and well into their 80s.

George's message of spiritual seeking was seemingly at odds with those of the controllers of Organised Society. And so, fortuitously, (as they would have seen it,) an intruder, Michael Abram, managed to break into George's Friar Park home near Henley on Thames on the night of 30th December 1999. The state-of-the-art security system was found to have been conveniently switched off, and his household staff were on leave.

George was awoken by the sound of breaking glass. Upon being confronted Abram fell on top of George on a staircase and proceeded to stab him around 40 times. (There is symbolic significance to the first names of the attacker and victim here, given that the Order of St. Michael and St. George is a mark of chivalry within the British honours system!)

Though George survived the event he died just under two years later of lung and brain cancer, thought to have been exacerbated by the attack, in which his lung was punctured. The address on his death certificate was listed as 1971 Coldwater Canyon in the Hollywood Hills. (Coldwater Canyon is a short distance from the much fabled Laurel Canyon, of which, more elsewhere!) This was later corrected to the address of a $4 million French country-style manor in Beverly Hills, however, said to have been owned by **Courtney Love** and once leased by "Paul McCartney."

By the time of George's death his bandmate John had been dead almost 20 years. Many who don't accept the official explanation that he died senselessly as a result of Mark Chapman simply having been a "deranged fan," assume that John had become a thorn in the side of the Establishment through his highly visible anti-war sentiments and support of leftist political ideologies.

It's no secret that U.S president Richard Nixon had attempted to get him deported several times, and Lennon had complained of being under constant surveillance by the FBI. His death in December 1980 occurred right before the Reagan administration, (with vice-president George HW Bush standing to be the *real* power broker in that regime) was due to take office the following month.

Is there more to know about Mark David Chapman? Well, there's only ever one answer to a question like that in a book like this, isn't there?!

Chapman is said to have been hanging around Manhattan's Dakota Building, in which Lennon and **Yoko Ono** lived, all day on 8th December 1980. In the early evening as the pair headed out to a recording studio, he was photographed as Lennon signed a copy of his new '*Double Fantasy*' album for him.

Some hours later, as John and Yoko returned by limousine, Chapman is said to have assumed a marksman's position and fired four shots into Lennon's back as he walked towards the Dakota's entrance lobby, with Yoko trailing some distance behind. The official account has it that the Dakota's doorman managed to get the gun away from Chapman and asked him if he knew what he had done, to which Chapman supposedly replied, "I've just shot John Lennon." Chapman then calmly leafed through a copy of J.D. Salinger's '*The Catcher In the Rye*' novel as he waited for the police to arrive, making no attempt to escape.

'*The Catcher In The Rye*', besides having been mandatory reading in English classes throughout American schools for decades, has been identified as a trigger text in an aspect of the CIA's MK-ULTRA mind-control project — specifically the programming of '*Manchurian Candidate*'-style assassins to carry out murder assignments, often retaining no memory of why they had killed after the event. (Another trigger is the dreamlike symbolism in the '*Wizard of Oz*' movie and its song '*Somewhere Over The Rainbow*,' and sure enough, a '*Wizard of Oz*' placemat was among the items left behind by Chapman in his hotel room for the police to find.)

According to author and researcher Joseph Atwill, the '*Catcher*' book also serves as a metaphor for its main character, Holden Caulfield, being initiated into the various degrees of freemasonry. The book features prominently in the Amazon Prime documentary '*A Clockwork Shining*' by Ryder Lee and Jay Weidner, (in which I was honoured to be featured as one of the talking heads,) which posits that the plotline of Stanley Kubrick's movie treatment of Stephen King's '*The Shining*,' really tells of an MK-ULTRA "real world" experiment taking place at its remote hotel location.

John Lennon: A walking contradiction

https://www.freemalaysiatoday.com/category/leisure/entertainment/2020/12/05/remembering-john-lennon-shot-to-death-40-years-ago/

Creator: Free Malaysia Today | Credit: Free Malaysia Today

Copyright: © Free Malaysia Today, 2025

In this regard, Chapman emerges as a probable subject of this type of programming — perhaps a new strand of it timed to remove a couple of undesirables, given that a few weeks after the Lennon slaying a young man named John Hinckley Jr. attempted to kill Ronald Reagan, by then American president. Reagan survived, denying Bush his first presidential stint by default. Hinckley was also reading a copy of '*The Catcher In the Rye*' at the scene.

A further curiosity is that Hinckley and Chapman bore a striking resemblance to each other at the time, and both looked somewhat similar to Stephen King. (Again, intricate human planning, or the result of the "matrix" arranging itself according to its coding?) Reagan was reportedly on Chapman's list of famous people that he wanted to kill, as was Paul McCartney, (perhaps he was a little late for that one?,) and **David Bowie** himself claimed that he was "second on his (Chapman's) list."

Ryder Lee and Jay Weidner point out the curiosity of the Lennon and Reagan events occurring within months of the release of '*The Shining*' in late 1980, particularly if their theory about the movie's true meaning is accurate. (Other "coding" connections come from Chapman having been raised in the Georgia city of Decatur, not a million miles away from the name of the Dakota outside of which he would accost Lennon, Lennon's own name being similar to that of the Russian leader Lenin, both characters portrayed as having been "working class heroes," and Lennon having been pictured in the '*Magical Mystery Tour*' film of 1967 next to a sign for a travel company bearing the slogan "the best way to go is by M&D Coaches" — MDC being the very initials of the man who would, 13 years later, apparently send him on his ultimate journey.

Plus, in a strange parallel between himself and the man he would go on to apparently kill, Chapman married a Japanese-American woman, Gloria Abe, in 1979. (His allotted handler, perhaps, as many have suspected Yoko of being to John?)

In Chapman's background we find *yet another* individual to have been raised within a military family. Hailing from Fort Worth, Texas, Mark's father, David Chapman, was a staff sergeant in the United States Air Force. Well, he was never going to be a plumber, was he?

So often it is the sons and daughters of military personnel who are used in social and scientific experiments. Accordingly, we get Mark's childhood account of his fantasising "about having God-like power over a group of imaginary 'little people' who lived in the walls of his bedroom." His father is said to have been violent towards his mother and emotionally cold towards Mark. Mind-control is born out of trauma. Did Mark's begin this early on? He had been plagued with mental health problems, attempting suicide at least twice, prior to the Lennon event.

By his teenage years, Chapman had apparently converted to the Presbyterian Christian faith, and had begun working as a summer camp counsellor at his local YMCA, as well as getting involved with the World Vision charity, a known "front" operation for the CIA. For a time he studied at Covenant College in Georgia. In this regard the name of the location, Lookout Mountain, becomes a curiosity when the military base of the same name in LA's Laurel Canyon, a known centre of operations for MK-ULTRA, gets thrown into the mix.

By 1977 Chapman had relocated to Hawaii, which has more military bases than any of the U.S. states, and an ideal location for mind-control facilities given its remoteness. In his book '*Weird Scenes Inside The Canyon*' Dave McGowan mentions that **John Phillips** of the **Mamas & The Papas** spent several months in Hawaii gearing up for their incoming music career, apparently writing many of their songs. Was he receiving MK-style programming whilst there — particularly if McGowan's suspicion that he was also being prepared to be a mind-controlled assassin is correct?

The following year, Chapman went on something of a world tour akin to that of a rock band. I hope he got a T-shirt listing all the dates. We are told that his YMCA connections allowed him to gain free or discounted accommodation. But even so, the question of how he could afford to move between Tokyo, Seoul, Hong Kong, Singapore, Bangkok, New Delhi, Beirut, Geneva, London, Paris and Dublin, in rapid succession, in those pre-budget airline days, becomes a valid one. Unless the trip was paid for by some undisclosed sponsor?

Chapman had also selected Russia as his destination for a YMCA exchange programme, but instead ended up in Beirut, Lebanon. Beirut is a key CIA base of operations, (and is where all three of spy Miles Axe Copeland's sons were born prior to being put to use in the music industry — most notably **Stewart Copeland** as drummer in the **Police** . . . the "Police," geddit?! By the way, further keeping it all in the family, it turns out that Miles' brother, Hunter Armstrong Copeland, married the mother of Courtney Cox-Arquette. Courtney, we are told, got picked from the crowd "at random" by **Bruce Springsteen** to come up on stage and dance with him in the video to his '*Dancing In The Dark.*' Well, it happens.

Similarly, Chapman was staying in Manhattan's Sheraton Hotel at the time of Lennon's death. Who paid for that then, as it wouldn't have been cheap?

Chapman arrived in New York from Atlanta in November 1980, but prior to this had made an earlier visit in late October which, he claims, is when he had initially planned to kill Lennon. What prevented him from following through? According to some it was the result of his having resisted his MK programming. This would have become apparent to his handlers, so it's reasonable to assume that efforts to reinforce his conditioning would have taken place before he was sent on his second attempt.

And this is where three lost days in Chicago appear to come into the frame. Right before arriving in New York for the second time, Chapman had stopped off in the Windy City. Official lore has it that he was there for only one day, yet the book '*Who Killed John Lennon?*' by British lawyer Fenton Bresler claims he was there for three. Is it plausible that the motive for his Chicago stop-off was to have his programming ramped-up? Are there any covert facilities of this nature in that city?

It turns out there is a notorious spot known as Homan Square. This sinister location is described as an interrogation facility shared by the police and the CIA, and as something of a "black hole" where many who go in are never heard of again.

As an article on '*The Guardian*' website from 2015 recounts:

> "*Brian Jacob Church, a protester known as one of the 'Nato Three,' was held and questioned at Homan Square in 2012 following a police raid.*
>
> "*Homan Square is definitely an unusual place,*" *Church told the 'Guardian' on Friday. "It brings to mind the interrogation facilities they use in the Middle East. The CIA calls them black sites … When you go in, no one knows what's happened to you.*"

> *"The secretive warehouse is the latest example of Chicago police practices that echo the much-criticized detention abuses of the U.S. war on terrorism. While those abuses impacted people overseas, Homan Square — said to house military-style vehicles, interrogation cells and even a cage — trains its focus on Americans, most often poor, black and brown."*

Sounds like just the kind of place where no-one hears you scream in which "off the books" black-ops might take place. Was Chapman forcibly detained and "treated" here before he was sent on to complete his mission? And do comments given by Chapman himself after Lennon's murder reinforce this?

According to Fenton Bresler's book, while Chapman was being held in custody following his arrest, as well as having been visited by psychiatrists including Milton Kline who had been an MK-ULTRA doctor, he was allowed, against protocol, to receive incoming phone calls. It was after one such call that Chapman allegedly changed his plea to "guilty," the initial plan having been for him to seek an insanity plea. Could he have been instructed to do so by a handler on that call? Indeed, he spoke afterwards of being instructed by "a little voice inside his head." (See the 1977 Don Siegel movie '*Telefon*' for further insights into how this all works.)

In more twists and turns than a game of Snakes and Ladders, Dave McGowan's book mentions that just days before Lennon's murder, Chapman had approached the occult film-maker and affiliate of the Church of Satan and Process Church of the Final Judgement, Kenneth Anger, (also a close associate of Beatles "rivals" the Rolling Stones,) and offered him a gift of some live bullets. In other tellings of the story Chapman is claimed to have said, "these are for John Lennon." The meeting is reputed to have happened in Hawaii.

This story is reinforced in several other books, including '*Rock Music: The Citadel of Satan . . .* ' by Alex Maloney, who writes:

> *"Six weeks before John Lennon was shot, Mark David Chapman was attending a film lecture given by Kenneth Anger in Hawaii. Lennon's killer met with Anger after the lecture and pumped (Anger) with questions about John and Yoko."*

In 2020, British former television producer David Whelan used his time under enforced lockdown to re-visit the fine detail of the Lennon murder, the results becoming his book '*Mind Games: The Assassination of John Lennon,*' published in 2024. In it, Whelan recounts Chapman's testimony given during his early days in incarceration, before the medical "experts" who would diagnose him as "schizophrenic" and "psychotic" would arrive.

Chapman's words read like those of a man who has had his thoughts tampered with, but still not entirely successfully. They are also consistent with the multiple personality disorder invariably brought on by MK-ULTRA.

> *"I never wanted to hurt anybody. My friends will tell you that. I have two parts in me. The big part is very kind. The children I worked with will tell you that. I have a small part in me that cannot understand the big world and what goes on in it.*
>
> *"I fought against the small part for a long time. But for a few seconds the small part won. I asked God to help me, but we are responsible for our own actions. I have nothing against John Lennon or anything he has done in the way of music or personal beliefs. I came to New York about five weeks ago from Hawaii, and the big part of me did not want me to shoot John. I went back to Hawaii and tried to get rid of my small part, but I couldn't.*
>
> *"I then returned to New York on Friday December 5th. I checked into the YMCA on 62nd Street. I stayed one night. Then I went to the book store and bought 'The Catcher in the Rye.' I'm sure the large part of me is Holden Caulfield, who is the main person in the book. The small part of me must be the devil.*
>
> *"I went to the building ... I stayed there until he came out and asked him to sign my album. At that time my big part won and I wanted to go back to my hotel, but I couldn't. I waited until he came back. He came in a car. Yoko passed first and I said hello. I didn't want to hurt her. Then John came ... I took the gun from my coat pocket and fired at him. I can't believe I could do that.*

"I just stood there clutching the book. I didn't want to run away. I don't know what happened to the gun, I just remember Jose kicking it away. Jose was crying and telling me to please leave. I felt so sorry for Jose. Then the police came and told me to put my hands on the wall and cuffed me."

The "Jose" he refers to was Jose Perdomo, the doorman working at the Dakota's main entrance that night. A claim has persisted for years that he was in fact a black-ops assassin on the payroll of the CIA who had infiltrated the Dakota staff, and the excellent researcher Ole Dammegard has pointed out that an individual with such a name was part of a crack team known as Operation 40, which was involved in many unofficially sanctioned projects including, but by no means limited to, the Bay of Pigs invasion in Cuba.

According to this line of thinking, it was actually this Perdomo who slayed Lennon; Chapman had merely been programmed to *believe* that he had done it and to therefore take the rap.

Though official reports maintain that Lennon was shot from the rear, medical personnel who examined his body insisted that he had been shot from the front, adding weight to the "Chapman didn't do it" theory. So, when Jose asked Mark if he knew what he had done and Mark replied "I just shot John Lennon," this would have been confirmation that the plan had worked.

However, whether down to the secrecy with which the information has been guarded, or to the namesakes merely being a "coincidence," no verifiable evidence has come to light to prove that the doorman was the same guy as the Bay of Pigs assassin.

Just as with George Harrison's normal security measures having been lacking when they were most needed, Whelan's book tells us that Lennon's main security detail, Doug MacDougal, had been suspended from duty until the day after the assassination by . . . Yoko Ono.

Yoko had been routinely in charge of John's security operations, which is about as reassuring as hearing that Jimmy Savile has been hired as the new child-minder. Even if MacDougal *had* been on duty that night though, can he really have been trusted to have prevented the killing given his own background as a FBI agent, and with his partner having allegedly been involved in the covering-up of the Martin Luther King assassination conspiracy?

The Dakota Building - if walls could speak...

It would be remiss of me here not to bring up the comments made to me by Ann Diamond when she guested on my '*Good Vibrations*' podcast in 2021. As well as having been a childhood test subject for MK-ULTRA experimentation at Montreal's McGill University under the psychopathic doctor Ewen Cameron, (where she claims she encountered a young, pre-fame **Mick Jagger** in the same facility,) Ann maintains that she was in a relationship with singer-songwriter **Leonard Cohen** for many years, and that Leonard led a double life, acting also as a spy in the employ of the CIA and Mossad.

Armed with this information, the lyrics to Cohen's '*In My Life*' take on a potential new dimension:

> "*I finally got my orders,*
> *I'll be marching through the morning,*
> *Marching through the night,*
> *Moving cross the borders,*
> *Of my secret life.*"

No-One's Dad's a Plumber

Ann says that, as well as being in London when **Jimi Hendrix** was murdered in 1970, (see '*Musical Truth 1*',) Cohen was suspiciously present in New York at the time of the Lennon event, (though Ann muddies the waters by stating that she considers that the Lennon shooting could have been a staged hoax:)

> "*There are reasons to believe that he didn't die, that he faked his death. I also think that Leonard was there that night. I think a lot of people were there, like with Kennedy. It was like a party, like a gathering. People got together; they knew something was about to happen.*
>
> "*He also spoke to a woman who told me that he came to see her in 2005 and he said 'I shot John Lennon,' and he said 'I did it for you.' And she didn't know what to think of that. Now, what I think is he <u>thought</u> he shot John Lennon, or he was there possibly under some form of hypnosis. But I suspect it was all some kind of 'double fantasy' game and that Lennon knew and had a double in place.*"

Certainly, as with McCartney, there have long been claims that there were at least two "John Lennons." This is a theory to which Mike Williams subscribes, and the name Colin Unwin, seemingly a musician born in Manchester in 1947, is one suggested for the actor playing Lennon in his latter period. But for the purposes of this book's findings I will continue to assume that there was only ever one Lennon and that he was killed. My mind can't handle another McCartney-scale mindfuck at this present time!

Lennon wasn't the only musician with whom Chapman seems to have had an unhealthy fixation. He also felt drawn to the American singer-songwriter, producer and musical boundary-pusher **Todd Rundgren**. Chapman was wearing a promotional T-shirt for Rundgren's '*Hermit of Mink Hollow*' album when he was arrested, and had left a copy of another album among the items in his Manhattan hotel room. Of that move, Chapman later commented:

> "*I left 'The Ballad of Todd Rundgren' in the hotel room... I can't describe what it meant. It was so poignant. I was always trying to get people to listen to him.*"

On this front it could be argued that Rundgren was the *real* obsession of Chapman's, not Lennon, whom he came to see as a "phony" in sympathy with the Holden Caulfield character.

Chapman's two greatest obsessions did not see eye to eye. One of the most headline-making aspects of Rundgren's career was his public spat with Lennon. In an interview for the February 1974 edition of '*Melody Maker,*' Rundgren began, seemingly spontaneously, complaining about John Lennon, accusing him of being a fake revolutionary simply out to make money, bringing up Lennon's striking of a waitress at LA's Troubadour club, and calling him a "fucking idiot."

Lennon penned a riposte employing his characteristic acerbic wit, calling his nemesis "Turd Runtgreen," which '*Melody Maker*' published in its September edition. Among John's caustic (and rather incoherent) comments were:

> *"I never hit a waitress in the Troubador. I did act like an ass, I was too drunk. So shoot me!*
>
> *"I guess we're all looking for attention, Rodd. Do you really think I don't know how to get it, without "revolution?" I could dye my hair green and pink for a start!*
>
> *"Anyway, however much you hurt me darling; I'll always love you."*

Lennon was just emerging from his "lost weekend" period spent in Los Angeles which had involved drink, drugs and unruly behaviour. He had been in an intimate relationship with May Pang, his and Yoko's secretary, something Yoko herself had suggested as a way of patching up their failing marriage! I suspect few other wives would be so accommodating. Very suddenly, Yoko summoned him back to New York, and a year or so later John entered his "house husband" isolation period in the Dakota following the birth of their son Sean in October 1975.

Some time later, Rundgren said:

"John and I realised we were being used, and I got a phone call from him one day and we just said, 'let's drop this now'."

The episode certainly did Rundgren's subsequent career no harm, it still being brought up by fans and interviewers several decades on.

Resources:

George Harrison book revealed Beatles musician's sarcastic response after being stabbed 40 times:

- https://www.independent.co.uk/arts-entertainment/music/news/george-harrison-death-cause-beatles-b2456658.html

The Guardian: The disappeared: Chicago police detain Americans at abuse-laden 'black site':

- https://www.theguardian.com/us-news/2015/feb/24/chicago-police-detain-americans-black-site

David Whelan on Substack:

- https://davidwhelan.substack.com/p/mark-chapman-unplugged

Book Review: Mind Games: The Assassination of John Lennon :

- https://libcom.org/article/book-review-mind-games-assassination-john-lennon

Daily Mail: Could the man jailed for John Lennon's murder be INNOCENT?:

- https://www.dailymail.co.uk/news/article-11995191/The-man-jailed-John-Lennons-murder-INNO-CENT-claims-bombsehll-documentary.html

Read John Lennon's hilariously bitchy letter to Todd Rundgren:

- https://faroutmagazine.co.uk/john-lennon-bitchy-letter-todd-rundgren/

John Lennon on 'The End of The Lost Weekend':

- https://www.johnlennon.com/news/john-lennon-on-the-end-of-the-lost-weekend/

The Ballad of Mark Chapman and Obsession With Todd Rundgren:

- https://www.kindamuzik.net/features/article.shtml@id=8099.html

John WINston Lennon = Colin UnWIN:

- https://www.youtube.com/watch?v=sEMLHfYHpFY

Good Vibrations Podcast #231 — Ann Diamond — MK-Ultra & Leonard Cohen

- https://www.spreaker.com/episode/gvp-231-ann-diamond-mk-ultra-leonard-cohen--52714510

CHAPTER 6

ALL IS MIND

As previously surmised — and it's not as if there's any shortage of evidence — music and entertainment and the presence of mind-control go hand-in-hand. Programming is applied to many, if not all most household-name artists to ensure they stay "on-script," performing on-cue and pushing many an agenda in the process.

> "Through the wall something's breaking,
> Wearing white as you're walking,
> Down the street of my soul."
> Laura Branigan: 'Self Control'

> "Remember, some of the most celebrated artists are born into the industry starting with a programme; they suffer ritual abuse and trauma in order to pass that same trauma and abuse to the fans that worship them. Almost every artist is an actor of some sort, passing along a message they were told to slip into the songs they distribute."
> Electric Being in an Instagram post, 2024.

As MK-ULTRA mind-control survivor Cathy O'Brien commented in her 2025 interview with me:

> "It's a slave society agenda and mind-control is key. Mind-control is a scientific formula — whether it's of an individual, a nation, a classroom, a military, or the world."

This being the case, there is no way that the man considered the first rock 'n' roll superstar, **Elvis Presley**, would have been allowed to have had the prolific and influential career that he did without being kept on an extremely tight proverbial leash. Suspicion in this regard has to fall on his manager, "Colonel" Tom Parker. "Manager" is often a euphemism for "handler."

Parker's real name was Andreas Cornelis van Kuijk, and much ambiguity arises regarding his background. He was Dutch, and is said to have arrived in the United States "illegally" when he was 20 years old. There are large gaps in his official biography. The honorary "Colonel" tag is said to have been given by Jimmie David when Parker had assisted him to become governor of Louisiana.

Though it seems highly likely that Elvis himself was mind-controlled, the same may also be true of Parker, since handlers often undergo programming themselves. Parker underwent two years of military service in the 64th Coast Artillery at Fort Shafter, Hawaii, (see Chapter 4 for more of suspicion on Hawaii,) and shortly afterwards re-enlisted at Fort Barrancas, Florida. His biography tells us that:

> *"He was punished with solitary confinement, from which he emerged with a psychosis that led him to spend two months in a mental hospital. His condition caused him to be discharged from the army."*

Solitary confinement is one of the techniques used in MK-ULTRA, and those of us fortunate enough to have never undergone it can only imagine the effects it has on the mind.

A key promotional picture of Presley and Parker together has a portrait of two dogs mounted on the wall behind. The larger of the dogs appears to be a representation of "Nipper," the emblem of the HMV brand. The smaller dog is wearing a top hat.

Is it possible that this widely-circulated photograph could be offering us a clue?

Operation Top Hat was a project conducted by the United States Army Chemical Corps at Fort McClellan, Alabama in 1953. It involved the testing of biological and chemical warfare methods, with army personnel used as test subjects.

We can only speculate without firm evidence, but could Parker have been subjected to something similar to Top Hat/ MK-ULTRA prior to his "discovering" Elvis in 1953, and could the picture represent him as being subservient to RCA, the label to which he signed Presley?

Agent Elvis?

Elvis is said to have died on 16th August 1977, aged 42. In 2024 the researcher Ole Dammegard, who specialises in exposing state-organised psychological operations and assassinations, released a webinar in which he proposed that Elvis was actually a secret DEA-agent appointed by President Richard Nixon, his status as a travelling performer acting as the perfect cover for spy operations. Curiously, this very idea formed the narrative of an animated Netflix series which aired in 2023 titled '*Agent Elvis.*' The show was co-produced by Elvis' ex-wife Priscilla.

Agent Elvis?

https://picryl.com/media/elvis-presley-recording-artist-actor-460976

Reportedly, Elvis was a patriot who was heavy on law enforcement and concerned about America's social descent, not least through the avalanche of street drugs coming through organised crime networks, and so volunteered for the role. His focus fell on the Chicago mobster Sam Giancana, and Carlos Gambino of the notorious Gambino crime family, both of whom are said to have been involved in the JFK assassination.

When the Mob began to suspect a mole in their network, suspicion first fell on **Frank Sinatra**. A hit was ordered on him, but miscommunication resulted in Frank's mother being taken out instead when a private plane she was travelling on crashed into a mountain in January 1977.

Later that year, with the assistance of his colleagues in the intel community, Elvis was forced to fake his death and go into hiding. He may have taken on the pseudonym Jon Burrows. The numerous claims of his having been spotted in the ensuing years may not be so wild-eyed and crazy after all. (See **Kirsty MacColl**'s '*There's A Guy Works Down The Chip Shop Swears He's Elvis.*')

A popular internet rumour of the past few years is that Presley, having faked his death, resurfaced under a new guise — Robert Wayne Joyce, the pastor of a small church in Benton, Arkansas. One of Joyce's favourite activities is to sing in the style of Elvis, often performing his songs, during his sermons. According to some, he was present at the funeral of Elvis' daughter Lisa-Marie in 2023.

Joyce does not seem to have a provable back history prior to around 2010.

A common objection to the idea that Elvis, after decades in hiding, could have re-invented himself as Joyce, perhaps having grown tired of living in anonymity and missing singing for a crowd, is that Joyce appears too young. At the time of writing he was officially in his 70s, whereas Elvis would have turned 90. In this regard, though, we must remember that celebrities — particularly those who may be affiliated with military intelligence — have access to the very best make-up and alternative health regimes that the rest of us don't.

Naturally, "conspiracy" theories have circulated regarding Elvis' twin brother Jesse, who, we are told, was delivered stillborn 35 minutes before him. Some have speculated on whether Jesse could have actually survived and that both played the public role of "Elvis."

Jesse provided a source of morbid fascination for Australian artist **Nick Cave**, whose album '*The First Born Is Dead*' was a direct reference to Jesse. Cave also recorded a track titled '*Tupelo*' named after Elvis and Jesse's home town, and again referenced the dead twin in his extremely dark novel '*And The Ass Saw The Angel.*' Cave has been unlucky on the family front; he lost a twin son himself. Arthur and Earl had been born in 2000. In 2015 Arthur fell, or jumped, from cliffs near Brighton and died. The inquest found that he had LSD in his system. Another son, Jethro, his child with Beau Lazenby, died in May 2022 aged 31. He had been diagnosed as schizophrenic.

Jimi and the Prince

Another rock music name got associated with the world of military mind-control in 2024, when a woman named Rachel Caruso published a video in which she claimed that her uncle, Paul Caruso, was one of **Jimi Hendrix**'s main handlers. She alleged that Jimi was a multi-generational MK-ULTRA slave.

Though his official biography tells us he came from working-class roots, Rachel, (who says she was subjected to satanic ritual abuse by her family herself,) alleged that he was descended from an "Illuminati" bloodline, and hand-picked to be an influential counter-cultural figure. Hendrix was softly-spoken, shy and sensitive in private, she maintains, his edgy, rebellious image having been a carefully-crafted facade.

As discussed in '*Volume 1*' Hendrix was assassinated on the orders of his "manager," Michael Jeffery — in reality a British military intelligence operative. Though the general consensus is that it was decided Jimi was worth more dead than alive owing to the fortune to be made from his music catalogue, Rachel claims that Jimi had undergone a spiritual awakening and begun to unravel his programming, which had marked him out for removal.

She also states that stories of Hendrix's drug addiction were systematically circulated to cover up the abuse he received at the hands of her uncle, and the manner of his death. A link to her video is in the Resources notes at the end of the chapter.

Worth a mention here is the blog article posted by Sandra Barr on the truthseeker444 blogspot page from 2016, in which she lists a number of eerie parallels between the lives and deaths of Hendrix and fellow musician **Prince**. Again, the full article is linked to at the end, but to summarise her main points:

> "*1. Purple Rain/ Purple Haze. Both stars had a fondness for the colour purple.*

2. Prince was a Jehovah Witness, Hendrix's birth name was Johnny Allen Hendrix — JAH — which is one of the shortened versions of Jehovah, and one of his biggest hit singles was "All Along The Watchtower." The Watchtower Society is the name of the governing body of the Jehovah Witnesses.

3. Both men had serious issues with people and corporations within the music industry who were ripping them off, and claiming ownership of them and their music.

4. Both men were speaking out about political issues, and against the Establishment.

5. Both men were funding "subversive" groups; Hendrix was supporting The Black Panthers, and Prince had donated £50,000 to a 9/11 truth group.

6. Both men were musical geniuses who died under very mysterious circumstances.

7. Both men at the time of death, were taking their music in a more spiritual direction.

8. Prince recorded an album called 'Rainbow Children.' Hendrix made an album and film just prior to his death called 'Rainbow Bridge.'

9. Immediately after death, the mainstream media embarked on a global campaign to besmirch and defame their reputations. With Hendrix they said he had committed suicide, and that he was a heroin addict who choked on his own vomit while stoned. With Prince they said he had full-blown AIDS, and that he was a drug addict.

10. Both men were reported to be suffering from influenza just prior to their deaths."

Could they have shared another trait in common, in that they had both begun to break their lifelong mind-control and regain some of their memories, and were their fates the direct result of having achieved this?

Situationist Comedy

Genres and musical labels are of little importance when it comes to the industry's true objectives. Sure enough, two names from a completely different scene, but sharing familiar characteristics, are **Bill Drummond** and **Jimmy Cauty**, better known as the **KLF**, the **JAMs (Justified Ancients of MuMu**) and the **Timelords**.

As the first two acts, the pair had numerous hit singles during the high point of the UK's Rave scene, becoming the best-selling singles act of 1991. Drummond was the driving force, and no secret was made of his strong interest in the occult. The pair claimed that their output was inspired by '*The Illuminatus! Trilogy*,' three books by Robert Anton Wilson and Robert Shea, described as:

> "*A satirical, post-modern, science fiction-influenced adventure story; a drug-, sex-, and magic-laden trek through a number of conspiracy theories, both historical and imaginary, related to the authors' version of the Illuminati.*"

Drummond and Cauty embraced Discordianism, Dadaism and Situationism, the latter being an "anarchic" social movement with its roots in France, and concerned with re-defining what might be considered "art." Other notable adherents to Situationism from the music world include band managers **Malcolm McLaren**, **Bernie Rhodes** and **Tony Wilson**. Situationist stunts from the KLF included their dumping a dead sheep on stage at the BRIT Awards. At the height of their success they deleted their entire back catalogue, and burned a million pounds in cash in a boathouse on the island of Jura, Scotland.

While these *could* be considered envelope-pushing "anarchic" statements, they might also be interpreted as the actions of two individuals under extreme forms of mind-control ... or other occult influences, given their extra-curricular interests. The videos to their singles may offer some cause for concern, given the over-obsession with robed figures presiding over large groups, with cult-like overtones.

In many ways, Drummond and Cauty's antics represent a rave-generation reboot of the activities of the British punk band **Crass**. This collective were noted for their avant-garde artistic expressions, anti-authoritarian stance — at least on the surface — and political activism, and might therefore be viewed as having pushed similar agendas with the same kind of objectives. (An entire chapter on the possible ulterior motives of the Punk and New Wave genres was in this series' second volume.)

Crass were instrumental in establishing the Stonehenge free music festival, and the traveller movement (cult?) it helped to spawn. The group claimed to have been monitored by the intelligence services. If this is true, might they therefore have been recruited for social-engineering purposes?

Special Delivery

Popular music has long been used as a vehicle for delivering messages to the mind. This occurs not only through frequencies and subliminal sounds — whether backmasked or otherwise — but also through visuals.

There are few better examples than those offered by **U2**'s giant-scale performance at the Sphere venue in Las Vegas shortly after it opened in 2023. This was described as '*V-U2, An Immersive Concert Film*,' directed by Morleigh Steinberg and the group's own The Edge, (real name David Howell Evans.) Its promo crowed proudly about using "vibrations so guests can 'feel' the experience." With all the electronics involved there would have been a whole load of radiation from EMF frequencies flying around the stadium also.

The show felt like mass mockery, with words and phrases flashed in split-seconds from the massive screen. Among the more obvious ones were: "Hell; Blackmail; Doubt; Weaker; Napalm; Disease; Ignorance is Piss; Death; Who Cares; Danger; Pussy; Victim of Yourself; Sex; Fascist; Jesus Wept." And of course no such exercise would be complete without our old friend... "666." Great "concert," huh? Rock 'n' roll, baby!

What was happening here was the same process as when someone watches television for extended periods. It's fair to assume that the majority of those in the so-called "western world" do, which goes a long way to explaining how large populations can have their thoughts and behaviours modified so easily such as in, oh, I don't know... the Co(n)vid scamdemic, perhaps?

The flicker rate emitted from TV lowers a viewer's brainwaves into into an alpha state, normally associated with meditation or deep relaxation. They are literally being hypnotised, all the while believing that they are simply unwinding from a tiring day with some "harmless entertainment." This is how advertising works, and why corporations pay millions to have their products featured on TV.

What, then, might have been getting put into the minds of those at the U2 concert who *weren't* consciously aware of how this phenomenon works?

The controllers continue to exploit all opportunity for mass mind-control — and possibly black magic(k)/ witchcraft — presented by large-scale music events. Those such as the Super Bowl Half-Time Show, the Grammys and the MTV VMAs, plus England's Glastonbury Festival, and now even the Eurovision Song Contest, benefit not only from the audiences in the venue absorbing the occult rituals they have become, but also the worldwide TV viewers tuned in.

Those *not* achieving TV coverage are becoming noticeably more esoteric, meanwhile. As one of my correspondents commented:

> *"There's definitely a kind of cult indoctrination methodology to modern music festivals, particularly of the EDM/ Rave variety. You're trapped in a compound, often deprived of sleep and/ or food, you're subject to the extremes of weather and you're bombarded with noise that impacts directly on the limbic system, and is accompanied by light shows that directly manipulate autonomic brain function.*
>
> *"... Let's be perfectly clear about this: very few of those subjected to this kind of entrainment will ever become psycho-killers or demonic vessels. But a plurality — if not a majority — will eventually become passive, indolent and depressive. I'm old enough to have seen it happen before."*

One good example is the annual Coachella Festival in California. In 2023, three giant statues called "the Messengers" stood at the gates and greeted celebrants as part of an "art installation." This put me in mind of what is said of the bizarre Burning Man Festival in the Nevada desert, covered fully in '*Volume 2*,' attendance of which has become a rite of passage for those in California's IT industry. Of the artistic side of Burning Man we are told that participants:

> "...create all the art, activities, and events. Artwork includes experimental and interactive sculptures, buildings, performances, and art cars, among other media. These contributions are inspired by a theme chosen annually by the Burning Man Project."

Attendees of the 2023 event found themselves facing unexpected challenges when sudden rainstorms hit the site close to the <u>military-owned</u> land (hello??? clue??) named Black Rock City where Burning Man is held. These conditions were unheard of at the time, and smack of military-controlled weather manipulation technologies such as cloud seeding, (see the video to **Kate Bush**'s '*Cloudbusting*' for a great demonstration of how this works!)

The desert sand at Black Rock City is of a quite distinctive constitution, and the biblical downpours turned the ground into sticky, clay-like mud, meaning no vehicles could get in or out. This stranded attendees for many days, with dwindling food and water supplies and poor sanitation—a situation similar to what we hear of the mythical Woodstock concert of 1969.

A few managed to get out, including EDM producer **Diplo** and actor/ comedian Chris Rock, who walked through six miles of mud before being picked up in a fan's truck. British DJ **Carl Cox** was stranded there for days, but put on a brave face on his social media posts, claiming that everyone was having fun and making the best of things.

Were the Burning Man crowd being used as experimental guinea-pigs for a weather-testing exercise, with further social studies of their communal experiences being closely monitored? An open mind cannot rule anything out.

All 'Sirs' Together

I mentioned earlier the claims of Ann Diamond regarding Leonard Cohen having doubled as a Mossad and CIA spy. Additionally, Cohen's song '*First We Take Manhattan*' was reportedly used as a form of torture for Palestinian prisoners, according to Mosab Hassan Yousef in his book '*Son of Hamas*':

> "Through the thick steel door, I could hear loud music playing in the distance — the same tape, over and over and over again, I used the mind-numbing repetitions to help me gauge time. Again and again, Leonard Cohen sang:
>
> 'They sentenced me to twenty years of boredom,
> For trying to change the system from within.
> I'm coming now; I'm coming to reward them.
> First we take Manhattan, then we take Berlin'!"

Ann's musician links don't end with Cohen, however, as she further claimed that she got to know a young, pre-fame Mick Jagger at McGill, whom she knew then as "Michael." Buried beneath the layers of systematic trauma, she was able to recover memories of having been flown to London in June 1963 at the time of the Rolling Stones' first single launch. Perhaps the intention had been to pair her off with Jagger in an arranged relationship, before the plan was switched to Cohen instead.

She says that in April 1965, just after she had turned 14, the Stones began their first major North American tour in Montreal, at that time the Jazz and entertainment capital of Canada. At her mother's invitation, Mick Jagger visited their house one day, but soon afterwards Ann was taken back to McGill and given massive electro-shock "treatment" to try and erase all memories of the encounter.

Years later, in 1977, friends connected to the music manager Robert Stigwood curated a reunion between Ann and Mick. Ann feels that her interactions with Jagger may have inspired many of the lyrics in the Stones' famous songs.

Jagger became a 'Sir,' of course, and this prefix is an indicator of those who have served their masters the most faithfully. Another one is Sir **Cliff Richard**, (real name Harry Webb.) An early image of Cliff posing with Sir Jimmy Savile, and Savile holding a pendulum as if hypnotising him, has long given cause for concern. As has Cliff's unlikely association with the Kray Twins, and the homosexual/ paedophilic MP 'Lord' Bob Boothby.

In the beginning Cliff was marketed as something of a British Elvis, but in the 1960s, as rock 'n' roll's popularity began to wane, we are told he converted to Christianity. Was this a sincere move . . . or could it have been a carefully calculated one to endear him to a new audience of God-fearing blue-rinse grans, and to divert attention away from some of his more dubious links?

A Reverend named David Winter is known to have played a prominent role in Cliff's conversion, coaching him in interviews and behind the scenes at concerts. Winter wrote sleeve notes for Cliff's '*About That Man*' release. Despite this, he does not get a mention in Cliff's main auto-biography. A strange omission for someone who had played such a major role in his life path?

Unless Winter was cover for an individual named Bill Latham, who was the *real* guiding force behind Cliff's Christian makeover? Latham moved in with Cliff in the 1960s, and they lived together for around 30 years. Handler? More? Cliff and Bill co-authored a book in 1988 titled '*Single Minded.*'

Cliff and a man named Nigel Goodwin went on to set up the Arts Centre Group in Waterloo, London, for christians working in the performing arts. According to a tenant who lived above the AGC headquarters, Nigel Goodwin's office door was regularly pick-axed by groups of teenage boys, and the place ransacked. What might they have been looking for?

In a video interview to mark the 50th anniversary of ACG, 80s singer **David Grant** made the comment "talk about no turn unstoned," the reverse of "no stone unturned."

Stones are associated with freemasonry, and masons are known to communicate in coded speech. Might Grant's comment shed some light on the true nature of the operation?

Despite identifying as born-again christians, David and his wife Carrie have three girls who have all "chosen" to identify as "trans" or "non-binary." I'm confused. Does this not rather imply that their God made three mistakes then, and that mere humans are able to put it right?

David, also a Fame Academy coach, was awarded an MBE in 2019.

'Ye, Jay and M.I.A

It's fair to say that **Kanye West** has never been one to shy away from controversy. The mainstream has him down as being outspoken and eccentric, and has focused on many of his "epic rants."

The most infamous occurred during a concert in Sacramento in late 2016, where Kanye addressed the crowd for 15 minutes or so and appeared to be calling out Jay-Z, for whom he had previously worked as a producer, as some kind of mind-control handler. Following the rant, Kanye found himself being forcibly handcuffed to a gurney and led away for "psychiatric evaluation."

At this point, it should come as no surprise that this phrase is another euphemism for having programming topped up at the lab, and that Kanye ticks many boxes for having been an MK slave throughout his career, including his being placed in an arranged relationship with Kim Kardashian. The mainstream claims that he suffers from bi-polar disorder to explain his extreme behaviour.

Kanye may have been ahead of the curve in hinting at Jay-Z's crimes, since both his name and that of his wife **Beyoncé**, (another arranged relationship) got called out by singer **Jaguar Wright** and pundit Candace Owens in the wake of the allegations against **Sean 'P Diddy' Combs**.

Added to this was the accusation from singer/ rapper **M.I.A.** that Jay-Z, who had signed her to his Roc Nation management in 2012, was involved in a campaign to prevent her from seeing her child who, she claims, was stolen by the state.

Though British-born, M.I.A has spent most of her career living in America, and in 2009, tied herself in to "the Establishment" by giving birth to the son of Benjamin Bronfman, whose father was the former CEO of Warner Music Group, and who had ties to the Lehman banking family. The pair separated in 2012.

In early 2024, she claimed in on-line posts that her son was living with people convicted of sex trafficking:

> *"I'm not allowed to see my child for stealing food when I was 18, when I was poor, yet ur (sic) government is OK with my child being with family convicted for child trafficking and sex cults OK (sic)."*

And in further messages:

> *"Biden won't let me see my child. The longest processing is ment (sic) to be 2 months and it's already been that."*

And:

> *"My first custody battle was 2013. My child was four. I was managed by JayZ (sic) who ultimately was paid by Bronfmans.*
>
> *"... The day I was served, 4 (sic) my child, Rock (sic) Nation stopped all communication with me and all my emails to JayZ (sic) asking for help was (sic) wiped from my inbox."*

In interviews and posts, M.I.A., has made comments that we can assume would not go down too well with the Establishment, and might well lead to her "cancellation." Such as her stance in 2020 that she would "choose death" rather than take a Co(n)vid vaccine, her post two years later asking why celebrities pushing vaccines aren't made to pay for lying, that the rollout of 5G technology was extremely harmful to human health, and that her fight to regain her child involved:

> *"The entire cess pool of US government and all global banking institutions and now Israels (sic) war and military indusyrial (sic) complex and a bunch of pedos (sic.)"*

She claimed that she was denied a U.S. visa due to her support for WikiLeaks founder Julian Assange, and her calls for a ceasefire between Israel and Palestine.

Yep. I guess that would do it.

How Many 'Ye's?

The idea that there has been more than one individual playing the public role of "Paul McCartney" will be a familiar one to readers of these books, (understatement of the millennium) If one accepts that this dynamic has indeed taken place, and that the controllers have ultimately got away with it... are we really to believe they wouldn't have conducted similar stunts elsewhere? This state of affairs may have been going on more widely than even the most vigilant of researchers would have realised.

The "Joe Biden" that occupied the White House from January 2021, (in between tripping over steps, walking in circles, forgetting what realm he was occupying, sniffing childrens' hair and pooping his pants on the golf course,) did look markedly different to the Joe Biden who served as Barack Obama's vice-president during his first term.

You won't find many pictures of Biden from that period because most have been scrubbed from the internet, though you might find a British actor named Struan (an anagram of Saturn) Rodger, looks rather familiar in some latter-day pictures of him. His IMDB page is here:

https://www.imdb.com/name/nm0734654/

There seem to have been at least three **Madonna**s publicly paraded since 2020. One, who appeared in a photoshoot with pink hair and gripping a knife between her teeth, looked no more than 30 at a time when Madonna was supposed to be 65.

Another, who performed in Colombia in 2022 alongside singer **Maluma**, (in black and white-striped mind-control trigger trousers,) seemed more convincing age-wise, but appeared too short and dumpy, and was barely capable of even the simplest dance move.

The one who appeared around a table with fellow degenerates like **Lil' Wayne** and **Jack Black** to announce her upcoming '*Celebration*' tour in 2023 did look like the real deal, displaying her distinctive gap tooth. What the purpose was in temporarily using "doubles," therefore, is anybody's guess.

And so . . . back to Kanye. A video emerged in 2022 said to be of him sitting in his car, claiming that "Hollywood' killed his mother, Donda, and that the ritual sacrifice of family members is a regular part of A-list celebrity life. I can't disagree with the claims. The only problem is that this did *not* appear to be the original Kanye West. Fellow rapper **Jadakiss** may not have been joking, therefore, when he commented in an interview that:

> *"I've met five or six different Kanyes. The first four was awesome. The last two was a little bit . . . "*

There seems to have been a concerted effort to link Kanye's name with extreme controversy as, around the same time, he was said to have "sparked fury" by appearing in a T-shirt bearing the face of Norwegian black metal singer and convicted killer **Varg Vikernes**.

Mainstream articles reminded readers of Kanye's earlier remark that he would go "Death Con 3 on Jewish people," that he had made further "anti-semitic" comments, and that he had hosted an album listening event wearing a Ku Klux Klan-style black hood throughout, (so, to be fair, no-one can be sure it was really him.)

In an interview in late 2022, Kanye complained about the stranglehold that he said "Jewish Zionists" had over the majority of black music artists. When it was suggested in response that he should visit the Jewish Holocaust Museum, he replied by saying "they" should visit Planned Parenthood, ("our Holocaust.") Planned Parenthood is a eugenics operation concerned with population reduction. Bill Gates' father was one of the founders, alongside Margaret Sanger, (cited as a major personal influence by Hillary Clinton,) who, at the 1939 launch of her "Negro Project" wrote:

> "We do not want word to go out that we want to exterminate the Negro population."

An extremely helpful piece of output from Kanye — assuming it really came from him — occurred when he re-posted a message he had received from Harley Pasternak, who claims to be a kind of personal trainer, or mentor to celebrities. Harley had written:

> "I'm going to help you (sic) one of a couple ways. First, you and I sit down and have an (sic) loving and open conversation, but you don't use cuss words, and everything that is discussed is based in fact, and not some crazy stuff that dumb friend of yours told you, or you saw in a tweet.

> "Second option , I have you institutionalized again, where they medicate the crap out of you, and you go back to Zombieland forever. Play date with the kids just won't be the same."

Nice guy, huh?

Kanye — if we assume it was him — prefaced the re-post by writing:

> *"What should be obvious by now is that I was raised to stand for my truth regardless of the consequences. So I will say this again. I was mentally misdiagnosed and nearly drugged out of my mind to make me a manageable, well-behaved celebrity."*

Can it be put any plainer, and, apparently, straight from the horse's mouth? And yet *still*, the abuse of celebrities continues. When *even* the P. Diddy case hasn't caused public uproar and demands for the sick beast that is the current entertainment industry to be shut down... what will it ever take?

Resources:

LOOK WHAT U2 JUST DID TO THE AUDIENCE AT THEIR CONCERT INSIDE THE SPHERE!:

- https://odysee.com/@SixthSense-Truth-Search-Labs:0/LOOK-WHAT-U2-JUST-DID-TO-THE-AUDIENCE-AT-THEIR-CONCERT-INSID:e?fbclid=IwAR0FtTbn3u9skHKPeq1_mU-HqFCFD-6-NROwUSCHWvrFJ3ijXM26D0GKu2I

Ole Dammegard shares deep insights on Elvis Presley's mysterious death that don't add up:

- https://www.bitchute.com/video/3DX8PJ7u6aZU

Bob Joyce Age Comparison:

- https://www.youtube.com/watch?v=npobe1AuQak

Pastor Bob Joyce's official website:

- https://bobjoyce.org/

Pastor Bob Joyce denies internet rumours:

- https://www.youtube.com/watch?v=IGPTca3MBTI

Elvis & Bob Joyce — Who Am I Voice Comparison:

- https://www.youtube.com/watch?si=Oq62jFRel5VTAD-f0&v=RXeXWTwzKPQ&feature=youtu.be

Rachel Caruso — Jimi Hendrix: Mind-Controlled Slave:

- https://foxyfox.substack.com/p/jimi-hendrix-mind-controlled-slave

Prince, Jimi Hendrix & The Simpsons:

- https://truthseeker444.blogspot.com/2016/05/prince-jimi-hendrix-simpsons.html

Diplo and Chris Rock Escape Burning Man Flooding By Catching a Ride in Fan's Pickup Truck :

- https://variety.com/2023/music/news/diplo-chris-rock-escape-burning-man-fan-truck-1235712449/

'A Certain Girl' by Ann Diamond;

- https://www.amazon.co.uk/Certain-Girl-ANN-DIAMOND/dp/0557022932

The Arts Centre Group 50th Anniversary:

- https://youtu.be/tSH-D52SLEI

Cliff Richard's 'secret relationship' exposed: 'We had to keep a low profile!'

- https://www.express.co.uk/celebrity-news/1354239/cliff-richard-news-relationship-girlfriend-uk-singer-summer-holiday-book-the-dreamer-spt

David & Carrie Grant's three daughters now identify as "trans" or "non-binary":

- https://www.dailymail.co.uk/femail/article-9982455/Carrie-Grant-says-three-children-born-girls-identify-trans-non-binary.html

Cliff Richard pays touching tribute to Bill Latham:

- https://www.dailymail.co.uk/news/article-11586227/He-changed-life-Cliff-Richards-tribute-friend-manager-lived-30-years.html

M.I.A. shares anti-vaccine views on Twitter: "I got different kinds of receipts":

- https://www.thefader.com/2022/10/13/mia-anti-vaccine-alex-jones-tweets

Jadakiss says he's met 4 or 5 Kanye Wests:

- https://www.instagram.com/reel/CuswwsuO4C0/?igshid=MzRlODBiNWFlZA%3D%3D&fbclid=IwAR3CyDvobdZJj5z7dYcznlE3WglEc52AjTLUJWRiqlD3uYQ1hcS4qBCjgv8

Kanye West says his mother was sacrificed by Hollywood:

- https://www.youtube.com/watch?v=UYoFGnkqhfo

Kanye West rants about Jewish Zionists and The Industry:

- https://www.instagram.com/reel/CjyR-IfDJ8B/?igshid=MDJmNzVkMjY%3D

Vigilant Citizen: Did Kanye Expose Hollywood "Personal Trainer" Harley Pasternak as an MK Handler?

- https://vigilantcitizen.com/latestnews/did-kanye-expose-hollywood-personal-trainer-harley-pasternak-as-an-mk-handler/

Daily Mail: Kanye West sparks fury wearing shirt with neo-Nazi killer on it:

- https://www.dailymail.co.uk/news/article-12985107/kanye-west-t-shirt-neo-nazi-tribute-varg-vikernes.html

CHAPTER 7

SEX AS A WEAPON

Ritual abuse goes hand in hand with music and entertainment. It should never have been this way, but the evidence speaks for itself.

> *"Oh, father,*
> *If you never wanted to hurt me,*
> *If you never wanted to live that way,*
> *Why am I running away?"*
> *Madonna: 'Oh Father'*

> *"This kind of life,*
> *Wasn't meant for the good girl.*
> *Try as I might,*
> *In the end, it's a cruel world."*
> *Lana Del Rey: 'Hollywood's Dead'*

Trauma-based mind-control has an even darker and more disturbing cousin. The two go hand in hand and it can be difficult to establish which particular process an affected individual has undergone.

This is the world of Satanic Ritual Abuse — SRA. It's way more common in the "entertainment" world than the average punter would ever consider. It's so widespread, in fact, that it appears to be a required component for "success" once you cross a certain line.

Cathy O'Brien, an MK-ULTRA survivor and co-author of the landmark book *'Trance Formation of America,'* shed some light on this dynamic during my podcast interview with her in 2025:

> *"Trauma is the basis of it. And they found through research there's no trauma more horrific on the human mind than the sexual abuse of a child prior to age five when their brain is still forming. So additionally, occultism, satanic ritual abuse is way up there in traumatic events on the brain.*

> *"For the same reason they did it in the Disney movies right from the get-go. We imported the Nazi techniques into the U.S. Walt Disney was associated with Werner Von Braun, head of NASA. What does childhood fantasy-land have to do with NASA and MK-ULTRA mind-control?"*

The signs are easy to spot when you know what you're looking for. When you do, you see it everywhere. As the mystic, philosopher and master freemason Manly P. Hall commented:

> *"When the human race learns to read the language of symbolism, a great veil will fall from the eyes of men."*

The Price of Fame

Perhaps we should start with the testimony of a woman who never did become famous, before we go on to study those who did. Her story gives an insight into the process that so many familiar names will have undergone.

Anneke Lucas was born into an outwardly respectable family in Belgium, where her stepfather was a village mayor. Unfortunately, Belgium, (as with so many other nations,) is infested with institutionalised paedophilia, as the public came to learn from the revelations surrounding the Marc Dutroux case in the mid-1990s.

Sure enough, Anneke claims that her mother trafficked her into a paedophile network where she was sexually abused. Those doing the abusing, as is always the case, were "fine, upstanding pillars of the community" such as politicians, government officials, judges and clergymen. The head of the network, she has said, was Paul Van Buenens, the Minister of National Defense and two-times Prime Minister of Belgium. When guesting on episode 96 of the *'Cosmic Matrix'* podcast, Anneke said that Van Buenens passed her on to a well-known billionaire:

> *"I would say that man took an interest in me and then had me mind-control trained in order for me to become his personal sex slave. He was creating a platform for me to be a famous French actress and*

singer from age nine to ten. I was being trained for those things all the time."

For whatever reason, she never became either of those things. But her revelations give an insight into how actors and pop stars are selected, created and systematically placed into the public eye, with mind-control in place to ensure that, in most cases, they become nothing more than puppets performing to a handler's cue.

Someone who would appear to have undergone a similar childhood to Anneke, but who obviously *did* become a celebrated pop star, is **Britney Spears**. The now-infamous 2003 ABC Primetime interview with Diane Sawyer, (linked to in the Resources section) gave a glimpse into what happens when programming temporarily breaks down. Interestingly, it begins at 22 minutes and 11 seconds into the show, (22 + 11 = 33 — masonic signalling?) and cruelly, the show's producers left the breakdown in the final edit of the show, then Sawyer moved the interview on as if nothing had happened.

Some years later, Britney was placed under the "conservatorship" of her father, James, in a story which reached the mainstream and did at least force the public into acknowledging that something was desperately wrong, if not with the entire industry, then at least in Britney's life. In her 2023 memoir '*The Woman In Me*,' Britney presented James Spears as a failed businessman and alcoholic who terrified her as a child.

The "conservatorship," which denied her freedom of movement for 13 years, seems a euphemism for SRA-style abuse, James having proclaimed "I am Britney Spears now." Britney was forcibly detained in "institutions," and medicated against her will, with every aspect of her daily life surveilled and controlled. Romantic interests were required to undergo background checks and blood tests, and made to sign NDAs and to disclose their sexual history before a first date. Britney wrote:

> "The insanity of this system kept me from finding basic companionship, having a fun night out or making new friends, let alone falling in love. It was just the worst thing that could possibly ever happen to my music, my career and my sanity."

After she objected to a new dance move suggested for her Vegas residency, she was sent to a solitary "rehabilitation" facility for two months where she was dosed with lithium, denied access to her family, and given set walking and sleeping times. She was unable to dress or bathe in private.

Britney seemed to hit the nail on the head when she commented:

> "I began to feel like I was being ritually tortured. If the idea of my being in that place was to heal, that was not the effect."

She lists socialite Paris Hilton and actress Lindsay Lohan as close friends. These two tick all the boxes for being SRA victims themselves, and tellingly, have both been in and out of "rehab." It becomes clear that "rehab" is code for a mind-control programming facility.

This has to raise a pertinent question regarding one of **Amy Winehouse**'s most famous songs when she spoke of "them" trying to make her go to "rehab' and of her saying "no, no, no." The song's co-writer and producer **Mark Ronson** insisted it referred to Amy addressing her drug and alcohol addiction. But, based on his family background, trust in his motives is a little thin on the ground for me. Is it more likely that the song in fact refers to a mind-control institution of the type to which Britney and so many others would have been admitted?

Alanis Morissette left little room for speculation when she commented in a 2021 Alison Klayman-directed documentary titled '*Jagged*' that:

> "Almost every woman in the music industry has been assaulted, harassed, raped."

She added that this phenomenon is even more ubiquitous in music than in the film industry, and that women fail to speak out for fear of losing their careers if they do, or of not being believed.

She stated:

> "It took me years in therapy to even admit there had been any kind of victimisation on my part. I would always say I was consenting, and then I'd be reminded like, 'hey, you were 15, you're not consenting

at 15.' Now I'm like, 'oh yeah, they're all pedophiles. It's all statutory rape."

In 2017, **Kaya Jones**, (real name Chrystal Neria,) a former member of the **Pussycat Dolls**, alleged via her Twitter account that members of the dance troupe-turned pop band were pimped out as prostitutes by record executives, plied with drugs, and forced to perform sexual favours as a condition of their continued success. Jones left the group in 2004 shortly before their breakthrough hit '*Don't Cha*.' Of that period she commented:

> "How bad was it? Bad enough that I walked away from my dreams, bandmates, and a $13 million record deal. We knew we were going to number one."

Jones further claimed that she had been pressurised into terminating her pregnancy when aged 19 if she wanted to continue performing with the group. Her comments clearly touched a nerve as, the following year, Pussycat Dolls' management sued the UK's '*Daily Mail*' for publishing her comments. In a scathing response, the group's manager Robin Antin described the article as:

> "Intentional, reckless and malicious...false and defamatory statements made by a disgruntled, unreliable and biased person looking for her 15 minutes of fame."

If Jones' claims had been an isolated incident perhaps Antin's rebuttal could be readily accepted. Jones repeated her claims again in 2024, however, in the wake of the allegations being levelled at **Sean 'P Diddy' Combs**, stating:

> "It's sad that it took yet another celebrity case to get people to understand the kind of exploitation that occurs."

The Rule of 13

According to many survivors of SRA, including the partner of one I've interviewed for the podcasts, the lifelong abuse of victims gets "topped up" in 13-year intervals. (Interesting that Britney Spears' conservatorship under her father was for 13 years, and Fritz Springmeier, one of the foremost researchers into this subject area who suffered a spell in prison in exchange for his efforts, has stated that "standard" "Illuminati" mind-control produces a 13 x 13 grid of 169 personalities.)

Those unfortunate enough to be born into a satanic family will take part in a 13-month ritual. The next will be at 13 years of age, then 26, 39, 52 and 65. Each, reportedly, is to entwine the victim further to dark forces, and on each, a victim 13 years younger than the subject is offered up as a sacrifice, representing the death of the subject's younger self. The 65th birthday ritual is a significant one as many do not live long beyond this.

I was told that each ritual is related to the five "I wills" of Satan located in the Bible, in Isaiah 14: 13-14. This is because satanists twist and pervert everything, so they work closely with the Bible to create rituals that stand for the exact opposite of what it expounds.

(It's interesting that **Paul McCartney/ Billy Shears** wrote and performed a song titled '*I Will*' (an identity clue — "I, Will?") for the **Beatles'** *White Album*.')

Survivors often find themselves summoned back to their families after years of being left alone, and having assumed they were free of their cult. Sadly they never are. This will be the case with many entertainment A-listers. My contact spoke of having had interactions with **Madonna**, who turned 65 in August 2023. This was during the period where various "doubles" of her — most of them highly unconvincing — were being paraded in public.

Where all this takes on a disturbing link to music industry activity is in a handful of pop videos from the 1980s. There will be many more, but these in particular came across my radar, and received some astute analysis from my SRA survivor friend and his partner, who has worked to systematically de-programme him, often at great cost to herself.

Laura Branigan: When "art" imitates life?
*https://itoldya420.getarchive.net/amp/media/
laura-branigan-c-1982-f7ba0b*

Their findings indicate that the video directors and those who ultimately controlled the artists, knew exactly what they were doing, all under the guise of "art."

Video Killed the Video Star

First off is a video I mentioned in '*Volume 2.*' The promo for **Laura Branigan**'s '*Self Control*' in 1984 was notable for being directed by a well-known name from Hollywood — William Friedkin, director of, among many other movies, '*The Exorcist*' and '*The French Connection.*' The video quite clearly depicts Branigan as a mind-controlled slave, dissociating from reality and interacting with various creepy characters, including a masked figure portraying her handler. Friedkin died in 2023 aged 87. Branigan died at the early age of 52 in 2004 of a reported brain aneurysm.

'*Self Control*' appears to be closely connected to the video for the 1985 single '*Duel*' by the German band **Propaganda**. Directorship here is credited to **Paul Morley** who was a renowned music journalist before setting up ZTT Records alongside producer **Trevor Horn**. This was the label which housed **Frankie Goes To Hollywood** and the **Art of Noise**, (of which Morley was a member,) alongside **Propaganda**. Morley married the lead singer from the band, **Claudia Brucken**, in 1985.

As my contact observes:

> "Both of the videos have the same theme. Both show D.I.D (Dissociative Identity Disorder) and sex kitten programming. In both videos the main singer is wearing a purple scarf. Coloured scarves are used right from the beginning to programme a baby and child.
>
> Different colours have different meanings.
>
> "Both run/ walk through a corridor of hands grabbing at them. This is them running through their mind and identities trying to take them. In the Propaganda video the corridor with the hands shows a child holding a baby doll, but at the end she becomes an adult, then an old woman. This is showing that right from baby to old age there is no escape from the identities in your mind.
>
> "Both feature/ focus on a flower. Flowers again are used in programming, and each programmer/ handler will use certain flowers in their programming. In the Propaganda video, when the usher drops the drugs into the drinks, she actually touches the rose on her tray first. The rose is the trigger rather than the drug. It switches identities. At the beginning of the video she steps out onto a rose on the ground.
>
> "Each feature a doll. This is sex kitten programming. In one you can clearly see the doll has a broken eye. In the other you only get to see one eye. In the Laura Branigan video, during the debauched dancing/ cavorting scene, there is an animal skin cloth. Again, sex kitten programming. These debauched dancers are probably representing different identities.
>
> "Laura's video goes from day to night programming. That's the host (day) getting taken over by an identity (night.) As she sings 'you take

my life, you take my self control,' she has a woman (an identity) stroking her hair."

Decades on, the same depictions of hands reaching out to molest their victims appeared in the video to the song '*Hypnotized*' (!) by the electronic dance music producer **Anyma** featuring vocals by British singer **Ellie Goulding**. Most of the video focuses on Goulding's face as it becomes blatantly obvious that it symbolises her mental breakdown under trauma inflicted by a handler. As well as the sea of hands, (with single eyes embedded in them,) we see her head being fractured into different compartments until she literally "gives birth" to a new version of herself hatching from the top of her head. Can it get any more blatant?

This video formed part of a new "futuristic multimedia experience" for Las Vegas' creepy Sphere venue, its exterior at the time dressed up to show a giant single eyeball surveying the city. The intention of the "immersive" experience would have been to immerse those in attendance in forms of mass mind-control themselves. '*Vigilant Citizen*' published an excellent article in 2025 breaking down more of the symbolism, which is linked to in the Resources section at the end.

A video equally deserving of such precise analysis is that of '*It's A Hard Life,*' the 1984 single by **Queen** from their '*The Works*' album. Directorship here is credited to Tim Pope who comes with a suspect résumé. Emerging from a banking family and having attended various upper-crust schools, he got featured early on in London's '*Evening Standard,*' (you know, like you do,) who presented him as "Tim Pope, aged seventeen, who wants to be a film director." He went on to work with HyVision, a company which trained high-profile politicians in how to conduct themselves in TV interviews, thus cementing his Establishment credentials.

The Queen video — said to be Freddie's idea in homage to the 'Pagliacci' opera — takes place in what appears to be a Rothschild-style mansion with an "*Eyes Wide Shut*"-style "elite" masked ball in full effect. (These really happen; do a Google Image search using the phrase "rothschild ball 1972" for some interesting results!) The band have remarked that they hated making this video and that it remains something of an embarrassment. They joked that **Freddie Mercury**'s red costume, aligned with several single eyes, made him look like a giant prawn. Jokes aside, there are some unsettling themes going on, as my contact further elucidates:

> "Right at the beginning the scene is set with the stairs in the shape/ form of a ziggurat temple. At the bottom of the stairs, in line with the blood flow, is a marked-out square on the chequered floor. This represents a portal.
>
> "Freddie's red costume is covered in eyes. Yes, you can look at it as the 'all-seeing eye,' but it's more likely to represent 'all eyes are on/ watching you.' He has pheasant feathers. These represent renewal and resurrection, the balance between the physical and spiritual worlds. Pheasant feathers are often used in ceremonial dress and religious rites. At 41 seconds Freddie turns to walk down the stairs. This side of his costume represents a slashed/ cut (sacrificial) body with strands of blood flowing.

There is much more analysis of the ritualistic elements of these scenes to be had. However, one element of my survivor friend's breakdown chilled me to the bone.

> "At 2:51 a woman in black, the High Queen witch, who until now has been sitting on the balcony watching the proceedings, comes down the stairs, and the camera zooms in to focus on her foot treading and pushing down on Freddie's foot. I noticed this straight away as very significant. It represents 'you cannot run and escape.' I think this was the sign, to those in the know, that Freddie was destined to be sacrificed."

The following year, Freddie put in his career-defining performance at the Live Aid concert, but was reportedly already ill. He died in November 1991 after several years of gradual wasting away. We are told he became a victim of HIV/ AIDS, but many researchers suspect victims of this "gay plague" to in fact have died from the "side-effects" (so, effects then,) of the pharmaceutical drugs, (not least the one known as AZT,) administered to "treat" the "virus."

In summing up:

> "*This is, to us, a full depiction of a satanic ritual and party, and the people who know, would know!*"

Altered States

A video from four years' previous depicts a very similar scenario. In the Mike Mansfield and **Adam Ant**-directed promo for **Adam & The Ants**' UK number one single '*Prince Charming*,' Adam acts out the rags-to-riches story of Cinderella, being transformed from a lowly servant to a dandy prince when the Fairy Godmother appears and waves her wand. This represents his dissociating and switching personalities.

The Godmother is portrayed by British actress Diana Dors, (real name Diana Fluck from Swindon,) who was marketed by her first husband Dennis Hamilton as something of a British version of Marilyn Monroe, in the same sexy "blonde bombshell" vein.

This is another representation of Beta Sex Kitten programming, one of many derivatives of MK-ULTRA. Diana was portrayed on the iconic sleeve to the Beatles' '*Sgt. Pepper*' album. She is on the right-hand side of the picture close to actress Shirley Temple. This has been interpreted as them symbolising the doors ("Dors") to the "temple" in yet more masonic communication from this most intricate of images. Dors died three years after this video, in 1984, of cancer.

The mansion setting has a black-and-white chequered floor, again suggesting the involvement of freemasonry. There are more masked ball guests straight out of '*Eyes Wide Shut*.' At the end of the video Adam is seen shattering a mirror. Broken mirrors, or windows, represent the fractured mind of the subject, allowing for the programming-in of different personalities or "alters" by a skilled handler.

He morphs rapidly into three celebrities — Clint Eastwood, Rudolph Valentino and **Alice Cooper** — then back to his dandy prince persona. (In the original version of the video he also becomes Marlon Brando's '*Godfather*' character, but for some reason this was cut from the main version in circulation.)

We are being told that Adam, (real name Stuart Goddard) is dissociative. The official story to explain his erratic behaviour, which has resulted in spells in "mental institutions," is that he suffers from bi-polar disorder, but to my thinking this is far more likely to be down to programming. His father, Leslie Goddard, had served in the Royal Air Force, (check!) In 1987 he was jailed for two years, and accused of having been a part of a paedophile network which also involved Jimmy Savile, (check!) At the time, Leslie lived in Pimlico, close to the Dolphin Square apartments where the VIP child abuse ring is said to have been based.

Adam's mother, meanwhile, was a domestic cleaner, and among her various clients was... **Paul McCartney**! Nothing unusual about that, of course. Adam *just happened* to "bump into" Paul in the studio while recording an album and had a picture taken with him. You know, like you do.

Those paying attention were getting handed a major clue when singer **Hazell O'Connor**'s career was kick-started with her central role in the Brian Gibson-directed movie '*Breaking Glass*' in 1980. Curiously, Dodi Al-Fayed is listed as one of the co-producers. The narrative depicts the brief rise to fame, followed by the spiralling into psychosis, of a singer in a post-punk band. Can the character's last name of Crowley really be put down to just random choice?! The story depicts how artists are utterly under the control of managers/ handlers, and how mental illness is often the inevitable result. The title speaks for itself in terms of mind-dissociation. Hazell herself seems to have been the product of trauma, having been raped in Morocco when she was 17.

In the video to the main song from the film, '*The 8th Day*,' O'Connor appears to pay homage to the Transhumanist robot from Fritz Lang's 1927 movie '*Metropolis*.' The song, penned by Hazell, seems to demonstrate knowledge of Theosophical teachings and is sung from the point of view of a demi-god, (Demiurge?) who wishes to create a new, technologically-based reality, with lyrics like:

> "*In our image, let's make robots for our slaves.*
> *Imagine all the time that we can save.*
> *Computers, machines, the silicon dream.*"

The technology then seems to turn on humanity — a predictive-programming warning?

> *"On the eighth day machine just got upset,*
> *A problem man had never seen as yet.*
> *No time for flight, a blinding light,*
> *And nothing but a void, forever night."*

She also appeared to be in a mind-controlled trance in the video to her song '*Decadent Days,* (alternatively known as '*D-Days.*')

More speculation, but a friend wrote in to question whether O'Connor's singer's character, with the first name of Kate, could in part have been based on Kate Bush, given that Bush's own career had sky-rocketed a couple of years before. I wrote much on Kate's life, music and career in the last book and she fulfills more tenets than most when it comes to a candidate for trauma-based mind-control. In a photographic book published by her elder brother, John Carder Bush writes of Kate:

> *"Under the costumes is my eight-year-old sister, still at the age when she believed Gandalf lived in a rock garden in Old Bexley, in love with her pets and beginning to discover that lonely world of self-to-be."*

A dissociated mind surely is a lonely place to be in.

Curiously, both Bush in '*Them Heavy People*' and O'Connor in '*D-Days*' refer to the "Whirling Dervishes," a group of Sufis who practice a form of physically active meditation. How would two young English singers know of such a group if not high-level initiated in some way? Spinning, or "whirling," is another mind-control state brought through hypnosis, (see **Kylie Minogue**'s '*Spinning Around*' and **Dead or Alive**'s '*You Spin Me Round (Like A Record.)*'

On to another telling video from the early 80s "New Romantic" era and, would you credit it — it's *another* one featuring an "elite" costumed ball with black-and-white checkerboard flooring! Hard to believe, I know. (Note to all music video directors — other designs of flooring are available.)

'*Vienna*' by **Ultravox** was directed by Australian film-maker Russell Mulcahy, an individual who is clearly high-level connected, and who worked extensively on videos for **Duran Duran**. '*Vienna*'s storyline appears to show a woman under mind-control becoming a programmed assassin. It begins showing a pale horse emerging out of the mist, symbolic of impending death. At the end, the woman shoots a man running after her as she moves towards a figure representative of her handler.

The beginning and end of the video show pillars, hinting at masonic links. A later video by Ultravox, '*Hymn*', depicts a Faustian-style soul-selling deal being made by each of the band's members in exchange for success in their respective fields. The video is said to have been directed by the group's **Midge Ure** and **Christopher Cross**. The sleeve to the single features a masonic arch, square and compass. If Ure is not a freemason I'm Madonna.

Besides Ultravox, Ure was involved in the group **Visage** alongside appropriately-named enigmatic frontman **Steve Strange**. Their best-known single, in the charts at the same time as '*Vienna*,' was '*Fade To Grey*.' Much of the ambiguous nature of 80s pop hits has been put down merely to artistic pretension, but with the benefit of hindsight and the ability to conduct and share the research, it seems most of it actually constitutes occult signalling. Only those schooled in secret-society and mystery-school teachings would have been able to decipher the symbolism at the time. These days any of us can do a crash-course and be decoding it in a flash.

'*Fade To Grey*' appears to depict a sacrificial ritual of the type conducted by the notorious occultist Aleister Crowley. He reportedly stated that once an entity is invoked through a particular ancient ritual, it stays a short while before it "fades to grey" and disappears. The lyrics appear to describe the fear of a sacrificial victim on an altar or 'platform,' ("one man on a lonely platform, one case sitting by his side, two eyes staring cold and silent, shows fear as he turns to hide.")

The 'case' is what the knives are carried in. It is said that the line "feel the rain like an English summer" should really be read "feel the *reign* like an English *Sumer*, an alternative name for Babylon from where the ritual originated.

Not quite Smashey and Nicey on '*Top Of The Pops*' any more, is it? I only wish it were.

The video was directed by **Godley & Creme** who had previously been members of the group **10cc**, and became the leading figures in music video production in the 1980s.

Steve Strange is another box-ticker. Born in South Wales, he came from a military family, (yawn,) before entering the London nightlife scene as the frontman for the Blitz Club in Covent Garden, the go-to spot in the early days of the New Romantic movement. He was the costume-designer for **David Bowie**'s clown-themed '*Ashes To Ashes*' video.

Strange died at the age of 55 from a reported heart attack while on holiday in Egypt. Interestingly, his real name was Steve Harrington, and this is the name of the character portrayed by Joe Keery in the hugely popular Netflix TV series '*Stranger Things*.' Strange/ 'Stranger'/ Harrington? Coincidence?? (There also turns out to be a DJ on the Soulful House circuit named Steve Harrington — not to be confused with Steve Arrington, the 1980s singer.)

A further great example of an 80s video bearing no relation to the lyrics, is the second to **REO Speedwagon**'s '*Can't Fight This Feeling.*' On the surface the song is a romantic ballad. Why, then, does it hint at lifelong SRA, the video beginning with a baby, then showing him growing to a boy, a teenager, a young adult, a married man spawning a child of his own, then an old man? Perhaps the lyrics refer to the complex relationship between the host and the core personality of an SRA victim, rather than to an emotional relationship?

There's nothing horrific to be seen, but the motifs all have meaning — an abundance of teddy bears and dolls, creepy figures with translucent faces, then the old man walking through a doorway at the end, symbolising one of the doorways of a fractured mind. This video was directed by John Jopson, who has also worked on Hollywood movies.

A handful of music videos feature — for no apparent reason — children being kept in cages. One is the Simon Milne-directed visual for **Duran Duran**'s '*Union of the Snake.*' A far more alarming one is the video for German metal band **Rammstein**'s song '*Engel,*' (meaning "angel" — what kind?!) In this one the children, who mouth the lyrics to the song, have panda-style black rings around their eyes. This is said to be a symptom of adrenochrome-extraction. What is this *doing* in a music video?

Attention of all the wrong kind was directed towards the band's lead singer **Till Lindemann** in 2023, when a number of women claimed that they had been groomed for sex during concerts. Reportedly, the group employs a Russian "casting director," Alena Makeeva, who scouts for girls to stand in "row zero" during concerts, marking them out for attending pre-and after-parties. Makeeva has posted pictures of herself with artists like **Nick Cave**, **Marilyn Manson** and **Iggy Pop**, and claims to have had affairs with some of them.

Director credits for the '*Engel*' video go to Hannes Rossacher and Norbert Heitker, known as "Titty Twister." (Classy.)

Bringing things up-to-date — just to show that the agenda really hasn't changed in 40 years — in 2025, **Lady Gaga** released her "comeback" single '*Abracadabra*.' The title should give us a clue, given that it's a favourite phrase of magicians and sorcerers, (roughly translated from the Hebrew meaning "as I speak I create.")

The song's video is loaded with dark occult and Kabbalistic symbolism, with Gaga even admitting to '*Elle*' magazine that it "contains a spell":

> "*The song has a spell in it. And I imagine that our negative backtalk or when people are hard on you in your life, the world is hard on you, that's almost like a spell. You can get seduced and you can start to believe it.*"

It's not as if viewers are not being warned. And it further serves as mockery of Gaga's claim, a few years ago, that she was tired of being exploited by the industry and was now going to go her own way and make her own independent statements through her music. That went well then.

Cathy O'Brien has her own views on why so many depictions of things she herself went through get systematically placed in music videos:

> "*So, these subliminals, which people are becoming more and more aware of now, affect the subconscious mind. When our conscious mind is distracted by trauma, or whatever — even harmonics, which is why music is used, it leaves the subconscious wide open to being easily-led and manipulated. Without a conscious mind filter, these subliminals*

that come in like that are conditioning the mind to accept this crime against humanity as something that should be.

"We have all been affected by subliminals, and the more we understand Neuro Linguistic Programming, the language of the subconscious, the more we understand that repetitive media narrative, like, three times and it goes into the subconscious, we get programmed, and our subconscious is what drives our thoughts, and ultimately our actions.

"So that sacred space there, we need to learn to keep a protection on it. and awareness is key. Knowledge is our defence against mind-control at all levels."

*

Clearly, none of this is happy stuff, and it can take a strong constitution to be able to look at it. But for as long as knowledge of SRA and the rest remains only within the realms of the "alternative" media, most members of society would scoffingly dismiss it all as wild fantasy.

And, for as long as that reaction prevails, the abuse continues. This is *not* what music is supposed to be about.

How can we *ever* move forward from this stalemate situation so that new generations can be saved from the abuse, and the perpetrators held to account?

Resources:

Anneke Lucas on episode 96 of the 'Cosmic Matrix' podcast:

- https://player.fm/series/the-cosmic-matrix/the-healing-journey-of-a-child-sex-slave-anneke-lucas-tcm-96-part-1

From 22' 11'. Britney Spears dissociates from reality on Diane Sawyer ABC Primetime show, 2003:

- https://www.youtube.com/watch?v=FyI6PTuLYgw

The Post Millennial: Alanis Morissette says she was victim of statutory rape:

- https://thepostmillennial.com/alanis-morissette-says-she-was-victim-of-statutory-rape?utm_campaign=6448712/23/21

Washington Post: Alanis Morissette makes multiple allegations of statutory rape:

- https://www.washingtonpost.com/business/2021/09/10/alanis-morissette-rape-hbo/

The Guardian: Pussycat Dolls sue Daily Mail owner over 'prostitution ring' story:

- https://www.theguardian.com/music/2018/may/23/pussycat-dolls-sue-daily-mail-over-prostitution-ring-story-kaya-jones

Former Pussycat Dolls member Kaya Jones claims group was a 'prostitution ring':

- https://tribune.com.pk/story/2500839/former-pussycat-dolls-member-kaya-jones-claims-group-was-a-prostitution-ring

Fox Nation: Ex-Pussycat Doll exposes horrifying music industry abuse:

- https://www.youtube.com/watch?v=fez-YdKhci0

Pussycat Dolls' Kaya Jones Says She Was Pressured to Have an Abortion While in Group :

- https://www.etonline.com/pussycat-dolls-kaya-jones-says-she-was-pressured-to-have-an-abortion-while-in-group-202572

BBC News: Rammstein fan Shelby Lynn alleges she was groomed for sex:

- https://www.bbc.co.uk/news/uk-northern-ireland-65843882

Rammstein — Behind the Scenes:

- https://www.welt.de/vermischtes/article245688134/Till-Lindemann-and-Rammstein-Behind-the-scenes.html

Rammstein 'Engel' video:

- https://www.youtube.com/watch?v=x2rQzv8OWEY

Adam & The Ants: 'Prince Charming' video:

- https://www.youtube.com/watch?v=9p__WmyAE3g

Ultravox: 'Vienna' video:

- https://www.youtube.com/watch?v=xJeWySiuq1I

Laura Branigan: 'Self Control' video:

- https://www.youtube.com/watch?v=RP0_8J7uxhs

Propaganda: 'Duel' video:

- https://www.youtube.com/watch?v=nnQ2zOmb6Hg

Queen: 'It's A Hard Life' video:

- https://www.youtube.com/watch?v=uHP-qgzUVLM

Hazel O'Connor — Decadent Days (1981 music video):

- https://www.youtube.com/watch?v=NWhK_UoxCVg

Hazel O'Connor — Eighth Day HQ:

- https://www.youtube.com/watch?v=O-c99rkQlV0

The Hazel O'Connor Story — Interview by Iain McNay:

- https://www.youtube.com/watch?v=eouVo9Y_Xs0

Former U.S. President Bill Clinton in an "Illuminati" mind-control trance:

- https://www.bitchute.com/video/jCaaXyEZMRs/

Vigilant Citizen: MUSIC BUSINESS Ellie Goulding and Anyma's "Hypnotized" Turns Monarch Mind-control Into a Futuristic Experience:

- https://vigilantcitizen.com/musicbusiness/ellie-goulding-and-anymas-hypnotized-turns-monarch-mind-control-into-a-futuristic-experience/

NME: Nick Cave's son Jethro Lazenby has died, aged 31:

- https://www.nme.com/news/music/nick-caves-son-jethro-has-died-aged-31-3221399

Vigilant Citizen: "The song has a spell in it": The Occult Meaning of Lady Gaga's "Abracadabra":

- https://vigilantcitizen.com/musicbusiness/the-song-has-a-spell-in-it-the-occult-meaning-of-lady-gagas-abracadabra/

CHAPTER 8
THE PRICE OF FAME

When comments are made about music "speaking to the soul" and "lifting the spirits," it pays to be cautious as to which souls and spirits we might be talking about.

Any conspirator looking to manipulate huge swathes of the masses would be falling seriously short were they not to exploit the amazing opportunities offered by entertainment and popular culture. These are the *perfect* vehicles through which to infiltrate the collective subconscious mind, and to insert messages which will go on to drive the thoughts, perceptions and behaviours of those susceptible to the tricks. Which, as all the evidence has shown, is the vast, overwhelming majority.

We're into the realms of the spiritual, supernatural and dark occult here which, regrettably, has always been part and parcel of the corporate music industry, and some on the inside would argue that getting such messaging delivered through stealth was the very reason for this institution being set up in the first place.

A mind which assumes it's merely getting some harmless fun and distraction with which to unwind and relax, is one wide open to being puppeteered by skilled practitioners. It's in the subliminal part of the mind — that which lies below the threshold of conscious thought, and therefore, informed analysis and judgement — where all the magic(k) occurs. (Aleister Crowley made the distinction between "magic" and "magick," the former being mere illusion, or sleight of hand as practiced by the likes of Derren Brown or David Blaine for showmanship purposes, but the latter constituting the manipulation to achieve, in Crowley's words, "the art and science of causing change to occur in conformity with the will.")

It's always useful when someone who has been on the inside comes forth as a whistleblower to reveal what it is they were a part of. Understandably, such characters are few and far between. We do have the testimonies of Lance Collins, otherwise known as John Todd, of his time working in the music industry to go on, (see '*Volume 1.*')

Though not employed specifically in the business, there are also the multiple revelations of Mark Passio, through the huge catalogue of work on his whatonearthishappening.com site. Mark was inducted personally by Anton LaVey into the Church of Satan, and was a part of other occult groups, before his conscience kicked in and caused him to leave and instead expose the plans of his former associates which had so shocked and outraged him.

A name we might add to their ranks is that of Zachary King.

He was born into a Baptist home, but started practicing satanic black magic(k) in the 1970s at the age of ten. He later became a satanist, attaining the topmost position of "High Wizard of the World Church of Satan." Despite this grounding, he converted to Catholicism in his early 40s in 2008, and, like the others mentioned, became a whistleblower, revealing many of the great secrets to which he had been privy.

In a 2024 interview with the '*Radio Immaculata*' YouTube channel, King related how, as High Wizard, he had been foremost in making *all* "pop stars, rock stars, rap stars etc," throughout the whole era of 1987-99. He spoke of the "Warehouse Deal," whereby wannabe pop stars show up in the warehouse district of Hollywood and Los Angeles. All are told that, if they want to be famous, this is where they have to go.

In the "Warehouse Deal," when the High Wizard enters, there may be thousands of aspiring pop and rock stars waiting. King mentioned that the official video for the song '*Like A Pill*' by **P!nk**, shows an actual High Wizard four times. The key question posed is: "what are you willing to do to be famous?" Here, the only "correct" answer is an unconditional "anything." Any other answer containing provisos is certain to result in rejection over a maximum of 12 months, in three-month stages when the same question gets repeated.

But if an aspirant gives the "correct" answer, the High Wizard hands them what is called the "Tier Two Card," which is a plain white card containing a phone-number, and tells them:

> "*You call that number, do what they tell you, and I will see you on MTV in six months.*"

Zachary mentioned that one such case was a musically-untalented young man whom he made a member of **NSYNC** or the **Backstreet Boys**, ie, of one of the two biggest U.S. boy-bands of that era.

King added that contemporary pop concerts feature actual demons interacting with the crowd, and in the performances.

His testimonies back up entirely the notion of the "Faustian Bargain," a trope associated with the music industry, just as with the Hollywood movie world, since its very inception. Those of a conditioned mindset like to chalk up the claims of artists having "sold their souls for fame and fortune" as meaning they simply had to sacrifice some artistic integrity, and bow to the requirements of their new corporate bosses, as a condition of their career.

As many a performer themselves has admitted, however, soul-selling occurs in a far more literal sense than a metaphorical one than many would ever realise, and the list of celebrities who have admitted to undergoing this process — usually with great regret attached — is endless.

Some such regrets are expressed in their lyrics, but many in throwaway comments given in interviews. There are more names from the rap and hip-hop field in the list than from any other genre.

Jay-Z's is a name which consistently comes up in this regard, with his wife **Beyoncé** usually included in the same sentence. Former NFL star Larry Johnson didn't mince his words when he commented on the '*Fearless*' podcast in December 2024:

> *"It's obvious they've been controlled by satanism. I'm not really scared to say that. We all know, Luciferians, Freemasons and all occult knowledge that was dragged up from Egypt, have now surfaced itself in American society. Obviously, they're not serving the same Most High God that I am."*

Johnson made the comments whilst recounting his having attended a late-night party in Colorado hosted by the couple, where he was shocked to see young children suddenly arriving at 11pm.

In early 2023, a former bodyguard of both Beyoncé and **P Diddy**, Ron Smith, commonly known as "Uncle Ron," publicly accused Jay-Z, his client's husband, of consistently drugging her to keep her under control. In a video message addressed at Jay-Z, he commented:

> "Hardly nobody know, but I'll say it, man. Yeah, Beyoncé's on drugs. She's been on them for a long time. And you keep her that way. Y'all worship what you worship to stay on top. But there's one thing about me, bro. I can't be bought."

Ron's video message was deleted from his platforms soon afterwards. But in September 2024, with the Diddy allegations in full swing, he re-surfaced on TikTok, with claims that Jay-Z and Diddy may have been involved with the murder of rapper **Notorious BIG/ Biggie Smalls** in 1997, commenting:

> "Jay-Z and Diddy wanted Biggie killed, bottom line. Here's a man that wanted to leave Bad Boy. He wanted to do his own thing. He mentioned several times that he was tired of being used and abused, that he was bigger than Bad Boy himself.
>
> "Jay-Z wanted him out of the industry, period, so he could take over and be the biggest Hip-hop artist around."

Within 24 hours of posting his video, Uncle Ron turned up dead, though his passing wasn't reported publicly until around a month later. The official cause of death was given as pneumonia.

Swiftly does It

Accusations of her pushing satanism and witchcraft through much of her on-stage symbolism followed **Taylor Swift** around during her '*Eras*' tour of 2023/ 24. (Her single '*Karma*' was released on 1st May, Beltane, 2023.)

Swift got promoted more than any other artist during the early 2020s, at one point being proclaimed "the most famous person in the world." For some reason, she had been deemed more important than any other pop princesses, despite being in her 30s, a good ten years older than most competitors, by that point. (The claim that she is the illegitimate daughter of Zeena LaVey, daughter of Anton LaVey, the founder of the Church of Satan, has not been categorically proven despite, arguably, something of a resemblance between the two.)

One claim of dark energy being conveyed through her concerts, came from a priest who performs exorcisms, Father Dan Reehil, who commented to the '*Daily Star*':

> "Even if her intent was not to practice any witchcraft or do any of the incantations, she is probably attracting a lot of demons to her concerts.
>
> "… That's where the problem can lie, because then you have these little girls who literally sort of worship her, who are now putting themselves in a position where they could be attacked by demonic forces."

Though doubtless coming from a place of genuine concern, Father Reehil seems to be missing the point that such rituals are hardly performed innocently or unwittingly.

A voice firmly of the view that Swift's shows were an accurate reflection of the music industry's true intent, was that of **Shane Lynch**, formerly of the Irish boy band **Boyzone**. In 2024, Lynch, having become a born-again Christian, gave an interview to the Irish '*Sunday World*' newspaper in which he spoke of the evil nature of the industry of which he had been a part.

He commented:

> "I think when you're looking at a lot of the artists out there, a lot of their stage shows are satanic rituals live in front of 20,000 people, without them realising and recognising. You'll see a lot of hoods up, and masks on, and fire ceremonies.
>
> "Even down to Taylor Swift, one of the biggest artists in the world. You watch one of her shows, and she has two or three different demonic rituals to do with the pentagrams on the ground, to do with all sorts of stuff on her stage.
>
> "But to a lot of people it's just art, and that's how people are seeing it, unfortunately."

His comments largely echo those of **Brian Harvey**, formerly a member of **East 17**, who has been outspoken about the sick nature of the music business for several years, and has stated that he is in fear for his life as a result of what he knows.

Souls Going Cheap

The soul-selling process was satirised by American comedian Trevor Moore of the collective The Whitest Kids in a 2015 video. Though obviously a spoof, the routine, depicting Moore's character entering into a deal in exchange for engineered fame, was completely on-the-money based on the testimonies of those who have gone through the process. (The video is linked to in the Resources section at the end of this chapter.)

In the early hours of 7th August 2021, Trevor Moore died after falling from the second-storey balcony of his Los Angeles home, aged 41.

I have been contacted by many former singers, musicians and producers since starting this work, all of whom say they have experienced the process outlined in the Trevor Moore video.

All of them concur that, once offered "the deal," there is still the opportunity to say no and walk through the door. The occultists only want those who are desperate enough for the rewards. The general view seems to be that anyone who rejects the offer, and goes away to try and alert others as to what they have witnessed, will simply be dismissed as "crazy." Perhaps this would have been the case some years ago, but awareness of these scenarios now seems to have penetrated mainstream consciousness, becoming the butt of many jokes.

Some mainstream flaunting of the concept came from the 1978 single *'Follow Me'* by French singer **Amanda Lear**. Though the official accounts claim the song is about a girl being seduced by "the devil," (and rejecting his advances on the alternative reprise version,) the lyrics make their real meaning quite clear:

> *"Faust was right, have no regret.*
> *Gimme your soul, I'll give you life,*
> *And all the things you want to get.*

"I'll sell you fame, merry-go-round,
Maybe to hell.
I am the key to your problem, so follow me.
"Unbelievable, maybe.
You'll have a new identity,
For a second of vanity."

In 2023, the song was chosen to accompany a worldwide advertising campaign for Coco Chanel's *'Mademoiselle'* fragrance, along with a one-minute video, but this did not feature the section of the song which includes the suspect lyrics.

One singer reached out to me to say that she had been brought from Australia to Britain, where she had been promised that she was going to be made "the next **Madonna**," becoming signed to Siren Records, a subsidiary of Virgin, in the 1980s.

She says she was sent to New York and Philadelphia to work with well-known producers on an album. She recorded two singles and videos which, she was surprised to see from the final cut, got loaded with "Illuminati" symbolism. When her controllers sensed that she wasn't desperate enough for the fame, she says she was promptly dropped.

At the age of 27, she says she experienced a mental breakdown, and only then realised that she had been a subject of MK-ULTRA and satanic ritual abuse. She came to discover that she emanated from one of "those" important bloodlines, and had been groomed from childhood to be a future pop star. It seems even those from the "right" families are considered disposable if they don't co-operate with the agendas set for them, or if the programming hasn't been effective enough.

Another insider confirmed that "parties" of the type portrayed in Stanley Kubrick's *'Eyes Wide Shut,'* (and, we are hearing, having occurred at many of the "freak-offs" hosted by **Sean "P Diddy" Combs** at his various mansions,) are a very real thing. She spoke of having been invited to one such event at a hotel, where young hopefuls wanting to get signed to a label were made to participate in "humiliation rituals" by having sex with industry executives. These are a condition of "success," and are invariably filmed for future blackmail potential.

It's a Family Affair

If claims of Faustian bargains and '*Eyes Wide Shut*'-style parties are too much for most in society to be able to accept, a subject area likely to receive even more scoffing dismissal, is the suggestion of the ritual sacrifice of family members in exchange for fame and fortune.

Just because it may sound "fantastic" upon first hearing, this doesn't necessarily stop it from being true. And being descended from an "important" bloodline family doesn't seem to negate this dynamic for many.

Celebrities certainly don't seem to be the luckiest when it comes to the untimely deaths of those close to them; **Mariah Carey**'s mother, Patricia, and sister, Alison, both died suddenly on the same day in 2024. No cause of death for former opera singer Patricia, who was 87, was released. She passed away just hours after Alison, aged 63, had died of complications from liver cancer.

In 2020, Alison had made the public accusation, via the New York Supreme Court, that her mother had taken her to satanic rituals when she was a child, and had allowed her to be sexually abused by strangers, leading to extensive post-traumatic stress disorder. She sought to sue her mother as a result.

Similar claims had earlier been made by Alison, and Mariah's brother Morgan, in 2017, when he had said that Mariah had also been present at such events during her childhood.

Alison's documents mentioned "middle-of-the-night satanic worship meetings that included ritual sacrifices." In an interview with '*The Sun*' newspaper, she further recalled:

> "*The ceremonies or rituals were always between 2am and 4am, and they weren't every week as far as I can remember — just certain dates... everyone would wear long robes with black hoods.*"

The video, (bearing no relation to the lyrics,) to Mariah's song '*It's Like That*,' is set in an "elite"-type mansion, with an '*Eyes Wide Shut*'-style masked ball in full effect, complete with a black-and-white checkerboard floor. The song was lifted from Mariah's 2005 album '*The Emancipation of Mimi,*' (her nickname.) The title doesn't necessarily reflect the way things turned out.

It appears that Alison had been passed over in favour of Mariah. Alison had commented in 1995 that she longed to be a famous singer. Instead, while her younger sibling basked in fame and wealth, Alison became a prostitute and drug addict.

I recall that, at the time, little credence was given to the title of the movie '*A Certain Sacrifice*' starring **Madonna**, filmed while she was still an unknown in 1979, but released fully after she had broken through to stardom. (While she may pass as an acceptable singer, Madonna's acting skills have always left a lot to be desired, making it abundantly clear that she didn't beat all rivals to gain her film roles through natural talent alone!)

As has been the case with many a music video, alarming signs can fly under the radar for decades before being truly recognised for what they are. And so it was when a 2023 article on the excellent '*Vigilant Citizen*' website, drew attention to the fact that the movie's storyline features a genuine sacrifice for fame and fortune being made.

As the article concluded:

> "*While 'A Certain Sacrifice' is an objectively awful movie, it is quite interesting from a 'historical' perspective. In less than an hour, the movie manages to put on screen several obsessions of modern pop culture, such as satanic rituals, blood sacrifices, sexual slavery, and very bad music.*
>
> "*In other words, it is a rather accurate reflection of the mindset of the entertainment world — a system in which Madonna became an important figure. Indeed, after the filming of this movie, Madonna would be known for combining shocking sexuality, (for the time,) and pseudo-satanic imagery — all of which were depicted in 'A Certain Sacrifice'.*"

Reportedly, Madonna tried to ban the movie from being released, offering up $5,000 to buy its rights, but unsuccessfully. VC speculates as to whether that could be down to the film's contents, going so far as to question whether it actually constitutes a snuff film, containing a very real sacrifice.

Her character, Bruna, shows clear signs of having been ritually abused, and of being a Beta sex kitten. She is shown being raped at knife-point by her "lovers" — a man, a woman, and a transgender woman — then again in a diner bathroom by the man who will become the film's sacrifice, a character named Raymond Hall. Dashiell, who appears to be Bruna's handler, kidnaps Hall and takes him to a theatre, where he is to be the "star" of a satanic ritual sacrifice.

As the VC article surmises:

> *"There are rumors of this scene being an actual sacrifice. According to a Reddit thread, Satanic Ritual Abuse survivor Fiona Barnett claimed that 'A Certain Sacrifice' is actually a snuff film. Some internet sleuths even looked up the actor playing Hall, (his real name is Charles Kurtz,) and could not find any information about him, leading them to believe that he might have actually died in the making of this movie."*

Who Wants It?

Something which still amazes me, is the relish with which some artists seems to have settled into their soul-selling roles. Though it could be argued that, were there any shreds of regret they would be reserved for their private moments away from the cameras — or that only those who had shown a genuine enthusiasm for pushing satanism, or had been adequately mind-controlled to have embraced it, would have made it through — still, I wonder how these individuals can be so devoid of the humanity and conscience which would keep the rest of us from ever being able to do things of the nature that *they* evidently do.

Billie Eillish, for example, wrote on her Facebook page in 2016:

> *"Why does anyone ever trust me lol im satan (sic.)"*

Rapper **Lil' Nas X**, when promoting his "Satan Shoes," produced by MSCHF and modelled on Nike's Air Max 97s, did so with apparent glee at being able to put his name to such a product. 666 pairs were released, and the early ones were marketed as containing traces of real human blood drawn from members of the launch team. *Who is OK with that?!*

Perhaps the most worrying indictment on where humanity's collective consciousness is at is the fact that the shoes, costing $1,000 a pair, sold out instantly.

A similar idea was put across in a 2021 video for the Premier Guitar platform, when musician **Steve Vai**, who had previously played in **Frank Zappa**'s band, spoke of "some of the fun, creative things you can do" before introducing his "DNA guitar."

This, he stated, was the idea of guitar manufacturer Ibanez, who wanted him to "mix my blood in the dip for this short run of guitars." He said he went to his local hospital and extracted vials of his blood for insertion into the instruments. He added:

> *"In 100 years, if they get cloning down and if they can take the pieces from this blood and take the DNA from it and clone me and make another Steve Vai..."*

Wherever and however the industry finds them, it would appear there's never any shortage of those prepared to continue pushing its sick agendas in exchange for five minutes of engineered fame, that has had nothing to do with any natural skill or talent that they may, or may not have.

On the subject of blood-infused shoes, meanwhile, it doesn't take much imagination to assume that the lyrics to an early song by **Elvis Costello**, *'(The Angels Wanna Wear My) Red Shoes,'* may have been hinting at the deal Costello, (real name Declan MacManus,) may have made for his own successful career:

> *"Oh, I used to be disgusted.*
> *Now I try to be amused.*
> *But since their wings have got rusted,*
> *You know the angels wanna wear my red shoes.*
> *"But when they told me,*
> *'Bout their side of the bargain,*
> *That's when I knew that I could not refuse.*

And I won't get any older."

Should we be concerned? Could these lyrics speak of Costello's own "bargain" and his learning to cremate his sense of care? Could there even be darker overtones through his reference to "I won't get any older," with regard to a certain substance occurring in the human body which is said to bring longevity and stave off the effects of ageing when consumed? (It begins with an A.)

The infatuation with this particular hue of footwear was continued by **Kate Bush** on her 1993 album '*The Red Shoes.*' We are told that the title song was inspired by a fairy tale written by Hans Christian Andersen, in which a young girl becomes controlled and forced to dance by a pair of red leather shoes. Bush's lyrics include:

> *"She gotta dance, she gotta dance, yeah,*
> *And she can't stop 'till them shoes come off.*
> *These shoes do, a kind of voodoo.*
> *They're gonna make her dance 'till her legs fall off.*
> *Call a doctor, call a priest."*

Occasionally, (though not often enough,) a well-known artist does us a big favour by revealing the inner workings of the industry based on their own experience. Researchers like myself and others can often feel as if we're banging our heads against a brick wall in trying to communicate such information, only for a recognisable insider to reveal the very same detail, but getting an instant "oh my God!" reaction from millions.

This happened when **Altiyan Childs**, who had been a winner on the Australian version of '*The X Factor,*' released a five-hour video in 2021 detailing what he described as "the world's secret religion." In it, he outlined the secret-society hierarchy which binds together not only all strata of the entertainment industry, but all other facets of Organised Society also. None of it was detail which had not been heard before, yet because his name came with the '*X Factor*' cachet attached, he was automatically guaranteed attention.

When being interviewed by Piers Morgan in the wake of her friend **Whitney Houston**'s untimely and mysterious death, singer **Chaka Khan** described the music industry as "demonic," stating, perhaps more literally than metaphorically, that it, "sacrifices people's lives and essences."

Dave Grohl of **Nirvana** and the **Foo Fighters** is one who would appear to have no problem with engaging in occult ritual. In his auto-biography '*The Storyteller: Stories of Life and Music*,' Grohl revealed that, early in his career, he had performed a ritual in homage to **John Bonham**, the long-deceased drummer with **Led Zeppelin**.

Grohl was asking for great musical proficiency, strongly aligned with the "crossroads" trope first associated with the ill-fated blues musician **Robert Johnson**.

Grohl wrote:

> "*The altar was set. The candles were lit. The ritual was prepared. I quietly sat down on the floor facing the makeshift shrine that I had constructed by hand with scrap wood and leftover model paint, cleared my mind of all thoughts, and began to pray. I don't know exactly who I was praying to, but I did know exactly what I was praying for. Success.*
>
> "*... There must have been some intangible, mystical element at play, I thought, and I was desperate to tap into that, so I performed my primitive rite with the intense, earnest conviction of a seventeen-year-old with nothing to lose.*
>
> "*The flickering candles at each corner of the board spilled their yellow light on to the cold concrete floor of my carport, illuminating the symbols I had drawn to summon the spirits that would guide me to my destiny: the John Bonham three-circles logo and the number 606, two emblems that held deep significance in my life.*"

The Devil's in the Detail

It seems a part of some artists' "deals" involves them openly pushing satanic symbolism in their shows. Whereas in decades past this used to be more subtle and below-the-radar, in the 2020s, it truly felt as if the industry's dark overlords had gone, "you know what? Fuck it! Let's go all-out and shove this stuff right down these idiots' throats. They're so profane they won't even notice!"

Sam Smith's performance at the 2023 Grammys, (sponsored by vaccine manufacturer Pfizer!) which saw him dressed as a typical depiction of "the devil" complete with horns, spoke for itself, and drew the ire of conservative politicians in America including Ted Cruz.

The video to her 2023 song *'Paint The Town Red,'* begins with **Doja Cat** removing one of her eyeballs, before dancing on the head of a horned creature as she sings, hinting at "the deal":

"Bitch, I said what I said. I'd rather be famous instead."

Dressed in a blood-red robe, she then cavorts with a Grim Reaper skeleton in a black robe, (the colours of satanism,) complete with a scythe, before growing horns and becoming an entity herself.

Florence and the Machine were selling T-shirts on their 2023 tour bearing the slogans *"Dream Girl Evil"* and *"Demon Daddy,"* along with an array of pyramids. To promote the group's appearance at the upcoming *'Dance Fever'* event, **Florence Welch** posted on her Instagram:

'They come to drink, they come to dance, to sacrifice a human heart."

At a performance in New York in 2022, a "fan" threw a fake severed hand on-stage, to which Welch commented, "thanks, I'll eat this later." In another reference to the Faustian bargain, the group's 2009 song *'Rabbit Heart (Raise it Up,)'* contains the lyric:

"You made a deal, and now it seems you have to offer up."

Then:

"I must become a lion-hearted girl, ready for a fight,
Before I make the final sacrifice.
We raise it up, this offering,
We raise it up."

Some years earlier, **Madonna** had performed at the 2019 Eurovision Song Contest alongside **Quavo**. Besides her act presciently "predicting" the "pandemic" and mask roll-out which would occur the following year, she was also wearing an inverted crucifix.

Though there are disappointing comments along the lines of "cool!" and "OMG, I love her!" to be found below such video postings, at least they are now being balanced out by more encouraging ones, indicating that the flagrant nature of what is now being passed off as "entertainment" is finally being correctly identified by many as satanic and ritualistic.

The controllers seem to feel the need to become more blatant with every passing year, and I'm *not* convinced it amounts solely to arrogant mockery. As they continue to do so, the veil they have so successfully held up continues to slip, and they expose their true nature for all (who choose) to see all the more.

Change the Channel

Certain songs have long stood accused, particularly among Christians, of standing as conduits for communicating messages. Indeed, the very word "music" is thought to derive from the Greek "*mousike*," meaning "the art of the muses."

In Greek mythology, the nine muses and daughters of Zeus, king of the gods, presided over music, song and dance. And according to some biblical interpretations, "Satan," or "Lucifer," (Christians often make no distinction between these two entities,) was in charge of musical choirs in Heaven before his fall from grace.

Two songs which have been endlessly analysed in this regard are, arguably, the two most played rock songs on FM radio stations of all — '*Stairway to Heaven*' by **Led Zeppelin**, and '*Hotel California*' by the **Eagles**. As well as both songs speaking of a lady shining light to show the way, both seem to offer similar messages about duality and choice.

In Zeppelin's:

> *"Yes, there are two paths you can go by, but in the long run,*

> *There's still time to change the road you're on."*

And:

> *'Cause you know sometimes words have two meanings."*

And in the Eagles':

> *"And I was thinking to myself,*
> *This could be Heaven, or this could be Hell."*

In '*Led Zeppelin: The Biography,*' '*Stairway to Heaven*'s writer, **Robert Plant** is quoted as having said:

> *"I was holding a pencil and paper, and for some reason I was in a very bad mood. Then all of a sudden my hand was writing out the words, 'There's a lady who's sure all that glitters is gold, and she's buying a stairway to heaven.' I just sat there and looked at the words and then I almost leapt out of my seat."*

More conspiratorial interpretations have been put on the song in recent times, suggesting it is foreshadowing the incoming New World Order agenda, or the new "aeon of Horus" spoken of by Aleister Crowley, and relevant because of guitarist **Jimmy Page**'s known infatuation with Crowley's teachings.

Could the talk of "a bustle in your hedgerow" and "a spring clean for the May Queen" be talking of population reduction in preparation for 2030 and beyond? And could the reference to, "be a rock and not to roll," be referring to freemasons, (stonecutters,) not faltering in their duty?

Eagles co-writer **Glen Frey** described the content of *their* song as:

> *"We take this guy and make him like a character in 'The Magus,' where every time he walks through a door there's a new version of reality. We wanted to write a song just like it was a movie."*

A less obvious artist to receive accusations of channelling occult messages from unseen realms, would surely be the housewife's favourite **Barry Manilow**. Yet, one of his most popular hits, a cover of a song written by former **Beach Boy Bruce Johnston**, and also covered by both **Captain and Tennille** and **David Cassidy**, appears to have been written from the point of view of what many would consider "the devil," or what Bob Dylan might deem "the Chief Commander."

The lyrics to '*I Write The Songs*' have parallels with a memorable scene from the 2018 movie '*Under The Silver Lake,*' where Andrew Garfield's central character encounters a wizened, apparently immortal old man, who claims to have been responsible for writing the majority of hit songs of the previous several decades, for which other songwriters and musicians had taken the credit.

The Johnston/ Manilow song tells us:

"I've been alive forever,
And I wrote the very first song.
I put the words and the melodies together.
I am music, and I write the songs.
". . . My home lies deep within you,
And I've got my own place in your soul.
Now when I look out through your eyes,
I'm young again, even though I'm very old."

It seems the closest we have to such a figure in contemporary times is the Swedish songwriter, producer and musician **Max Martin**. Since the 1990s, he is credited with having written multiple songs for a huge array of pop's heavy-hitters, first coming to prominence for composing a string of hit singles for **Britney Spears**.

In Episode 163 of the Christian-slanted '*LED Live*' podcast, the hosts make the case for a backmasked message being contained within Britney's Martin-penned '*. . . Baby One More Time.*' The claim is that the line, "when I'm with you I lose my mind, give me a sign," comes out when played in reverse as, "sleep with me, I'm not too young."

Backmasked messages are absorbed into the subliminal mind of the listener. Reportedly, the subconscious can discern messages, words or symbols in reverse; they do not need to be delivered in a linear, left-to-right fashion.

Sometimes, messages within songs can be missed for years, and it's only when their true meaning is pointed out that it becomes so obvious what they had always conveyed, and we can wonder how we ever missed it.

I've been playing and hearing **Soul II Soul**'s 1989 hit '*Back To Life*,' voiced by **Caron Wheeler**, for decades, and it was only in 2024 that the profundity of its lyrics hit me. The song's composition is credited to multiple writers, including, surprisingly, singer **Mary J Blige**, from a time before she had become famous, and Caron Wheeler herself.

Wheeler revealed that the song refers to a Near Death Experience she had undergone, where her consciousness had temporarily left her body, yet she had been advised by "spirit guides" that her time to fully pass over had not yet come, and she must return to her body and complete her "life mission." This despite her feeling indescribable peace and serenity where she was, and not wanting to come back.

This is a *classic* NDE scenario reported by multiple experiencers, and makes so much sense of the lyrics:

> "*Back to life, back to reality,*
> *Back to the here and now, yes,*
> *Show me how,*
> *Decide what you want from me.*
> *Tell me, maybe I could be there for you."*
> *Back to life, back to the present time,*
> *Back from a fantasy, yes.*
> *Tell me, now, take the initiative.*
> *I'll leave it in your hands until you're ready."*

In 1990, Wheeler released her solo single '*Living In The Light*,' which appears to subtly address her experiences further:

> "*Had to survive, living in the light.*
> *Had to stay alive, living in the light*
> *Have to survive,*
> *Living in the light.*

"... Stolen form the centre of the world, untimely departure. Somehow survived, living in the light.

"... Living in a light, (so bright had to guide you home.)"

Aleister Crowley: The original purveyor of the sex, drugs and rock 'n' roll lifestyle

Description: Aleister Crowley - 1929

Source: https://www.pinterest.fr/pin/670614200742066627/

Author: Unknown

https://commons.wikimedia.org/wiki/File:Aleister_Crowley_-_1929.jpg

You can Call me Al

Before signing off on this topic, (it will soon be over, I promise,) a quick return to the much-aforementioned Aleister Crowley.

On the cover of his 2023 book '*Marr's Guitars*,' former **Smiths** guitarist **Johnny Marr**, (born on Halloween of 1963,) is pictured next to a brick wall which bears Crowley's Thelema slogan "do what thou willst shall be the whole of the law," written in graffiti. Not by accident, I would suggest.

Toyah Willcox released an album and single titled '*Love Is The Law*,' in completion of the Thelemite slogan, in 1983. Of her extremely dubious past we are told that, during her time living and recording demos in a former British Rail warehouse known as "Mayhem," Willcox used to sleep in a coffin, (I'm sure we all have one lying around somewhere,) for lack of a proper bed. (One of **Peter Gabriel**'s theatrical tricks during his Genesis years was to arrive on stage in a coffin, in tribute to an earlier stunt portrayed by "shock" performer **Screamin' Jay Hawkins**.)

Another Crowleyian reference came from the naming of the **Red Hot Chili Peppers**' album '*Blood Sugar Sex Magik*.' ("Sex magick" was an interest of Crowley's through the belief that the manipulation of energy can be harnessed most powerfully during moments of sexual orgasm. Reportedly, no bodily fluid or excretion was out of bounds when it came to such rituals. I'll pass on that one, thanks anyway.)

Below the Radar

The two most common types of correspondence I have received since doing this work have come from concerned parents, worried about their son or daughter getting caught up in the industry's diabolical traps, and from aspiring artists feeling they have much to offer through their music, but bemused to hear that they'll never make it to a certain level without compromising their morality.

The old adages "there's no such thing as a free lunch" and "if it sounds too good to be true ... it is" didn't come about by accident.

My advice is for music-makers to, by all means follow their dreams, but to be aware that there is a threshold, above which they will no longer have a soul to call their own. This, undoubtedly, they will eternally regret. Decent livings can still be made in the lower reaches of the industry, flying below the radar, so to speak. Or better yet, through the wholly independent route.

I have been producing my '*Sound of Freedom*' conscious music podcast since 2013, which features meaningful message music from, generally speaking, artists who write, produce, perform and distribute themselves, or as part of a small, independent collective, with no corporate meddling in their content whatsoever.

What results is output often of equal, or superior standard to anything put out by the majors, with the benefit of the artist being free to express themselves in a completely authentic manner. Some of the songs I've featured have blown me away in terms of their lyrical and musical impact.

You can find the link to the complete Mixcloud archive of all the shows in the Resources section at the end.

Resources:

Zachary King YouTube interview archive:

- https://www.youtube.com/results?search_query=%22Zachary+King%22&sp=EgIYAg%253D%253D

P!nk: 'Like A Pill' official video:

- https://www.youtube.com/watch?v=JDKGWaCglRM

Radio Immaculata: Top Satanist's ASTONISHING Miraculous Medal Conversion w/ Zachary King:

Zachary King's website:

- http://www.allsaintsministry.org/Home.html

List of celebrities saying they sold their souls for fame and fortune:

- https://de.scribd.com/doc/110582344/They-Sold-Their-Soul-to-the-Devil

Trevor Moore — High In Church — Illuminati:

- https://www.youtube.com/watch?v=_574Rxxez2c

What Did Trevor Moore's Autopsy Reveal?:

- https://www.comingsoon.net/documentaries/news/1733139-what-did-trevor-moore-autopsy-reveal

You Won't Believe What They Did For Fame and Money:

- https://www.youtube.com/watch?v=Y1ByPgdH8h4

WHO ARE YOU COCO MADEMOISELLE? — CHANEL Fragrance:

- https://www.youtube.com/watch?v=AI-CwgHOCqc

Music & Witch Language: John Todd (Collins):

- https://odysee.com/@erinmoffett:3/music-witch-language-john-todd-collins:3

Inside Edition: Mariah Carey's Mourns Mother and Sister Who Died on the Same Day:

- https://www.insideedition.com/mariah-careys-mourns-mother-and-sister-who-died-on-the-same-day-88812

Independent: Mariah Carey's sister accuses their mother of alleged sexual abuse at 'satanic worship meetings':

- https://www.independent.co.uk/news/world/americas/mariah-carey-mom-sister-alison-lawsuit-mother-patricia-sexual-abuse-satanic-rituals-a9658656.html

Mariah Carey: 'It's Like That' official video:

- https://www.youtube.com/watch?v=uI2cwfluyNo

50 Cent Exposes Jayz & Beyoncé's Sacrifices For Fame:

- https://youtu.be/h8I6mpzAydw

A Tale of a Bodyguard: Uncle Ron on TikTok:

- https://www.tiktok.com/@official_uncle_ron/video/7189647436627856686?is_from_webapp=1&sender_device=pc&web_id=7439997407695472184

What Really Happened to "Uncle Ron"?:

- https://www.youtube.com/watch?v=vOTUQYYuZmM

Ex-NFL Larry Johnson claims children attended late-night rap party hosted by Jay-Z and Beyoncé:

- https://tribune.com.pk/story/2515559/ex-nfl-larry-johnson-claims-children-attended-late-night-rap-party-hosted-by-jay-z-and-Beyoncé

Vigilant Citizen: "A Certain Sacrifice": Madonna's First Movie That Ends With a Satanic Ritual Sacrifice:

- https://vigilantcitizen.com/musicbusiness/a-certain-sacrifice-madonnas-obscure-first-movie-that-ends-with-a-satanic-sacrifice/

Fact Check: Were the Grammys Sponsored by Pfizer?:

- https://www.newsweek.com/fact-check-were-grammys-sponsored-pfizer-1779143

Billboard: Sam Smith & Kim Petras' 'Unholy' Grammys Performance Deemed 'Satanic' & 'Evil' by Conservatives:

- https://www.billboard.com/music/awards/sam-smith-kim-petras-unholy-2023-grammys-satanic-evil-1235213736/

Doja Cat — Paint The Town Red (Official Video):

- https://www.youtube.com/watch?v=m4_9TFeMfJE&feature=youtu.be

Florence Welch thanks fan for fake bloody severed hand flung onstage :

- https://nypost.com/2022/09/22/florence-welch-receives-fake-bloody-severed-hand-from-fan/

Madonna, Quavo — Eurovision Song Contest 2019:

- https://www.youtube.com/watch?v=VG3WkiL0d_U

WAS LUCIFER A MUSICIAN? — The Teaching Psalmist Episode 6:

- https://www.youtube.com/watch?v=BEZ3qzKVElY

Song Facts: Stairway To Heaven by Led Zeppelin:

- https://www.songfacts.com/facts/led-zeppelin/stairway-to-heaven

CONVERSATIONS WITH DON HENLEY AND GLENN FREY by Cameron Crowe, August 2003:

- http://www.theuncool.com/journalism/the-very-best-of-the-eagles/

"I'm a human fax machine." Spirits telling artists what to write | LED Live • EP163:

- https://www.youtube.com/watch?v=l0DQmO62oRA

Altiyan Childs exposes freemasonry on the entertainment business:

- https://www.youtube.com/watch?v=6twHgHjHUek

Chaka Khan Reveals Dark Secrets of the Music Industry:

- https://www.youtube.com/watch?v=raOPADUCom4

Premier Guitar: Steve Vai Rig Rundown Trailer:

- https://www.facebook.com/watch/?extid=CL-UNK-UNK-UNK-IOS_GK0T-GK1C&v=925327898240785

Controversy Surrounds Taylor Swift's Eras World Tour with Accusations of Satanic and Witchcraft:

- https://youtu.be/fTKdNYCmk5o

Boyzone's Shane Lynch accuses Taylor Swift of performing demonic rituals at concerts:

- https://www.independent.co.uk/arts-entertainment/music/news/taylor-swift-boyzone-shane-lynch-satan-b2503007.html

Boyzone's Shane Lynch: 'The music industry is Satanic':

- https://www.premierchristianity.com/features/boyzones-shane-lynch-the-music-industry-is-satanic/16349.article

Caron Wheeler reveals 'Back to Life' was about her Near Death Experince:

- https://www.facebook.com/reel/865574035346398

Lyrics: Soul II Soul Featuring Caron Wheeler: Back to Life (However Do You Want Me):

- https://genius.com/Soul-ii-soul-back-to-life-however-do-you-want-me-lyrics

The Perimeter: David Bowie: Occult Hero:

- https://www.newsfromtheperimeter.com/home/2018/1/21/david-bowie-occult-hero?fbclid=IwAR0SAtQq-Dd_hnkk5aIK-w2Ptjwu27QMoPkcIq--rAebQvLE45tOTEO87jrw

Occult Symbolism and Pop Culture with Isaac Weishaupt

BONUS Studio 666 Film Analysis: Dave Grohl's Teenage Seance, Taylor Hawkins & Blood Sacrifice Theory!":

- https://www.tapesearch.com/episode/bonus-studio-666-film-analysis-dave-grohl-s-teenage-seance-taylor-hawkins-blood-sacrifice-theory/ESvYGGcfTpHk3j8GK3xVhi

The Economic Times: Taylor Swift is 'attracting demonic forces' to her concerts, warns exorcist:

- https://economictimes.indiatimes.com/news/international/us/taylor-swift-is-attracting-demonic-forces-to-her-concerts-warns-exorcist-know-why-he-has-advised-to-skip-her-live-performance/articleshow/106493069.cms?utm_source=contentofinterest&utm_medium=text&utm_campaign=cppsthttps://economictimes.indiatimes.com/news/international/us/taylor-swift-is-attracting-demonic-forces-to-her-concerts-warns-exorcist-know-why-he-has-advised-to-skip-her-live-performance/articleshow/106493069.cms?from=mdr

The Sound of Freedom conscious music podcast — complete archive:

- https://www.mixcloud.com/TheSoundOfFreedom/

CHAPTER 9

WHAT'S THE AGENDA, KENNETH?

"And I see your true colours shining through."
 Cyndi Lauper: 'True Colours'

"Things are going to slide, slide in all directions,
Won't be nothing,
Nothing you can measure any more.
The blizzard, the blizzard of the world,
Has crossed the threshold and it has overturned the order of the soul."
 Leonard Cohen: 'The Future.'

It's dumbfounding to me as I sit here writing this some years on, how few people in "polite society" seem to want to talk about the outrageous and unforgivable assault on our rights and freedom represented by the Co(n)vid scamdemic and associated agendas any more.

It would be understandable if this were down simply to them being heartily sick of having pored daily over the fine detail of what was being done to us in those times, as many researchers did. I strongly suspect, however, that it's more down to the notion that things have gone "back to normal," and that it was all a total nightmare but there's no sense in dwelling on it, and we might as well just get on with our lives and put it all behind us.

My feelings on the overall subject will be abundantly clear to anyone who has read '*Volume 3*' so I won't labour the point any more — except to say that Co(n)vid offered the *perfect* opportunity to see on which side of the fight for freedom everyone's favourite household-name musicians stood.

Almost without exception, as we saw, this was on the side of tyranny, 99 per cent of A-listers pathetically parroting the official line on everything. Not a set of balls or a backbone in sight. I only mention it again because the examples of owned assets continuing to push the propaganda have persisted, giving us further evidence by which their true allegiances can be judged.

The Rolling Stones: A Lifetime Actor's work is never done.
From left: Mick Jagger, Ronnie Wood, Keith Richards, Charlie Watts bow post-show 22 May 2018 in London.

Date: 22 May 2018

Source: StonesLondon220518-115

https://commons.wikimedia.org/wiki/File:Rolling_Stones_bow_post-show_22_May_2018_in_London_%2841437870275%29.jpg

Author Raph_PH

The **Rolling Stones** proved they were kept on the shortest leash of any pop poodles in 2022 when announcing that they were going back on the road following the scamdemic, with two concerts in London's Hyde Park... but with a condition; the band got to dictate what went into the bodies of their fans, or else no performance.

This was the *real* agenda lurking beneath the Co(n)vid hype — to induce the bulk of the world's population, under duress, to take unknown and provably dangerous substances into their bodies as, apparently, the "only way" to get society "back to normal," and all Establishment assets were employed to get the coercion achieved.

In their promo video, **Keith Richards** tells fans: "we've all had the shot, and you'd better get one too" whilst **Mick Jagger**, mincing flamboyantly, crows about wanting to keep it "a safe one," then says, "so, if you're not vaccinated, get tested." Richards adds, "if you want the masks on, put 'em on, it's no big deal."

They're the "bad boys of Rock 'n' Roll," don't you know!

Another question arises here: what the hell were these guys, all well into their 80s, still doing touring at their age? I'll be told "they miss the buzz," but really — why would you want to put in the hard slog of hitting the road when you're already a millionaire, and could have retired years earlier and lived out your remaining days quite comfortably?

The Stones stand as full confirmation that a Lifetime Actor's work is never done and that you may get the fame, the wealth, the women/rent boys, (depending on your preference,) the drugs and the 'Sir'-doms... but that there's always a heavy price to pay, and you won't have a mind to call your own from the moment you take the deal.

Fellow soul-seller **Peter Gabriel** was there to ensure the real agenda behind Co(n)vid got the right endorsements as he allied himself with 'The People's Vaccine' campaign, writing on his Twitter in 2021:

> *"The Peoples' Vaccine' campaign is calling on G20 leaders to lift patents, share vaccine technology and let developing countries make their own vaccines so everyone around the world has the chance to access the Covid vaccine."*

Pete, similar to the likes of **Sting**, **Bono** and **Bob Geldof**, presents himself as a "philanthropist" and a "political activist." This has also seen him be an associate of the World Economic Forum for decades, the organisation which sought to shape the human society which emerged out of the chaos of Co(n)vid in its own image and steer things several steps further to New World Order totalitarianism. Pete has been making trips to the WEF forums in Davos since the early 2000s.

(Speaking of Bono, the *Sunday World* carried a story of **Liam Gallagher** claiming that he and **Bruce Springsteen** once ruined Bono's day by sending him a picture of them dining together when they ran into each other in Ibiza. Reportedly, Bono suffers from a crippling fear of missing out, (FOMO,) and his wife called Gallagher to say he was distressed to see the pair enjoying themselves without him.

This would be funny were it not for the fact that, like Bono, both Gallagher and Springsteen were active in pushing official Co(n)vid and vaccine propaganda, the latter being another to insist that his fans get what the Sheep Farm lads refer to as the "three-dart finish" as a condition of coming to his shows. The **Kaiser Chiefs** did the same, earning themselves the nickname "The Pfizer Chiefs" in the process.)

Annie Lennox is another who has kept busy with the "activism" outside of her music. As late as winter 2024, she was helping re-ignite paranoia among hypochondriacs by posting a picture of herself wearing a face mask to her Instagram, with the caption:

> *"Back to wearing my mask again. There's a tide of COVID comin' through. I have friends who have been affected recently. I really don't mind wearing my mask if it helps me to avoid coming down with it. Stay healthy peeps!"*

I listed the very few honorary exceptions in '*Volume 3*' who had spoken out against the 2020/ 21 tyranny. It didn't take long. One name I missed was former Sex Pistol **Johnny Rotten/ John Lydon**. Though he certainly could have said more, he did at least indicate his opposition to being instructed to take unknown medical interventions as a condition of integrating back into society when speaking to '*Mojo*' magazine in an interview in 2020.

After discussing the onset of his wife Nora's dementia, and the personal and professional challenges this brought, at least a hint of his old, outspoken self was on display as he commented:

> *"On one hand, I'm very lazy, but on the other I love to work. I don't think locking us up is the answer, and now they're talking of shutting down everything again. I don't believe the death tolls — no one seems to be keeping proper statistics, can you believe?*
>
> *"And there's a lot of profit to be made from vaccines. Big money going on there! To bring in mandatory injections of vaccines, which they're*

talking about, for me that comes with serious issues. You don't have the right to pump chemicals in me if I don't want them. There is no great conspiracy, just headless chicken-dom.

"A few greedy, self-serving self-appointed people being completely incompetent."

It sure was disappointing that more from the Punk/ New Wave scenes did not speak up at a time when their voices were needed more than at any other in music history, given the way those genres have been promoted as "rebellious" and "anti-establishment." About as dangerous as a cosy night in with a cup of cocoa.

Don't Shoot the Messenger

It's often in what I refer to as a musician's "extra-curricular activities," rather than in their music, that we can discover all we need to know about their loyalties.

A name which repeatedly comes up in such conversations is **Roger Waters** of **Pink Floyd**. Many have highlighted Roger's apparent "anti-establishment" stance, particularly when it comes to his outspoken-ness about the Zionist regime of Israel and its murderous incursions into the neighbouring state of Palestine. Here is not the place to get into the politics and history of that scenario; that should be left to authors and researchers who are much more informed in such matters. But here *is* the place to question whether Roger may have been instructed to take such a stance in order to endear him to certain demographics, so that he would be trusted when delivering any message henceforth.

Roger certainly seems to fit the bill and, according to many, has taken a bold and brave stance and "said all the right things" when he has appeared on countless television and radio shows and podcasts — many of them hosted by the BBC, well-known for its unwavering support of Zionist Israel. In 2022 he told '*Rolling Stone*' magazine that he was on a Ukrainian "kill list," and had been targeted for "liquidation" after urging Kiev to make peace with Russia.

But, as aligned as many may feel with his views, and regardless of how much he seems to be "on the side" of so many regular people, we must ask ourselves a question. If Roger really *is* such a threat to the Establishment, and is spouting opinions which are a threat to the likes of the BBC and its allies... why would he have been given the airtime in the first place?!

We might ask the same of Russell Brand when, some years ago, he appeared on the likes of the BBC's '*Newsnight*' and '*Question Time*' bleating about the need for "a more egalitarian society" and a "revolution of consciousness." (That went well then.) Again, if Brand were the real deal, why would he have been given such high-profile platforms, with audiences of many millions, from which to spout such 'unpopular" views?

In the case of Waters we must remember that the band he was a part of has had a career spanning multiple decades, with multi-million-selling albums, and live shows attended by tens of thousands at a time. They were also instrumental in pushing the psychedelic counter-culture in London in the late 1960s, which has been shown to have been another social-engineering psy-op. "The Floyd," as they were known then, were the house band at London's UFO Club, a venue extensively involved in pushing psychedelic youth culture and co-owned by one of the main "faces" on the "London Underground" scene, John "Hoppy" Hopkins. He had emerged from Cambridge University as a nuclear physicist. A natural career path from that into music clubs, I'm sure readers will agree.

Coming back to more recent times, we must remember that Roger was promoting Co(n)vid mask-wearing, and in a 2020 interview, commented, "thank God for Anthony Fauci" before going on to praise "good people... like Bill Gates."

Someone as smart as Roger, who is capable of stripping away the lies and propaganda to get to the crux of what is happening in Israel and Palestine, is certainly capable of researching the true nature and motives of psychopaths like Fauci and Gates.

Mixed messages have been the order of the day with Waters; in the same concert he will laud Establishment propagandists George Orwell and Aldous Huxley, but also Wikileaks' Julian Assange. These cognitive dissonance-inducing stances mark him out as either naive and confused, (which, to be fair, Roger often appears to be — the aftermath of having been mind-controlled himself like his former bandmate **Syd Barrett**, perhaps?) or knowingly complicit. I suspect the answer won't be a clear one, and that each case warrants independent investigation.

As surmised elsewhere, there is a hierarchy within the music industry, and the likes of Roger Waters and Pink Floyd will be in the very top ranks given their longevity.

But what of contemporary artists? We can get a clue as to their likely rankings when we ask how many of them will still be around and getting talked about 50-60 years from now. Does anyone think that conversations along the lines of "Oh, Cardi B is great. I've loved her output for decades now. Her music has spoken to me in such a deep, profound way throughout my life," or, "the lyrical and musical complexity of Central Cee's last few albums have truly pushed the envelope of creativity in amazing new directions," will be taking place decades from now? It's a rhetorical question!

Artists in these times are disposable commodities who will be lucky to have a shelf life beyond a decade. Of course, they are used as mouthpieces to spout rhetoric and push agendas the same way as their forerunners always were. But they will be considered to be of far less value to their corporate overlords. Many will realise this, some only after experiencing a few years at the hands of the industry's manipulators, and occasionally this seems to cause the odd name to speak out about what's really on their mind, without fear of how it will affect their careers, since they've realised that they're not going to last much longer on that front anyway.

Former **Moloko** singer **Roisin Murphy** discovered this the hard way when feeling to speak out about puberty blockers as part of the Tavistock-grade "gender-fluidity" agenda in 2023. A good gauge of whether an apparently noble message has been delivered with the full approval of the Establishment, or whether it came from the individual mind of the artist concerned, can be seen in the aftermath. If the act continues unhindered, it was the former; if they get cancelled, it was "off-script."

Murphy had written on her private Facebook page:

> *"Puberty blockers are fucked, absolutely desolate, big pharma laughing all the way to the bank. Little mixed-up kids are vulnerable*

and need to be protected, that's just true. Please don't call me a terf (trans-exclusionary radical feminist), please don't keep using that word against women."

The first sign that she had hit a nerve came when ten hours' worth of her output, which had been scheduled for broadcast across two episodes of BBC Radio 6's *'6 Music Artist Collection,'* got dropped at short notice, to be replaced with output from rapper (and *'Top Boy'* actress) **Little Simz**. BBC scheduling staff had complained about the decision having been taken by bosses with no reason given. Some older shows featuring Roisin's output which had been available on the BBC iPlayer platform, were also removed.

Reporting on the story, the *'Daily Mail'* quoted an "insider" as saying:

"The BBC is supposed to be an impartial organisation so it is outrageous that Roisin can't express her view without being cancelled by our national broadcaster. It's like she has had her voice taken away from her. It basically means that she can't say what she thinks if she wants to appear on a licence fee-funded airwaves, (sic.) Whatever happened to free speech?"

It didn't end there. In the wake of her comments, Murphy's record label, Ninja Tunes, refused to promote her new album, *'Hit Parade,'* and two scheduled acoustic shows with signings at London's Rough Trade East were cancelled.

Writing on Twitter/ X, Murphy commented on the situation:

"I have been thrown into a very public discourse in an arena I'm uncomfortable in and deeply unsuitable for. The music I make is the core of everything I do and it's ever-evolving, freewheeling and unpredictable.

"For those of you that are leaving me, or have already left, I understand, I really do, but please know I have loved every one of you."

It was subsequently reported that all proceeds from the album would be donated to organisations that combat "transphobia."

To paraphrase George Orwell, "all social justice causes are equal, but some social justice causes are more equal than others." The trans agenda has been a hot potato for many years now, and is an area in which any artists who might have a tendency to be outspoken have had to tread extremely cautiously.

On reflection, a blurring of the genders has been pushed by music personalities for decades, **David Bowie**, **Marc Bolan**, **Prince** and **Annie Lennox** being examples which spring immediately to mind. Should we put these expressions down to creative artistry... or was society being primed for a much more insidious agenda which would have been known to be coming?

We've explored the social-engineering tactics of the Tavistock Institute. Perhaps we shouldn't be too surprised, therefore, to find that another operation under the same umbrella, GIDS (The Gender Identity Development Service,) based at London's Tavistock Clinic was, until 2022, the world's largest "gender identity" clinic for children. Perhaps surprisingly, it was ordered to close and move its operations when the service was deemed "unsustainable" following an investigation by, of all operations, the BBC's '*Newsnight*' programme! Among other activities, GIDS had been offering hormonal "treatment" for "gender-diverse youth" on the NHS.

Sam Smith had clearly been the principal name chosen to help popularise ideas of gender dysphoria, blending from being a he/him biological male at the start of his career, to insisting on they/them "pronouns" some years later, by which point his output had become undeniably satanic, as evidenced by his performance at the 2023 Grammys which saw him in a full blood-red "devil" suit. At the BRIT Awards a few days later he appeared in an inflated black rubber suit which made him look like a walking tyre.

By the following year, a painting of Smith, naked except for a toga, wearing angel wings and playing the harp between two pillars, (masonry,) was displayed at London's National Portrait Gallery. The picture, titled '*Gloria*' after his 2023 hit song, was part of the Gallery's "History Makers" section. They were entirely correct in that Smith's antics were "making history," but neglected to point out that it was for all the wrong reasons.

He ... sorry, "they," were far from alone, however. Many celebrities had, by this point, announced that they would be raising their children transgender or "gender-neutral." Those from the music world have included **P!nk**, **Adele**, **Beyoncé**, **Sting**, **Cher** and **Gwen Stefani**. Naturally, several Hollywood actresses are also in the mix.

When critical thought is applied, the notion that famous celebrities would *just happen* to decide to blur the genders of their children rather than, say, Barry at the local garage or Linda on the checkouts, with it *not* being part of an agenda, is ridiculous. Former **Beach Boy Mike Love** highlighted the absurdity of it all in 2023 when, prior to performing his song *'Surfer Girl,'* he hesitated on the grounds it was "gender-specific," hoping there was "nobody from Budweiser ... or the FBI" in attendance.

On reflection, we can find ideas of androgyny in many popular hits of decades past. **Lou Reed**'s *'Walk on The Wild Side'* left little to the imagination with lyrics like:

> *"Holly came from Miami, F.L.A.,*
> *Hitch-hiked her way across the U.S.A.*
> *Plucked her eyebrows on the way,*
> *Shaved her legs and then he was a she."*

Tucked away on the **Beatles**' "McCartney"-penned *'Ob-La-Di, Ob-La-Da,'* was a rather strange footnote to the apparently happy tale of Desmond and Molly:

> *"Desmond stays at home and does his pretty face,*
> *And in the evening, she's a singer with the band."*

Wait ... what? Why was *that* there?!

The **Kinks**' contribution was their song *'Lola'*:

> *"Girls will be boys and boys will be girls*
> *It's a mixed up, muddled up, shook up world ... "*

And this foreshadowed the same sentiments expressed a couple of decades later by **Blur** on *'Girls & Boys'*:

"Girls who want boys,
Who like boys to be girls,
Who do boys like they're girls,
Who do girls like they're boys.
Always should be someone you really love."

One take on just *why* all this slow-drip programming has been getting done in society, is the observation that the dark occultists see connection with original Source Creation, as coming through a "superman" entity, (spoken of by Aleister Crowley in his writings, and by Crowleyite **David Bowie** in one of his song lyrics.)

This represents an individuated unit of consciousness that is neither male nor female, acknowledging that gender and duality do not exist in the spiritual world. This is given as the reason why the Baphomet, (or Goat of Mendes,) is revered as one of their favoured motifs, since the figure embodies both masculine and feminine attributes. The creation of such "supermen" beings is only something they have in mind for their own class, however. They have a more sinister plan when it comes to the rest of the population.

Through encouraging Transgenderism, bisexuality and Transhumanism in wider society, the "elites" are seeking to blur the lines between the genders, thus creating a society of "neutral" humans much more aligned to the ultimate vision of a communistic One World Government presided over by an AI singularity.

Normalising Narcissism

When Generation X parents bemoan the quality of the music that their Millennial or "Gen-Z" children might be listening to, and insist "music was better in my day," they might — scientifically — be on to something.

The decline in both lyrical content and production styles is *not* simply down to subjective opinion; scientific studies have shown that these elements have been systematically degraded over the decades.

Former Rockefeller Foundation/ Planned Parenthood executive Dr. Richard Day was bang on the money when, in March 1969 he outlined, at what was supposed to have been a "secret" meeting, the cultural changes in Organised Society that were scheduled to take place during the decades ahead. According to Lawrence Dunegan, one of the doctors who attended the meeting and who publicly revealed what he had heard many years later, Day talked of how popular music was scheduled to "get worse":

> *"Lyrics would become more openly sexual . . . Older folks would just refuse to hear the junk that was offered to young people, and the young people would accept the junk because it identified them as their generation, and helped them feel distinct from the older generation . . .*
>
> *"This aspect was sort of summarised with the notion that entertainment would be a tool to influence young people. It won't change the older people, they are already set in their ways, but the changes would all be aimed at the young who are in their formative years, and the older generation would be passing. Not only could you not change them, but they are relatively unimportant anyhow. Once they live out their lives and are gone, the younger generation being formed are the ones that would be important for the future in the 21st century."*

Sure enough, in 2024, it was reported that a team of European researchers had analysed the words of more than 12,000 English-language songs across the genres of rap, country, pop, R&B and rock, spanning the period 1980 to 2020. Their conclusion was that song structures have not only been getting more simplistic, but there has been a recognisable trend towards lyrics becoming more narcissistic and nihilistic in theme. The results confirmed previous research which had shown a decrease in positive, joyful lyrics over time, and a rise in those that express anger, disgust or sadness, plus an increase in the use of words such as "me" or "mine," indicating a move towards self-obsession.

This all reinforces an observation made some years previous by the British researcher Paul Joseph Watson in his video titled '*The Truth About Popular Music*':

> "Researchers in Spain using a huge archive known as the Million Song Dataset, found that pop music has become blander. Based on studies of pop songs from 1955 to 2010, the team found that the diversity of transitions between notes, chords, melodies and other sounds, has diminished over the last 50 years.
>
> "The Spanish study also found that producers are baking volume into songs at the production stage, making them artificially louder. This over-compression has the effect of sucking all the dynamics out of a song."

What won't have helped things ... or will have, depending on whether you support the agenda or not ... is the application of artificial intelligence programmes in music-making. A.I. apps such as Kiln, MasterWriter and ChatGPT have become capable of writing entire songs from scratch with minimal human input. This, combined with digital, electronic production methods, explains why so much contemporary output seems to lack the "warmth" or human feel of songs from decades previous — because they are completely inorganic and artificial on every level.

In 2025, a coalition of British musicians released a "silent" album consisting only of sound from an empty recording studio, in protest at new UK government proposals to allow A.I. computer models to be "trained" using copyrighted content. The concerned musicians included **Kate Bush**, **Annie Lennox**, **Damon Albarn** and **Billy Ocean**.

These changes have occurred in tandem with all the others in Organised Society — automated phone and banking systems, cashless business payments, digital media, real-time monitoring and surveillance to "keep us safe," streaming music instead of buying physical formats. What links them all is the cold, soullessness of it all — as good an announcement of the true nature and intent of the controllers as it's possible to get.

Shades of Grey

A movement contemporaneous to Punk and New Wave in Britain was Two Tone, named after the scene's principal record label, and representing the unification of both black and white youth through music. It all seemed very noble on the surface... but is there more to know about the ultimate motives of this genre, as there is with so many others?

The researcher known as Wyvern the Terrible delved into this topic in a video and on-line article in 2024, beginning with an examination of Two Tone's founder. His street name of **Jerry Dammers** conceals his upper-class origins, named as he was Jeremy David Hounsell Dammers, having been born in India and educated at King Henry VIII private school in Coventry.

Jerry's father, Horace Dammers, would become Dean of Bristol Cathedral from 1973 to 1987. Horace attended the "elite" Malvern College where the likes of C.S. Lewis, Alan Turing and Chris Whitty were educated. Horace's great-grandfather had been Adjunct General to King George V of Hanover, who in turn was Queen Victoria's first cousin, and the last Hanoverian king.

This dynamic is very similar to that of the former BBC Radio 1 DJ **Tim Westwood**, whose father was also a bishop. Both Jerry and Tim's career paths are far from the natural ones one might assume those with their kinds of backgrounds would pursue. I'll be told that many young people rebel against their parents' value systems, and yes they do, and this would account for the odd example. But when it *keeps* happening it becomes a trend, and worth paying attention to by anyone who doesn't wish to be played like a violin.

Back to Horace Dammers, and we find that in 1972 he founded the Lifestyle Movement within the Church of England. As Wyvern observed:

> *"One of the main tenets... was to advocate for communal use of materials. Sharing cars, lawnmowers and household tools between neighbours, encouraging bicycles. It stated its opposition to Nuclear Power and over-reliance on aviation as means of travel."*

With the benefit of having lived through the madness of the 2020s, this sounds very much like messaging from the World Economic Forum with its "you will own nothing and be happy" credo, and very much like a form of socialism in line with the direction in which Britain was getting pushed.

Dammers also made the "progressive" move of welcoming ethnic minorities and those of other faiths into his ostensibly Christian church, which didn't go down too well with many of a more conservative nature. Though, again, noble-sounding on the surface, it also comes across as a blueprint for a form of communism which, in the long term, would be highly compatible with the so-called Kalergi Plan of cultural displacement as a method of undermining nations.

Given Horace's pushing of these agendas, is it conceivable, therefore, that these motives were passed on to his son, and that the multi-culturalism expounded by his record label could have represented more of the same? At the time of its launch, Britain had endured a decade of trade union action, the "troubles" in Northern Ireland, and general social strife, and Margaret Thatcher's Conservative party had just replaced Labour in government.

Jerry's vision was, reportedly, to create a kind of "punky-ska" sound aimed at unifying rival factions within youthful society. He once commented:

> *"I saw Punk as a piss-take of rock music, but couldn't believe people took it seriously. It seemed healthier to have an integrated form of British music, rather than white people playing Punk, and blacks playing Ska. Two-Tone was an integration of the two'."*

He was assisted in his creation of the Two Tone label by Bernie Rhodes, the manager of the **Clash**, and an adherent to the avant-garde Situationist International social movement. It was Rhodes, reportedly, who brought the **Specials** to the label as one of its first acts, and who defined the movement's look, its mix of "rude boy" and skinhead fashions, including tonic suits, loafers, pork pie hats and Abercrombie jackets.

Here, another aspect of Two Tone becomes relevant — a figure on the black-and-white checkerboard design which appeared as part of its main logo. Though the cover story would be that it represents the coming-together of black and white youth, the fact that this is also a design which figures heavily in the teachings of Freemasonry cannot be ignored. Given the Dammers family's heritage, it would be extremely unlikely that there weren't masons lurking within the ranks.

Wyvern makes the observation that the lyrics, penned by Dammers, in two of the songs by The Specials, can be seen as an attack on traditional family structures and the role of women as mothers. In '*Too Much Too Young*':

> "*You've done too much,*
> *Much too young.*
> *Now you're married with a kid,*
> *When you could be having fun with me.*"

With slightly darker overtones, the song might also be considered an advertisement for population reduction:

> "*Ain't you heard of the starving millions?*
> *Ain't you heard of contraception?*
> *Do you really a program of sterilisation?*
> *Take control of the population boom.*
> *It's in your living room.*
> *Keep a generation gap.*
> *Try wearing a cap!*"

Then, in the song '*Happy Marriage*':

> "*He wanted to be something, but now he never will*
> *She got him where she wanted and forgot to take her pill.*
> *And she thinks she'll be happy, hanging out the nappies,*
> *If thats a happy marriage, I prefer to be unhappy.*"

And, seemingly mocking married couples as being sheep:

> "*Married woman, married man,*
> *Where did you get that family plan?*
> *Mrs. Ewe and Mr. Ram,*
> *Where did you get that lovely lamb?*"

As Wyvern concludes in his article:

"Dammers' messaging seems to repeatedly smear the notion of settling down in a traditional family structure, and raising children within a marriage. One might conclude that this messaging appears entirely simpatico with the wider 20th century Deep State social-engineering agenda that his father's work also seems to have embodied, each within their own chosen demographic.

"...I'm not sure much of a conclusion is needed to this piece. It seems pretty evident to me that Dammers was more than just an 'angry young man with a record collection', and a central figure in a social-engineering project that masqueraded as a youth movement.

Ragtags and Gags

The industry seems to be structured as a hierarchy. Whilst bands like the Rolling Stones or anyone with a 'Sir' in front of their name would never be permitted to say anything anti-Establishment, those on lower strata — such as Lydon, for example — do seem to be allowed a certain amount of licence to speak their minds.

The danger is that so many of them will have been so system-entrained into believing The Official Version of Everything through decades-long careers — possibly with an avalanche of mind-numbing drugs involved — that they would be incapable of seeing the wood for the trees even if they *were* allowed to speak out. Many do seem rather dim. **Sir Rod Stewart** springs to mind, who, when outlining the attendance requirements for his 2021 Christmas party, commented:

> "It makes me angry, especially in America where they talk about 'It's my right, it's my freedom'. No it's not! Because you are a killer, and you can be killed. We have a big party at the house every year... It's dead simple. If you haven't been tested, if you haven't got the two vaccines and the booster, you can't come."

Ah well. Down to Wetherspoons it is then.

Former **Smiths** frontman **Morrissey** got a semi-honorary pass in my 2021 Roll Call. He only gave one interview during the Co(n)vid debacle, and this was conducted by his nephew, Sam Esty Rayner. As with anyone, opinions have remained divided as to whether Morrissey is the real deal or just another actor playing a role. I cautiously veer towards the former, and if this is the case, it would be understandable why he would have chosen not to be interviewed by the Establishment music press during those times.

In that interview he had commented:

> "More people are now forced into poverty which is another form of slavery, as is tax and Council Tax and all the other ways in which we are pinned down and tracked. Our present freedom is restricted to visiting supermarkets and buying sofas. The government act like Chinese emperors... 'We will allow you to live as we do if you behave yourself'."

At the very onset of Con(v)id, immediately prior to the first UK lockdowns, Morrissey had changed the backdrop slogan at one of his concerts from "you are the quarry" to "you are quarantined."

By the following year, Morrissey was ready to release his new album, '*Bonfire of Teenagers*,' and in an interview filmed at the London Palladium, again directed by his nephew, he was ready to vent on "diversity" within society — Cultural Marxism by any other name:

> "Diversity is people that you don't know... It's just another word for conformity... You don't see anything diverse anywhere. It's all conformity... when people talk about diversity they don't think about the great things that we <u>don't</u> have in common. Those things are ignored and they always made countries very interesting... Now they just want everything to be the same... It doesn't mean avant-garde, or let's make really interesting strange art, it means box everybody... diversity is a terrible word.

> "In the late '90s I was interviewed a great deal and I constantly spoke of a dumbing-down that was happening in England everywhere. Television, television commercials, everything to do with British life, it was just aimed at the moron. And that has absolutely happened now. I mean, if you watch British television commercials, they're insufferable."

As he toured the new album, he reserved some scathing remarks for the NHS when introducing his lament for the elderly, '*I Live In Oblivion.*':

> "*This passion play that we call life. When you come to the end you will be either shoved in a hospice, shoved in a home, or at the mercy of the NHS, which is a fate worse than life.*"

In the Palladium chat, he made the observation, "nothing's been injected into me." This was ostensibly a reference to how he was no longer of financial interest to the record corporations, but we can speculate as to whether it may have been a coded comm in reference to something else. Either way, Morrissey at least remains endlessly interesting to listen to in interviews, able to divert away from the on-message propaganda soullessly spouted by most of his contemporaries when not talking about their music.

Her Travesty

Another useful gauge of where a music-maker's allegiances lay came when we were told the Queen had finally passed away on 8th September 2022. All the Sirs who'd been given their ego-appeasing gongs getting on their knees to fawn and scrape, including "**Paul McCartney**," **Ringo Starr**, **Mick Jagger** and **Elton John**, was only to be expected. What may *not* have been was hard "rockers" like members of **Black Sabbath**, **Aerosmith**, **Billy Idol**, **Saxon**, **Stryper** and the **Offspring** lining up to pay their tributes, including **Def Leppard**'s **Joe Elliott** describing her as "a wonderful lady" who had displayed "dignity." Why Americans felt the need to get involved I don't know, but **John Bon Jovi** Tweeted that she had been "the ultimate example of service and duty."

Yes, but who *to*?!

An all-too-rare difference of opinion, however, indicating the capacity for critical thought and the courage to share it, came from American indie-folk artist **Phoebe Bridgers**, who messaged on Instagram:

> "*Today we mourn all the stolen, violated, and traumatized lives who were affected and destroyed during Qween (sic) Elizabeth II's reign.*"

> *"Today is a brutal reminder that war criminals will be honoured while entire populations and societies bear the battle scars of colonial genocidal violence, invasion, religious persecution, and white supremacy."*

Some royal sucking-up has been coming from the DJ world since the advent, beginning some years ago, of radio and club DJs being given MBEs and OBEs. Those to have gratefully accepted them include **Pete Tong**, (see the Gatekeepers chapter later in the book,) **David Rodigan**, **Trevor Nelson**, **Soul II Soul**'s **Jazzie B**, Drum & Bass pioneer **Goldie**, Kiss FM founder **Gordon Mac**, **Steve Lamacq**, **Jasmine Dotiwala**, ("services to broadcasting, music and equality, diversity and inclusion,") and the **Dreem Teem**'s **DJ Spoony**, (a BEM — British Empire Medal for "services to charity through music during the Covid-19 pandemic.")

Perhaps the most surprising comments came from **Norman Jay**, one of the founding DJs on London's Kiss FM pirate station in the 1980s, and a mainstay of the Notting Hill Carnival with his celebrated Good Times sound system. Following the receiving of his gong, he messaged:

> *"I never imagined in my lifetime that I would ever get to meet any member of the Royal Family, let alone the Queen. Things like that just don't happen to ordinary folk like me from a disadvantaged black working-class background."*

There seems to be such a disconnect when it comes to this line of thinking, with so few joining the dots to see that the polarity between the poor working class and the "elites" represented by the Royals, is *because* of the very *existence* of these institutions, and the activities of those from generations past which have hardly shown favour towards people of colour. I get that the hard-working pioneers in any field, such as Norman, are proud of their achievements, and welcome them being recognised, but still, having *nothing whatsoever* to do with an institution which has brutalised and enslaved populations is the only real stance which carries any virtue.

Trust the Scam

It had become abundantly clear by 2021 that the "Q-Anon" movement, with its notion that there were a powerful group of "White Hats" working behind the scenes — in collusion with Donald Trump in most versions — to take down the "cabal" and arrest and execute its perpetrators, amounted to nothing more than possibly the cruelest psy-op ever, giving as it did false hope to millions that "something was being done" about this world's malevolent control system.

The operation was timed to coincide with Trump's first U.S. Presidency bout, the first hints of it coming in 2017, (17 being a number endlessly associated with the phenomenon.) Attention was first paid to the idea as a result of a series of posts, or supposed intel "drops," on the on-line message boards 4-Chan and 8-Chan. The messages were cryptic and ambiguous in nature, and were always signed off with "Q." (Perhaps we should recall that Q was the letter assigned to James Bond's quartermaster. That's James Bond as in the British *military intelligence* operative!)

If there *really* were such a group, it would surely have shown its hand, with verifiable evidence offered to *prove* its existence, during the tyranny of 2021 and the medical genocide that followed in its wake. The author David Wilcock was promising years before the advent of Q that the "elites" were poised to be taken down by a benevolent task force of military types. As Diana Ross once sang, "and I'm still waiting." The Q operation has been shown to have effectively been a re-boot of a scheme known as Operation Trust ("trust the plan?") coming out of Russia at the time of the Bolshevik Revolution in 1917, (another "17.")

Here's where things connect — as they invariably do — back into the music game, and things get really intriguing. Many of the characteristics of the Q scam seem to have been foreshadowed in a stunt pulled by Pink Floyd, or those that control them, some years before.

What is considered to be the group's last "proper" album, '*The Division Bell*,' was released in 1994. When the group embarked on a massive tour to promote it, messages began getting posted to a Pink Floyd group on the old Usenet platform by someone identifying themselves as 'Publius.'

The messages, always ambiguous, suggested that the album, its artwork and lyrics held a deep secret and a challenge. Fans were sceptical, so Publius promised evidence. During one of their shows, the words "Enigma Publius" flashed up on the stage. The phenomenon became huge news among Floyd fans well into the 2000s, with lyrics and artwork being closely scrutinised for "comms," and the band denying any knowledge of it throughout. Eventually it all seemed to fizzle out.

Much of this may sound familiar to anyone who has studied the 'Q' phenomenon. Was this a dry-run for what was already known to be coming many years later, with Floyd fans being used as guinea-pigs to test responses?

Publius' sign-off was usually:

> *"Listen*
> *Read*
> *Think*
> *Communicate"*

The first letters of each word taken backwards give us 'CTRL' — meaning "control" on a computer keyboard.

Cinderella Fairy Stories

A general rule of thumb with which you'll never go far wrong is: be suspicious of "Cinderella Fairy Stories" to explain how certain artists became so successful so quickly. These are to be found everywhere, a classic example being Madonna's claim, in her monologue to her 1985 '*The Virgin Tour*' video compilation:

> *"I went to New York. I had a dream. I wanted to be a big star, I didn't know anybody, I wanted to dance, I wanted to sing, I wanted to do all those things, I wanted to make people happy, I wanted to be famous, I wanted everybody to love me. I wanted to be a star...*
>
> *"...I worked really hard, and my dream came true!"*

What she failed to mention is that, on her French-Canadian mother's side, one way or another she's related to: Abraham Lincoln, George

H. W. Bush, Camilla Parker-Bowles, Princess Diana, Marilyn Monroe, Hugh Hefner and Tom Hanks, as well as future successful actor Brad Pitt, and future successful politicians Barack Obama and Justin Trudeau. I guess it just slipped her mind. Easily done. (In the majority of cases it's on the mother's side that the interesting bloodline links of this nature come, the fathers — often providing the military connections — being relegated to little more than sperm donors.)

Ed Sheeran, his official biography tells us, independently released his first collection of work at the age of 13. Sounds plausible. I mean, what 13-year-old *hasn't*, right? We are told the beginnings of his fame came when he was noticed busking at train stations. It's nothing to do with his father being a lecturer and art curator with connections to Prince/ King Charles, you understand. When promoting the Martin Scorsese-directed movie '*The Irishman*,' actor Stephen Graham said he was convinced that Ed was related to Frank Sheeran, the gangland character being portrayed in the film by Robert De Niro.

And so, the same dynamic rears its head when it comes to the backstory of the British folk-rock group **Mumford & Sons**. Their guitarist, **Winston Marshall** — or Winston Aubrey Aladar deBalkan Marshall to give him his full name — is the son of Sir Paul Marshall, a tycoon with a net worth of £630 million who went on to become a co-owner of GB News.

His aunt, Penelope Jane Clucas Marshall, worked as a journalist for ITV News, and was a graduate of the London School of Economics. Winston, by his own admission, was a "Trustafarian." As '*The Guardian*' observed in 2010:

> "*There's nothing inherently wrong with musicians being privately educated. It's just a bit grating when one of them insists on going by the name "Country" Winston Marshall.*"

The parents of founder and singer **Marcus Mumford**, who holds dual British and American citizenship, were leaders of the evangelical Christian movement The Vineyard Churches. **Bob Dylan** was an early member. (Cult?)

Fulfilling the same Trustafarian archetype is producer, songwriter, DJ and socialite **Mark Ronson**, who also holds dual UK/ US citizenship.

He emanated from an Ashkenazi-Jewish family which had relocated from Europe and Russia, and had shortened the family name from Aaronson to Ronson. His father was a music manager and publisher, and his mother a writer, jewelry designer and socialite.

She re-married, to **Foreigner** guitarist **Mick Jones**, (not to be confused with the **Clash** member of the same name… who is a cousin of the former Conservative Transport secretary Grant Shapps!) Mark's sister **Samantha** also became a DJ, singer and songwriter.

Whilst living in New York City, Ronson befriended a young **Sean Lennon** as a childhood friend, (well, we've all done it,) and later enjoyed a rapid rise to fame as a DJ, getting hired to play at parties hosted by many celebrities and public figures. I know from experience that working your way up in the DJ game is a hard slog if you're really doing it off your own back, and these types of gigs only come if you're a "chosen one." (I'd have wanted to have played at one of these "elite" shindigs during my naive youth, but now, with my middle-aged cynicism and world-weary jadedness, I can't think of any worse place to be.)

His studio albums followed, which saw him collaborating with many popular names from the U.S. hip-hop scene, and he remains best-known for his 2007 album '*Version*,' which spawned his hit single with **Amy Winehouse**, '*Valerie*.'

Farming the Ants

If it's not abundantly clear to all by now that no artist or band would ever be allowed to make it to the top league without "approval" from the controllers of Organised Society — let alone be able to manage and fund themselves without the same kind of assistance — I honestly don't know what more evidence I could offer.

Examples of this factor are to be found everywhere — the **Beatles** would be arguably the best — but any band which became the flag-bearers for a particular genre would have been selected in the same way.

The early 1980s "New Romantic" scene is as good as any to examine. **Steve Strange** of **Visage** and **Boy George/ Culture Club** were among the poster children for this ambiguous post-punk scene, and have been discussed elsewhere. The most commercially successful of the early bands, meanwhile, was **Adam & The Ants**. There's more on Adam/ Stuart Goddard in the '*Sex As A Weapon*' chapter, but worth adding here is what appeared to be absolute confidence on Adam's part that his band would become as successful as they did, at the very time they did.

In an interview given to the '*Sound on Sound*' website in 2013, **Chris "Merrick" Hughes**, who was the drummer and producer for the group, before going on to a highly successful producing and songwriting career throughout the industry, recalled:

> "And Adam told me, 'mate, in six months time you won't have to carry your drums around and set them up. There will be people who'll do that for you. Six months from now we'll be household names. We'll walk off stage into cars and straight back to the hotel. This will be a breeze.'
>
> "Remarkably, he was right. Within six months, we were on 'Top Of The Pops.' I absolutely adore him for that and I cherish the day he made his prediction."

Was Adam just being braggadocious? Did he possess soothsaying abilities? Or was he merely relating what he had been told by other parties about his band being chosen ones for engineered fame and fortune?

This confidence in assured success seemed to be expressed in the lyrics to the single '*Kings of the Wild Frontier*':

> "A new Royal Family, a wild nobility, we are the family."

Early on, somehow, Adam became friends with Arnold Schwarzenegger before he had "made it," and landed a part in Arnold's film '*The Last Action Hero*' many years later, (though the scene didn't make the final cut.)

Adam also had a part in the nihilistic film '*Jubilee*,' chronicling the British punk trend of the time, alongside **Toyah Willcox** and other "faces" from the scene. For the first version of his band, then titled simply The Ants, Adam was managed by eccentric svengali **Malcolm McLaren**, who enticed members of Adam's band away to help form his new project, **Bow Wow Wow**. (This was fronted by singer **Annabella**

Lwin, and McLaren courted more of the controversy in which he seemed to delight by having her pose nude for a record sleeve when she was 14 years old.)

Within a month Adam had regrouped to put together the second iteration of his band, headed by **Marco Pirroni**, who co-wrote their two hit albums. This involved a totally different look and unique sound for the band, and by July 1980, a new record deal had been secured with CBS. Adam is credited with having chosen all the band's costumes, and having devised the storyboards for the elaborate videos to accompany the hit singles.

At this point, the fame and fortune that Adam had so presciently "predicted" happened just as he had said. He became a household name overnight after performing '*Dog Eat Dog*' on '*Top of the Pops,*' with the '*Kings of the Wild Frontier*' album appearing the following month and becoming the best-seller of 1981.

We might ask ourselves, therefore — *if* the group had been specially selected as (very temporary) leaders of their genre — what agendas was it they were pushing?

My best guess is that this came from their highly elaborate videos, most of which are credited to Mike Mansfield, (mainly known as a film director,) with input from Adam. As well as pushing the familiar themes of dissociation from mind-control which I cover elsewhere, many of them evoke scenes of "elite" balls of the type depicted in Stanley Kubrick's '*Eyes Wide Shut*' movie, involving as they do, occult ritual.

Scenes of this nature appeared in many New Romantic-era videos, and would appear to have been a ploy to get such themes and motifs embedded in the collective hive-mind of the viewing public. Possibly as a form of arrogant mockery, or possibly through fulfillment of the tenet by which the controllers seem to operate — of needing to tell us at all times who they are and what they do — albeit in cryptic, coded form that very few in the early 1980s could have been expected to have deciphered.

Adam has indicated that he is in "the club" on a handful of occasions where he has been pictured flashing up the "devil horns" sign, as well as the well-worn one-eye symbolism, (accentuated in his early days by his wearing of a patch over one of his eyes.)

Resources:

Music News: John Lydon pulled Public Image Ltd album because of his wife's Alzheimer's:

- https://www.music-news.com/news/UK/135499/John-Lydon-pulled-Public-Image-Ltd-album-because-of-his-wife-s-Alzheimer-s:

Yahoo News: Rod Stewart bans anyone who isn't triple-vaccinated from his Christmas party:

- https://uk.news.yahoo.com/rod-stewart-bans-anyone-isnt-170000842.html

Morrissey Interview 2022:

- https://www.youtube.com/watch?v=2WTH6288UG8

Phoebe Bridgers shares post mourning 'all the violated lives destroyed during Queen Elizabeth II's reign':

- https://www.independent.co.uk/arts-entertainment/music/news/phoebe-bridgers-queen-elizabeth-ii-death-b2163728.html

Blabbermouth: Rockers React To Death of the Queen:

- https://blabbermouth.net/news/rockers-react-to-death-of-queen-elizabeth-ii

Tavistock-Tone: The Specials, Jerry Dammers & The social-engineering Of 2-Tone:

- https://www.youtube.com/watch?v=VZx2HLcS1XQ

Song Meanings: The Specials: Too Much Too Young:

- https://songmeanings.com/songs/view/115308/

Rolling Stone: Roger Waters: I'm on a Ukrainian 'Kill List':

- https://www.rollingstone.com/music/music-features/roger-waters-ukrainian-kill-list-1234604081/

The Independent: Roger Waters claims he's on Ukraine's 'kill list':

- https://www.independent.co.uk/arts-entertainment/music/news/roger-waters-ukraine-russia-concert-b2195793.html

Pink Floyd: The 'Publius Enigma' riddle:

- https://en.wikipedia.org/wiki/Publius_Enigma

Angelfire: Messages Sent By Publius:

- https://www.angelfire.com/co/1x137/publius.html

Operation Trust:

- https://en.wikipedia.org/wiki/Operation_Trust

BBC News: Artists release silent album in protest against AI using their work:

- https://www.bbc.co.uk/news/articles/cwyd3r62kp5o

Irish Times: Has the BBC secretly cancelled Róisín Murphy for her views on puberty blockers?:

- https://www.irishtimes.com/culture/2023/09/23/has-the-bbc-secretly-cancelled-roisin-murphy-for-her-views-on-puberty-blockers/

Daily Mail: Art-lovers question why painting of controversial pop star Sam Smith naked except for a toga, wearing wings and playing a harp will be displayed in the National Portrait Gallery:

- https://www.dailymail.co.uk/news/article-13692651/question-painting-controversial-Sam-Smith-naked-toga-wings-harp-displayed-National-Portrait-Gallery.html

X: Mike Love claims he is afraid to perform 'Surfer Girl' because it is "gender specific", implies that he fears retaliation from the FBI and the Budweiser corporation. (2023):

- https://twitter.com/beachboysmoment/status/1678082877991559169?ref_src=twsrc%5Etfw%7Ctwcamp%5Etweetembed%7Ctwterm%5E1678082877991559169%7Ctwgr%5E351ab6d-4f8e364d73232f85d2301a5505061a2cb%7Ctwcon%5Es1_c10&ref_url=https%3A%2F%2Fwww.rumormillnews.com%2Fcgi-bin%2Fforum.cgi%3Fread%3D227261

The Guardian: Song lyrics getting simpler, more repetitive, angry and self-obsessed — study:

- https://www.theguardian.com/music/2024/mar/29/song-lyrics-getting-simpler-more-repetitive-angry-and-self-obsessed-study

The Highwire Podcast, Episode 368: A New Dawn?:

- https://rumble.com/v4q7rju-episode-368-a-new-dawn.html

CHAPTER 10

THE SICKNESS BENEATH THE SURFACE

Sean "P. Diddy" Combs. A titan of music, entertainment and baby oil. He didn't kill himself. You know, just in case…

https://commons.wikimedia.org/wiki/File:Sean_P._Diddy_2013.jpg

English: Sean P. Diddy in 2013

Date: 2013

Source: Cannes Moments: Sean Combs Reveals the Secrets of CÎROC's Success

Author: Cannes Lions Learnings

The eventual arrest and jailing of **Sean 'P Diddy" Combs** in 2024 brought the sordid nature of the entertainment business kicking and screaming into mainstream consciousness, as the public was forced to acknowledge what lurks beneath the glossy surface.

> *"Take that, take that, take that!"*
> Sean *"P. Diddy"* Combs on Notorious B.I.G's *'Hypnotise.'*

> *"I'm so very sickened,*
> *Oh, I am so sickened now."*
> Morrissey: *'Suedehead'*

There's little need to focus on every aspect of what **Sean 'P. Diddy' Combs** stands accused of, as the mainstream media has done a good job of that over the months, and there'll be *plenty* more to come as his trial progresses. We might ask ourselves why Diddy's activities became exposed at the time they did, though, given that the Establishment could easily have kept them covered up if they'd wished — just as they could have with the deeds of Jimmy Savile.

"They" seem to have no problem with throwing one of their own under the bus when it suits them. Perhaps this is all part of the "elite" favoured tenet of placing the truth in plain sight so we can never make the legitimate claim that we weren't, in some way told. The only difference between the above pair, of course, is that they waited until Savile was dead before "exposing" him. It seems depravity comes with a grading system.

And so it was that his former partner, (slave,) singer **Cassie Ventura** filing claims against Diddy in late 2023, accusing him of "a decade-long cycle of abuse, violence and sex trafficking," set into motion a chain of other accusations against Combs. He fast became dubbed "the Jeffrey Epstein of Hip-Hop" when it emerged that he appeared to have been running a blackmail operation for years via his lavish parties, (which he himself labelled "freak-offs,") where celebrities, politicians, business leaders and other well-known figures would be coerced into taking part in wild sex orgies, involving, allegedly, many women sex slaves who had been drugged, and in some cases, allegedly, children. Many others, in the wake of Cassie's claims, came forward to accuse Combs of having sexually, physically and psychologically abused them.

For many who had been observing Diddy's conduct ever since the 1990s, when he was known as "Puff Daddy" and had gained unprecedented levels of control over the hip-hop world through the Bad Boy

Records label facilitated for him by industry mogul Clive Davis, his apparent come-uppance was a welcome turn of events. Combs had shown himself to be a brutal psychopath in his business dealings. In his eye-opening book '*Dancing With The Devil: How Puff Burned The Bad Boys of Hip-Hop*,' former rapper **Mark Curry** detailed how any artist who signed to Bad Boy would end up regretting it as they became utterly exploited by Combs.

The most extreme example occurred when Christopher Wallace, known as the rapper **Biggie Smalls/ Notorious B.I.G.**, was gunned down in a hail of bullets in Los Angeles in March 1997. This occurred six months after "rival" rapper and former friend **Tupac Shakur** was killed in an almost identical drive-by shooting in Las Vegas. Amidst the slew of accusations aimed at Puffy in 2024 were the claim that he had been implicated in both murders. According to the '*Daily Mail*,' Combs was named 77 times in court documents related to the charges against Duane "Keffe D" Davis, who had been accused of murdering Shakur almost three decades on.

The unsealed indictment which was eventually brought against Combs in 2024 summed up what he was being accused of — and this is just what was allowed to leak through into the mainstream:

> "*For decades, Sean Combs, a/k/a 'Puff Daddy,' a/k/a 'P. Diddy,' a/k/a 'Diddy,' a/k/a 'PD,' a/k/a 'Love,' the defendant, abused, threatened, and coerced women and others around him to fulfill his sexual desires, protect his reputation, and conceal his conduct. To do so, Combs relied on the employees, resources, and influence of the multi-faceted business empire that he led and controlled, creating a criminal enterprise whose members and associates engaged in, and attempted to engage in, among other crimes, sex trafficking, forced labor, kidnapping, arson, bribery, and obstruction of justice.*"

These claims, plus the ones involving his "freak-offs," really are the tip of the iceberg, however, when it comes to what lurks beneath the glamorous facade of entertainment, and it would be a serious mistake to treat the Combs affair as an extreme one-off. Just as it always was with Savile.

The Camera Never Lies

Before we leave Jeffery Epstein (who didn't kill himself) alone, a link back to the music industry comes from the fact that he was in attendance, for some reason, at the 1985 Eurovision Song Contest; the video link is at the end of the chapter. Epstein went on to run similar operations to Puffy, reportedly involving the filming of famous and powerful people in compromising positions, then using the footage as leverage over them.

Perhaps both Epstein and Combs were taking their inspiration in this regard from a much earlier source. In Nazi Germany, Adolf Hitler reportedly had an Austrian-Jewish advisor named Erik Jan Hanussen. As well as being a mentalist and stage-performer who dabbled in clairvoyance, hypnosis, occultism and astrology, Hanussen was active in instructing Hitler on how to perform in public, and in how to achieve a dramatic effect through his persona.

An extra-curricular activity, meanwhile, was his organising "blackmail parties" aboard his yacht where future operatives and agents were filmed performing heinous acts, thus allowing them to be manipulated for the rest of their careers.

They Got Game

Diddy's wasn't the only name from the rap/ hip-hop world to get dragged through the mud in 2024, (though claims in the mainstream that he was ever any kind of "rapper" were an anathema to veteran fans of the genre, his "skills" consisting of little more than "uh-huh, yeah, that's right" dubbed over his artists' records ... one of whom had asked for it.) In the wake of the evolving scandal, Canadian "rapper" (another term used lightly) **Drake** found himself embroiled in similar claims.

Drake's real name is Aubrey Graham. Born in Toronto, he is half-Ashkenazi Jewish on his mother's side. His back story comes with the familiar rags-to-riches story attached. Aubrey started out as an actor before transitioning into a "rap" artist. His rise to fame was very swift following his signing to Young Money Entertainment, and he went on to eclipse **Jay-Z** as, arguably, the most prominent and successful name on the rap scene for many years afterwards.

Though no stranger to controversy generally, from claims of assault, drugs possession and copyright and music publishing infringements, the allegations of sex-trafficking and blackmail aimed at Drake were exacerbated considerably by a back-and-forth slew of "diss" tracks — always a staple part of hip-hop culture — between Drake and rapper **Kendrick Lamar**, who appeared to show knowledge of Drake's behind-the-scenes activities and to be determined to expose them. It came to a head on Lamar's Interscope Records-released track '*Not Like Us,*' in which he accused Drake of being a "certified paedophile," its lyrics including:

> "*Say, Drake, I hear you like 'em young.*"
> "*To any bitch that talk to him and they in love,*
> *Just make sure you hide your lil' sister from him.*"
> "*Tryna strike a chord and it's probably A-Minor.*"

(This is wordplay insinuating that Drake likes "a minor.")
This track appeared only hours after Lamar's previous dig at Drake, '*Meet the Grahams,*' in which he alleged that Drake was a sexual predator who signs known sex offenders to his OVO Sound label, and runs a sex trafficking ring out of his Toronto mansion known as the Embassy — a scenario alarmingly similar to the one connected to Puffy which the public was starting to hear about.

'*Not Like Us*' went on to win five awards at the 2025 Grammys — song of the year, record of the year, best rap song, best rap performance and best music video, bringing Kendrick's career total to 22. These are unlikely achievements for a "diss" record... unless it was all orchestrated hype and, for whatever reason, the controllers *wanted* Drake humiliated and more attention drawn to the dispute between them? Lamar also performed the song at the U.S. Super Bowl Half Time Show to a huge audience where ex-tennis pro Serena Williams, who had previously dated Drake, was featured as a dancer.

Another rap titan's name got dragged into the whole sorry mess in the wake of the Diddy affair, in the form of the aforementioned Jay-Z, real name Shawn Carter.

In 2024, a woman filed a lawsuit against Carter alleging that he and Combs had drugged and raped her at a New York MTV Music Awards after-party in 2000 when she was 13 years old. Jay-Z subsequently issued a new motion seeking to dismiss the lawsuit, citing inconsistencies in the woman's claims.

Many commentators have long suspected Jay-Z's marriage to **Beyoncé** of constituting an industry-arranged relationship, and of his fulfilling the role of her mind-control handler. She certainly appears to be in a dissociative trance in this video in which she rocks back and forth as Jay-Z sits idly by, seemingly oblivious:

https://www.youtube.com/watch?v=hY5Xndp2bQY

Rap and hip-hop culture — particularly in its glory years of the 1990s — was always marketed as a highly heterosexual genre, its A-list rappers full of machismo. The Diddy allegations, however, suggested that participation in gay sex rituals were a standard requirement for any rapper to make it big. Many names synonymous with alpha-male machismo found themselves accused of having partaken in such activities. One was the late Biggie Smalls/ Notorious B.I.G. Biggie and Puff look decidedly intimate in photos and videos of them from the '90s when viewed from a newly-informed perspective.

There's also the case of the "girl" being seduced by Biggie in the video to his song '*Big Poppa*' actually being a transgender named Shameka Lockett. Shameka also appears in bed with Biggie in the video to his song '*The Warning*,' and in the video to the remix of **Craig Mack**'s '*Flava In Ya Ear*' where **LL Cool J** raps "he she" as Shameka dances behind him, before adding:

> "*Blow-ticious. Skeevy. Delicious... But is he good?... Poppa love it when he does it.*"

Biggie himself in the song had opened with:

> "*Niggas is mad, I get more butt than ashtrays.*"

Lord Jamar, member of the popular '90s group **Brand Nubian**, weighed in on these songs and videos being seen through a new set of lens in a 2024 interview, observing:

> *"LL was one of my favourite rappers back in the day, and I hate that he's embroiled in this shit. But, when you get next to certain people, and baby oil starts splashing around, you're gonna get some on ya, man."*

Jamar was also candid about how the Diddy allegations had caused many to re-visit the output of Biggie Smalls from renewed perspectives:

> *"Very gay lines like, 'I don't care how good a woman looks, I would never give fellatio to her father because she's so beautiful'... He said he'd 'fuck Rupaul before he'd fuck those ugly-ass Xscape bitches'... 'liquor be digging me in my asshole'... he said, 'I'll fuck with niggas who kidnap your kids, fuck 'em in the ass, throw 'em over a bridge.*
>
> *"There's so much shit that Biggie said that people just overlooked at the time, and now when we fast-forward to where we're at and we hear about all the shit with Puff... it was bad back then, but it's really not ageing well now."*

Nothing's Gonna Change

A name not spoken widely since the late 1980s came forth in 2021 to reinforce sexual favours in exchange for success being the norm.

Singer **Glenn Medeiros**, who had a one-hit wonder in 1988 with 'Nothing's Gonna Change My Love For You' told the 'Celebrity Catch-Up' podcast that he had had many offers himself, but he had turned them down, leaving the music industry entirely a few years later and fading into obscurity through choice:

> *"You saw it everywhere... Would it have led to me being more successful in my career? Potentially. But I wasn't willing to do that. I had friends who specifically said, 'I am going to be moving in with this person because this person is going to be helping me with my recording career.'*
>
> *"Unfortunately most of the females and some of the males I met—it literally took them having to have relationships with others to be able to get to the top."*

In the same podcast he stated that the music industry is owned in very large part by organised crime gangs, with drug-pushing and the pimping-out of artists being just another day at the office.

> *"To me, between all of those things — the drugs, the pimping out of artists and also the sexual relations that were happening — it was the music industry that I saw."*

School's Out

The stories of institutionalised sexual abuse and violence which come attached to so many "elite" public schools, were echoed in claims made about Chailey Heritage and Craft School in East Sussex, related to the new-wave/ post-punk singer **Ian Dury**. He was unfortunate enough to have swallowed a mouthful of infected water at a lido as a child resulting in his contracting polio. Dury's condition had been so serious that he had not been expected to live. Regardless, he pulled through, and was eventually sent to "convalesce" at Chailey Heritage, a former workhouse which had been converted into a school for disabled children.

There, according to an article on the '*Dangerous Minds*' website, he suffered bullying and sexual abuse at the hands of other boys. Out of great pain and trauma comes great art, however, and Dury adopted the faux-cockney persona which would later colour his musical output as a coping mechanism at the school.

I'm reminded here of the story covered in the last book, of **Terry Hall** of the **Specials** and **Fun Boy Three**, who revealed late in his life that he had been abducted and sexually abused by a paedophile gang while on a school trip to France decades before.

Back to the Beeb

The BBC enters the frame once again when we re-visit the appalling story of **Ian Watkins**, former singer with the Welsh band **Lostprophets**, (and not to be confused with a different Ian Watkins, otherwise known as "**H**" from the pop group **Steps**.)

Watkins was sentenced to 29 years in prison in 2013 charged with multiple sex offences, including the sexual assault of young children and infants. At this point an unlikely name entered the frame in the form of Peaches Geldof, the second daughter of **Bob Geldof** and Paula Yates. Peaches was investigated by police later in 2013, when she was said to have Tweeted the names of two young women who had allowed their babies to be abused by Watkins.

The two were convicted of offences alongside the singer, but had an anonymity order in place to prevent the identities of either them or their babies becoming public knowledge. Somehow Peaches knew who they were. Among her series of Tweets she commented:

> *"The papers MUST name 'woman A & B' who offered up their own babies to this monster in the hopes of being close to their (majorly talentless) musical hero without a backward glance, as they are equal in their monstrosity.*

In April 2014, Peaches was discovered dead by her husband **Thomas Cohen** of the group **S.C.U.M.** at their house in Kent. The public was told that she had died of a heroin overdose in the same fashion as her mother, Paula Yates, was said to have done in 2000. She was 25.

Watkins himself had previously been in a relationship with Fearne Cotton, BBC Radio 1 and BBC TV presenter, (a fact which seems to be absent from both his and her Wikipedia entries.) In 2014, Cotton came under fire from child campaigner Sara Payne, the mother of murdered schoolgirl Sarah Payne, after Cotton had played a promo including the word "Megalolz" on her Radio 1 show. This, reportedly, was a phrase used by Watkins to make light of his crimes.

With some irony, Cotton had previously presented programmes aimed at children on the CBBC channel, and had been a regular presenter on BBC1's annual '*Children in Need*' broadcast. (Previous '*Children In Need*' shows had featured Jimmy Savile, Rolf Harris and Gary Glitter. Sorry, just remind me again — exactly *how* is this institution *still* in operation?!)

Fearne's grandfather's cousin turns out to have been Sir Bill Cotton (CBE,) a long-standing TV executive. Among the shows he commissioned for broadcast on BBC1 was... Jimmy Savile's '*Jim'll Fix It.*'

Cotton was a close friend of fellow broadcaster Holly Willoughby, who had worked on ITV's '*This Morning*' alongside former CBBC presenter Phillip Schofield.

The Teenage Tiptoe

Pop songs can become such earworms, working their way into the subconscious mind when the conscious is not engaged, that the real meaning of well-worn lyrics can go undetected, often for years, until pointed out.

Upon close inspection, many songs become highly suspect in this regard, hinting as they do at sexual attraction towards minors.

In '*I'm On Fire*' **Bruce Springsteen** leaves little room for ambiguity when he sings:

> "*Hey, little girl, is your daddy home?*
> *Did he go away and leave you all alone?*
> *I got a bad desire,*
> *Oh, oh, oh,*
> *I'm on fire.*"

It's a similar scenario with '*Girl, You'll Be A Woman Soon*' by **Urge Overkill**, featured memorably in Quentin Tarantino's '*Pulp Fiction*' movie and written by **Neil Diamond**:

> "*Please, come take my hand,*
> *Girl, you'll be a woman soon.*
> *Soon, you'll need a man.*"

Winger's song '*Seventeen*' makes its intentions clear:

> "*She said,*
> *I'm only seventeen,*
> *I'll show you love like you've never seen, oh,*
> *She's only seventeen,*
> *Daddy says she's too young but she's old enough for me.*"

We might also consider **Queen**'s song '*Tie Your Mother Down*' from the band's 1976 '*A Day At The Races*' album. The lyrics, credited to **Brian May**, include:

> "*Got my timin' right,*
> *Got my act all tight,*
> *It's gotta be tonight my little school babe.*
> *Your Mamma says you don't.*
> *Your Daddy says you won't.*
> *And I'm boilin' up inside.*
> *Ain't no way I'm gonna lose out this time, oh no.*"

How about '*Christine Sixteen*' by **Kiss**? About as subtle as a flying brick:

> "*I don't usually say things like this to girls your age,*
> *But when I saw you coming out of the school that day,*
> *That day I knew, I knew,*
> *I've got to have you, I've got to have you.*"

We should also question the motives of the song '*Thank Heaven For Little Girls*,' first performed by **Maurice Chevalier** and featured in the film '*Gigi*':

> "*Each time I see a little girl,*
> *Of five or six or seven,*
> *I can't resist a joyous urge,*
> *To smile and say,*
> *Thank Heaven for little girls*
> *For little girls get bigger everyday*
> *"... Those little eyes*
> *So helpless and appealing*
> *One day will flash and send you*
> *Crashing through the ceiling.*"

'*My Sharona*' by **The Knack** declares:

"I always get it up for the touch of the younger kind."

Have music audiences been having paedophilia slyly "normalised" right in front of their noses by these beloved rock icons?

(*'I'm The Leader Of The Gang (I Am)'* by **Gary Glitter** and *'Two Little Boys'* by **Rolf Harris** are song titles which have not aged well in the circumstances, while we're on it.)

Mention should probably be made here, in the interests of completism, of a couple of honourable exceptions. In **Union Gap**'s song *'Young Girl,'* singer **Gary Puckett** appears appalled to discover that his lover is in fact underage, meaning he can no longer be with her:

"With all the charms of a woman,
You've kept the secret of your youth.
You led me to believe you're old enough,
To give me love,
And now it hurts to know the truth."

Then, in **ABBA**'s *'Does Your Mother Know,'* a rare song sung by the group's Bjorn, he tells of almost falling for the sexual allure of a girl in a disco, before reminding himself that she's underage:

"You're so hot, teasing me.
So, you're blue, but I can't take a chance on a chick like you,
That's something I couldn't do.
There's that look in your eyes,
I can read in your face that your feelings are driving you wild,
Ah, but girl, you're only a child."

Neil Sedaka only just stays the right side of decency on *'Happy Birthday Sweet Sixteen.'*:

"Tonight's the night I've waited for,
Because you're not a baby any more.
You've turned into the prettiest girl I've ever seen
Happy birthday sweet sixteen."

As I mentioned in '*Volume 1*,' former BBC TV and radio presenter Ed "Stewpot" Stewart met his wife when she was 13 and he was 34, marrying her four years later, and fellow BBC DJ John Peel somehow got away with marrying his wife, Shirley, when she was 15 and he 26.

Disgraced singer/ producer **R Kelly**'s marriage to singer **Aaliyah** was annulled in 1994 when it was discovered that she was 15. He was 27. **Elvis Presley** met his future wife Priscilla when she was 14. Rock groupie Lori "Lightning" Maddox has stated publicly that she was in sexual relationships with **David Bowie**, **Jimmy Page** and **Mick Jagger** while still underage, and while they were all in their 20s, (though there are inconsistencies in the way she has told the stories over the years.)

Rolling Stone **Bill Wyman**, 33 years her senior, dated **Mandy Smith** from when she was 13, marrying her when she had reached 16. And at this stage few will surely be too shocked to hear that, according to the '*Who's Dated Who*' website, **Sean 'P Diddy' Combs** dated the mother of one of his seven children, Sarah Chapman, from when she was 13 and he was 10 years her senior.

He ought to be in jail! Oh, hang on . . .

When she was 14, '*Stranger Things*' actress Millie Bobby Brown told reporters of her close friendship with **Drake** and of how he gave her "advice about boys." When pressed to elaborate she replied: "that stays in the text messages."

He ought to be investigated! Oh, hang on . . .

Baby Talk

I tell you what; I'll be glad when my duty in reporting all this stuff is done and I can go and take a shower; you may feel the same from reading it. We're nearly done.

Just as we can ask how it was considered OK for record labels to release, and for radio stations to play, the above songs, so we can ask just who sanctioned an unbelievably sick picture for **Alice Cooper,** (Vincent Furnier,) to help promote his 1973 album '*Billion Dollar Babies.*'

With none-too-subtle hints at child sex trafficking, the image shows Cooper, flanked by his band, holding up a screaming and obviously disturbed naked baby. The baby has black rings around its eyes — a common symptom, we hear, of Adrenochrome extraction, (see previous book.) Several white rabbits are in the picture, along with stacks of cash.

Isn't it funny how Facebook were all "moral" when they deleted accounts that didn't go along with the official narrative during the Co(n)vid scam, yet morality and censorship are nowhere to be found when it comes to this one, with Cooper — or whoever controls his page — being able to post it freely on several occasions? Almost as disturbing as the image are the remarks from Furnier's starstruck fans. Did they find it at all troubling? No. Instead they made comments like: "I LOVE this photo, and every single song was so great! Thank you, Alice!"

Can A-list, household-name artists really be "philanthropists"? Or is their involvement in charities and "humanitarian" causes only ever going to be cover for the pushing of some "elite" agenda or other? Anyone who was taken in by the idea of **Madonna** having a big heart and just being full of love and care when she began adopting children from Malawi, would have had their illusions shattered when, in 2023, the Ethiopian World Federation urged its nation's president to look into the integrity of Madonna's charity, Raising Malawi.

The Federation requested that the president:

"... restrict her and her associates' accessibility to Africa and to African children as a precautionary measure until a thorough investigation is done into child trafficking, sex exploitation, sexual slavery, adoption reversal, threat of coercion, fraud, deception and abuse of power or vulnerability."

The group were particularly concerned about the content of Madonna's 1992 book '*Sex*,' which featured depictions of sado-masochism and featured gay porn stars, claiming that this should have flagged her up as unsuitable for adopting Malawi children, which she began to in 2006.

The petition cited concerns over David Banda, one of her adoptees, being made to wear female clothes, make-up and jewelry in public, with Madonna pictured holding his hand in a manner suggestive of them being lovers.

The Federation stated that:

> *"We firmly believe that Malawi has been robbed of its most precious resource — its children. In 2013, the country accused Madonna of 'bullying' state officials and making diva demands — and of citing her Raising Malawi charity as the reason for doing so."*

Perhaps an insight into the way Madonna *really* views babies comes from a '*Vanity Fair*' promotional image in which she is seen wearing a costume decorated with severed baby heads, as a demonic-looking entity cavorts behind her.

Suitable mother material, anyone?

Resources:

Deadline: Diddy Denied Bail: Sean Combs To Remain In Custody Until Trial On Sex Trafficking, Racketeering & Other Charges; Faces Up To Life In Prison If Convicted:

- https://deadline.com/2024/09/sean-diddy-combs-charged-sex-trafficking-racketeering-prostitution-1236091518/

Jeffrey Epstein in attendance at the 1985 Eurovision Song Contest — 34 seconds into this video:

- https://www.youtube.com/watch?v=4wkxfxGk0T8&t=659s

Programmed To Chill Podcast Episode 24: Esoteric Nazism Reexamined pt. 2, or, Hitler's Magician:

- https://www.podcast24.dk/episodes/programmed-to-chill/05-esoteric-nazism-reexamined-pt-2-or-hitlers-magician-BDsHq0rMc

BBC News: Drake sues for defamation over Kendrick Lamar song:

- https://www.bbc.co.uk/news/articles/cyv433le3vno

Gene Deal Reveals A Trans Woman Was Biggie's Love Interest In The "Big Poppa" Video:

- https://www.youtube.com/watch?v=tS1AdK-_Iyc

Shameka Lockett in the 'Big Poppa' video:

- https://www.tiktok.com/discover/shameka-lockett-big-poppa-video

Lyrics: Kendrick Lamar: Not Like Us:

- https://www.boomplay.com/lyrics/166296009

Singer Glenn Medeiros: 'Sexual favours were the norm in music industry':

- https://www.bbc.co.uk/news/entertainment-arts-56029660

Guardian: Peaches Geldof investigated over tweet naming mothers in Ian Watkins case:

- https://www.theguardian.com/society/2013/nov/28/peaches-geldof-tweet-ian-watkins-lostprophets
- https://www.independent.co.uk/news/people/news/fearne-cotton-criticised-by-mother-of-murdered-school-girl-sara-payne-for-broadcasting-the-word-megalolz-following-paedophile-ian-watkins-conviction-9093294.html

Ian Dury: sexually abused at Chailey Heritage care home?:

- https://dangerousminds.net/tag/Ian-Dury

Rolling Stone: Jimmy Page Dated a 14-year-old Girl While He Was in Led Zeppelin:

- https://www.rollingstone.com/music/music-lists/the-10-wildest-led-zeppelin-legends-fact-checked-153103/jimmy-page-dated-a-14-year-old-girl-while-he-was-in-led-zeppelin-153501/

Access Hollywood: 'Stranger Things' Millie Bobby Brown Says Drake Helps Her With Boys:

- https://www.youtube.com/watch?v=lYZPKh74Li8&t=36s

Pop 'N Hiss: Alice Cooper's Billion Dollar Babies :

- https://www.vintageguitar.com/59555/pop-n-hiss-alice-coopers-billion-dollar-babies-2/

Investigations into Madonna's Malawi charity:

- https://www.nyasatimes.com/ethiopian-world-federation-asks-president-chakwera-to-institute-investigations-on-integrity-of-madonnas-malawi-charity-raising-malawi/

Madonna 'Vanity Fair' babies image:

- https://www.instagram.com/sororitevintage/p/Cnmr06_pb6A/

DJ John Peel Poses As A Schoolgirl:

- https://www.gettyimages.co.uk/detail/news-photo/radio-dj-john-peel-poses-in-a-schoolgirl-uniform-5th-news-photo/155167056

CHAPTER 11

THE DEPARTED

The music industry has a fairly high casualty rate when it comes to its famous artists. You may have noticed.

> *"Hollywood's dead,*
> *"Elvis is cryin,'*
> *"Lennon, wake up,*
> *Cobain, stop lying there."*
>   Lana Del Rey: 'Hollywood's Dead'

> *"Hollywood and the industry are coming to an end soon. Dark times always turn around to good, happy times like night and day. Can't wait to see them take their last, ghastly breath."*
>   Commenter on Celeb Live YouTube channel.

If the same number of let's say, oh, I don't know... plumbers?... were to turn up dead, (particularly at the age of 27,) as musicians do, people would surely be asking "why are so many plumbers dying?!" But rock star deaths are so often chalked up as some kind of "overdose" attributed to the out-of-control lifestyles these musicians live. It's either that or loose allusions to "suicide" owing to the pressures of fame.

Ambiguity often pervades the circumstances, without a specific cause of death being presented. But it's ultimately gotten away with, the masses just accepting that such things are simply a routine part of this business. It's just another day at the industry office.

Body Count

The deaths of **Jim Morrison** and **Janis Joplin** entered rock industry mythology decades ago, and fans and researchers alike have pored obsessively over the fine detail of the incidents. Despite this, however, one name which has been conspicuously absent from most resulting accounts muddies the waters considerably.

An article published in 2021 by '*People*' magazine spoke of a charismatic French aristocrat named Count Jean de Breteuil, the dashing young heir to a financial fortune and a title, who seemingly infiltrated the music world to become a self-styled "dealer to the stars." The drugs he pushed came in never-ending supply, and he was never busted by law enforcement, instead using his "diplomatic status" to move gear around the world.

Breteuil seemingly worked his charms on Pamela Courson, the long-time partner of Jim Morrison, and struck up a friendship with her. Jim would appear to have objected to their relationship, and the fact that Breteuil had apparently got Pam hooked on heroin. The **Doors**' song '*Love Street*' is said to reference Courson's foreign shopping trips with Breteuil, containing the lyrics:

> "She has robes and she has junkies, lazy diamond-studded flunkies."

'*People*' claimed that Breteuil got involved in selling cocaine and particularly potent blends of heroin imported from Morocco, to faces on Los Angeles' music scene in the late 1960s. One is said to have been Janis Joplin, who was found dead of a heroin overdose in her room at the Landmark Hotel on 4th October 1970, aged 27. (Note to all musicians: other ages at which to die are available.) An obituary article on Soul singer **Bobby Womack** by '*Rolling Stone*' magazine revealed that he had been with Janis on the night of her death. She had declined his offer of cocaine, and told him to leave when her (unidentified) heroin dealer had shown up.

In how many accounts of Janis' life and death does Breteuil's name crop up?

His friendship/ relationship with Pamela Courson is what is said to have prompted Pam's decision to move to Paris with Jim Morrison, though the couple mostly lived at separate addresses due to the combustible nature of their strained relationship.

No-One's Dad's a Plumber

Jim Morrison: Death by Bathtub ... or an earned retirement for the Admiral's lad?

https://picryl.com/media/jim-morrison-1969-5d9ca3?__cf_chl_tk

The consensus account has it that Jim died in the bathtub of his apartment in the Le Marais district on 3rd July 1971, (two years to the day after **Rolling Stones** founder **Brian Jones** was found dead in the swimming pool of his country cottage, also aged 27.) Most accounts I've come across claim that Pam was alone when she discovered Jim unresponsive in the tub. It seems Pam's various comments have been wildly inconsistent, as well as her claims of Jim having used heroin for the first time during his time in Paris. Famously, no autopsy was ever conducted on his body.

The most extreme alternative take, however, has come from Sam Bennett, the manager of Paris' The Rock 'n' Roll Circus nightclub, in his 2007 book '*The End: Jim Morrison.*' His claim is that Morrison showed up at the venue in the early hours of 3rd July and met with two dealers working for Breteuil looking to purchase heroin for Courson.

Bennett says he later found Morrison dead in one of the bathroom stalls having OD-ed. Breteuil's associates insisted on moving the body and placing it back in Jim's apartment bathroom, he says, to avoid a scandal. Courson never made any mention of this turn of events.

In 2025, a new claim that Morrison had been able to fake his death came from a three-part series streamed on Apple TV titled '*Before The End.*' The motive for Jim wanting to disappear is given as his fearing imprisonment after being convicted of indecent exposure the previous year, plus his disillusionment at having been kicked out of the Doors. The documentary alleges that Jim may have become a maintenance man named Frank working in Syracuse, New York. "Frank" is interviewed and denies he's Morrison, but in a veiled way, saying:

> "I'm not Jim ... except I love the song by Jimmy Cliff: 'We all are one, we are the same person.' That's one way to look at it."

A couple of Morrison's exes, who were also interviewed, make cryptic comments alluding to the faked death, and a private investigator claims that Morrison's social security profile is still active and that he has traced it to the New York area. The series was created by Jeff Finn who is listed on IMDB as "an experimental artist, writer, musician and filmmaker," as well as being a "Doors superfan."

Meanwhile, another name from rock music's pantheon got caught up in Breteuil's fatal web. This was **Marianne Faithfull**, singer, actress, close **Rolling Stones** associate, and on-off girlfriend of **Mick Jagger**. (Faithfull herself was no random nobody, being descended on her mother's side from the Sacher-Masoch aristocratic bloodline from which the term "masochism" is derived. The Sacher side of the family have a hotel named after them in Vienna which was featured in the iconic movie '*The Third Man.*')

Faithfull had met Breteuil at a party in London, where he had already added **Keith Richards** to his client list. He was seemingly keen to meet her because of her connection to Jagger. Despite saying she took an instant dislike to the Count, she ended up in a relationship with him anyway, (rather ironic considering her surname!) and got hooked on his wares. She travelled with him to Paris after Jim and Pam had moved there.

Breteuil seems to have juggled his time in Paris between Faithfull and Courson, among other women. In her 1994 memoir "*Faithfull,*"

Marianne says she was in bed with him at *L'Hotel* when the phone rang some time after midnight on 3rd July. Breteuil told her the call was from Courson. After leaving in an agitated state he returned some hours later, woke a groggy Faithfull, and told her to pack at once as they were headed to Morocco.

Faithfull wrote:

> *"Jim Morrison had OD'd and he had provided the smack. Jean saw himself as dealer to the stars. Now he was a small-time heroin dealer in big trouble."*

I personally have trouble accepting that Jim really died in 1971 given the well-documented military connections of his father. As such, he becomes a prime candidate for death-fakery. But if we imagine for a moment that his death on 3rd July was real, it set into place a chain of subsequent sorry demises. Talitha Getty, an aristocrat who had been one of Breteuil's clients in London, died two weeks after Morrison, aged 30, of a suspected overdose. Breteuil himself died less than a year later on 25th June ("anti-Christmas) 1972, at the ripe old age of 22, succumbing to an overdose of his own goods. Pam Courson died of an overdose in April 1974, just weeks after she had been legally declared Morrison's heir.

Faithfull emerged as pretty much the only survivor from the scene. In a 2014 interview with '*Mojo*' magazine, she commented of Breteuil:

> *"He went to see Jim Morrison and killed him. I mean, I'm sure it was an accident. Poor bastard. The smack was too strong and he died. Anyway, everybody connected to the death of this poor guy is dead now. Except me."*

Faithfull did pass away at the age of 78, on 30th January 2025, after a long catalogue of health problems.

A pertinent question arises here . . . and it's not the first time its like has had to be asked. If the Count was the heir to a financial fortune and was of "elite" stock, why would he get involved in pushing fatal drugs to rock music's royalty, and in hanging around in late-night music clubs, instead of the palaces and mansions one might expect someone of his background to be at ... unless the infiltration and drug pushing was a mission, coming as a direct result of his family bloodline?

Taking the Michael

Rumours that many of the big-name music stars who are said to have passed away in recent years in fact faked their deaths and re-appeared briefly in public to drop cryptic clues, have proliferated the internet. Any researcher daring to go down such rabbit holes must first bear in mind that the web is full of click-baiters, attention seekers, money grabbers, charlatans and just plain crazies, so extreme vigilance and full reliance only on real evidence become essential to navigate this murky world.

Just as Elvis Presley is said to have become Pastor Bob Joyce and **David Bowie** is said to have re-appeared as industry executive Jack Steven, (though the "real" Jack Steven does seem to exist so was Bowie "playing" him in that famous Sky News clip?) so the idea has persisted that **Michael Jackson**, similar to Elvis, was permitted to fake his death and fade off into obscurity. (A further link between the "King of Pop" and the "King of Rock 'n' Roll" is the two-year marriage between Jackson and Elvis' daughter Lisa Marie.)

Before Michael faded into obscurity, so the theory goes, he made an appearance on Larry King's CNN show the morning after the death announcement under the guise of a conceptual artist, David Rothenberg, known as "Dave Dave." The story was that Dave had become an extreme burns victim as a child and had undergone reconstructive surgery. Many have suggested that Dave was in fact Michael under heavy make-up, and have claimed their voices matched. It's impossible to verify the rumours, however, particularly with Rothenberg himself having reportedly died in 2018.

A burns story resulting in possible facial disfigurement surrounds Michael himself — officially this time. In January 1984, while filming a Pepsi TV commercial, Jackson's hair caught fire when a pyrotechnic malfunctioned. We are told the crew responded immediately by pointing fire extinguishers at his head. A key point emerges here. If the extinguishers were of compressed CO_2 they would have caused extreme icy cold — enough, potentially to have caused severe damage to his face, and particularly the tip of his nose and possibly his ears.

Years of attempted reconstruction would presumably have followed for a star of such magnitude, therefore, the stories of him attempting to look less like his abusive father through cosmetic surgery, and then contracting a rare skin condition, possibly in place as diversion tactics. When he re-appeared, this marked the beginnings of his severe changes in appearance.

Perhaps ongoing attempts at reconstructive surgery were what gradually caused this, not least the change in skin colour, with his wearing of a hairpiece to cover his ears and any damage they may have suffered.

This would also have been a traumatic incident, potentially affecting his mannerisms and behaviours. He appeared very fragile in subsequent public appearances. *If* Michael became Dave Dave this *might* have been a psychologically beneficial tactic, as discussing a much more extreme burns case may have put his own, more minor situation, into some useful context, possibly helping him mentally heal.

Time seemed to have been running out for Michael in all kinds of ways. Just as Elvis had apparently got into hot water with The Mob, so Michael had incurred the wrath of certain Jewish groups through comments he had been making about Jewish control over the entertainment industry, and the inclusion of "anti-semitic" lyrics in '*They Don't Care About Us*' when he had sung "Jew me, sue me, everybody, do me. Kick me, kike me, don't you black or white me."

Was Michael breaking his programming? (MK-ULTRA survivor Cathy O'Brien claims he was inducted into the same CIA project as her.) Could the allegations of sexual impropriety with children be somehow connected, these events concocted to try and keep him in line?

If this is the case, and *if* he was able to fake his death and be retired off... at what cost did it come? Could it have involved him relinquishing the publishing rights to both his own back catalogue and that of the Beatles to the parties he had so enraged?

Fuel was added to the fake death rumour at the time of Michael's funeral, when some fans got suspicious of an unknown figure in attendance.

Michael's song '*Will You Be There*' was performed by singer **Jennifer Hudson** at the ceremony. It contained a spoken section, but attendees reported that Michael's voice sounded highly emotional with the word "pains" spoken instead of "pain" as on the recorded version. Some questioned whether the section could have been getting spoken in-person, live from behind the scenes.

Healing the Payne

Some artists' departures get tongues wagging and social media posts trending more than others, and the sudden demise of former **One Direction** member **Liam Payne** aged 31 on 16th October 2024 certainly did that. Of his many relationships the most high-profile was with former Girls Aloud singer **Cheryl Cole** with whom he had a son. Cole had been on the judging panel of ITV's '*The X Factor*' through which One Direction first found fame, (though their "success" would have already been pre-orchestrated.)

No-One's Dad's a Plumber

Liam Payne. The Industry Reaper strikes again.

File:One Direction NRJ 2014 2.jpg

Description

English: Liam Payne of One Direction at the NRJ Music Awards 15th Edition on 14 December 2013

Date: 14 December 2013

Source: Own work

Author: Georges Biard

Payne was reported as having "accidentally" fallen from the third-floor balcony of the CasaSur hotel in Buenos Aires, Argentina. He had travelled to the country with his girlfriend Kate Cassidy, reportedly to renew his U.S. visa and to attend a concert by former bandmate **Niall Horan**. Payne remained in the city alone after Cassidy returned to America.

The lines were blurred from the start when the communications director for the Buenos Aires Security Ministry reported that Payne "had jumped from the balcony of his room." An Argentine journalist named Paula Varela, however, claimed that he had accidentally fallen after fainting on the balcony, citing unreleased CCTV footage as her evidence.

The hotel's manager is reported to have made a call to emergency services mentioning, "an aggressive man who could be under the effects of drugs and alcohol," and adding that, "when he is conscious he is destroying the entire room and we need you to send someone." The '*Daily Mail*' reported a fan named "Rebecca" as having encountered Payne in the lobby of the hotel where he had said: "I used to be in a boy band — that's why I'm so fucked up."

The public was left with the impression that Payne had become yet another casualty of the pressures of celebrity life and had gone off the rails through drink and drugs, (despite his family's claims that he had been "clean" for some time.) This idea was fuelled by comments made by Payne's ex-girlfriend, Maya Henry, on an episode of '*The Internet Is Dead*' podcast aired just two days before Liam's death. She commented:

> "He would always play with death and be like, 'well, I'm going to die. I'm not doing well'."

Henry had earlier published a book, '*Looking Forward*,' detailing her alleged abuse at the hands of Payne. This contains the claim that Payne had messaged Henry's mother saying, "I'm not going to be around much longer."

Adding intrigue to the story is a man named Rogelio (Roger) Nores, who is thought to have been the last person to have seen Payne alive when he had met with him on the afternoon of his death at the hotel.

In his first podcast on the subject, researcher Joseph Morris revealed that Nores has a murky past, with connections to arms smuggling and financial misconduct. He also appears to be connected to Maya Henry's family, having been photographed with Maya's mother in 2021. Maya's father, Thomas J Henry, is a lawyer who seemingly defended the Nores family in some of the cases brought against them.

Morris further contends that staff at the Buenos Aires hotel confirmed that Maya herself was staying one floor above Liam at the time of his death, despite having made her first Instagram post in weeks just the day before, claiming to be in New York.

Shady characters are often seen hanging around with stars who are soon to meet their demise, as was the case with an individual named Raffles, who was around **Whitney Houston** in the days leading up to her death, and had earlier been hanging around **Michael Jackson**.

According to many, the 25 reported injuries on Liam's body are compatible with some kind of physical altercation having taken place before the fall. I'm reminded of similar claims having been made regarding **INXS** singer **Michael Hutchence** when he was found dead in a Sydney hotel room of what was said to be "suicide," and reports of some kind of disturbance occurring shortly before **Amy Winehouse** was found dead at her home in 2011 aged 27, of what was implied to be "substance abuse." She too is said by family to have been "clean" for some time.

Veteran researcher into the occult within entertainment, Isaac Weishaupt (a pseudonym!) went further in his Substack article of 19th October, suggesting that Payne's death may have represented a "blood sacrifice" to coincide with the "supermoon" that was present that night. The same dynamic may have been at play when *'Friends'* actor Matthew Perry died in October 2023 at the time of that month's "Hunter's Moon."

However fantastic and impossible the idea of ritual sacrifices within entertainment may sound upon first hearing, all the research that I and so many others have done — including eye-witness insiders who have worked within these industries — demonstrates that they are, unfortunately, very real. At their very top levels the controllers of these industries are dark occultists. Their satanic belief systems with all the ritual activity they contain, are very important to them, and drive much of what they do.

You can Check Out any Time You Like...

In other boy band news, "Death By Bathtub" struck again with singer/rapper **Aaron Carter**, the brother of **Backstreet Boys** member **Nick Carter**. Aaron was said to have drowned in his bath in northern Los Angeles on 5th November 2022, with the water jets still running. He was found by his housekeeper who called 911. He was 34.

The media reported that multiple cans of compressed air used for inhalant abuse were found in his bathroom and bedroom, as well as bottles of prescription pills. There was no suicide note. Though he had a son with one of his partners, and had dated celebrities Hilary Duff and Lindsay Lohan, Carter came out as bi-sexual in 2017.

Carter had earlier complained that members of his family, along with the Sony music corporation, were conspiring to kill him, that his brother Nick was "a rapist," and that he had had to go into hiding after a failed attempt to "swat" him. He had asked his fans to support a GoFundMe campaign to facilitate his safety. In a since-deleted video from 2019 he stated:

> *"Sony Records owes me $3.5 million. And they don't want to pay me. And it would be in their better interests, just like Michael (Jackson) told me. They owe me money and they're trying to kill me off.*
>
> *"There's been a lot of misdirection that I've had to do in order to protect myself."*

I've noted before how this realm seems to have a morbid sense of irony when it comes to the circumstances of artist deaths. The more I investigate such notions the more I am convinced that this is down to the computer-style "matrix" coding through which this reality operates, rather than it all being down to calculated human planning. I have been exploring these ideas in my "God' series of videos, the YouTube link to which is included in the resources section for anyone further interested… but I digress.

There was no better illustration of this dynamic than when **Pete Burns**, frontman of the '80s group **Dead or Alive** (what's in a name?) turned up dead as part of 2016's musician body count of a reported sudden cardiac arrest, aged 57. Decades earlier Burns had sung a song titled '*My Heart Goes Bang*' on his group's '*Youthquake*' album, with its lyrics:

> *"You, you, you take my heart and break it up. Get me to the doctor. My heart goes bang, bang, bang, bang."*

It emerged again when **Scott Hutchison**, the frontman of the Scottish groups **Frightened Rabbit** and the **Fruit Tree Foundation**, was found dead in the Firth of Forth near Edinburgh in May 2018. He was 36. This was seemingly down to suicide as Scott had been very candid about his battles with depression, and had Tweeted two messages indicating that he was about to take his own life.

Where the strangeness arises is in a song released ten years before on the Frightened Rabbit album '*The Midnight Organ Fight*,' titled '*Floating In The Forth*.' Certain lyrics seem to have foreshadowed Hutchison's ultimate fate, including:

> "*Am I ready to leap?*
> *Is there peace beneath,*
> *The roar of the Forth Road Bridge?*
> *On the Northern side.*"

And:

> "*These manic gulls scream it's okay,*
> *Take your life.*"

The song ends with the line:

> "*I think I'll save suicide for another year.*"

There are echoes of Hutchison's fate in the story of another musician... though with many complications in the narrative. This is the mysterious disappearance of **Richey Edwards**, guitarist and creative muse with Welsh band the **Manic Street Preachers**.

He vanished on 1st February 1995 after driving away from a London hotel on the day he was due to fly to America for a promotional tour. He was widely assumed to have taken his own life following a long period of depression, his car having been found abandoned near the Welsh side of the Severn Bridge.

The problem in establishing what happened to him comes from the fact that no body was ever found. The possibility arises, therefore, that he *could* still be alive having faded into obscurity. If he did achieve this it's difficult to know how it could have been pulled off without the complicity of the military intelligence services, since he would surely have been found by now otherwise.

There were constant rumours of his having been spotted in Goa, India, a popular location for those who wish to "disappear." The British investigative journalist Richard D. Hall took up the case in 2019 with an episode of his Rich Planet on-line TV series titled '*The Tragic Street Preachers.*' With the assistance of Richey's former best friend Richard travelled to France to follow up the possibility that Richey may have been living there under a new identity, but concluded that it was a false lead.

We should probably note Edwards' age at the time of his going off-grid... 27!

An all-too-familiar routine played out when 90s rapper **Coolio** began to speak out publicly about the true nature of the corporate hip-hop industry in 2022. He reinforced what many other whistleblowers had already claimed about how young, budding stars are lured into the industry's clutches by being made to attend gay sex orgies. In spite of its traditionally macho, alpha-male image, the hip-hop scene, he and others have claimed, is actually run by a "Gay Mafia." This was largely reinforced through the multiple allegations launched against Sean "**P. Diddy**" **Combs**.

Commenting on the '*Hip Hop Uncensored*' podcast, Coolio said:

> "I don't want to say political power, but the amount of social power that I was able to achieve, you would think that I would be a prime candidate to be a member of the Illuminati or a member of the elite society or whatever.
>
> "You would think that they would come at me, and I think they did. Sideways though. Nobody ever got at me directly and said 'we want you to join us and we're doing this.' That's never happened. But I will tell you, I've had motherfuckers come at me for some weirdo shit, like on some gay shit... and I was like, what? Why the fuck would I do that?"

On 28th September 2022 Coolio turned up dead. There are some familiar elements here. He was discovered "unresponsive" in a bathroom, (just like **Elvis, Avicii, Whitney Houston, Bobbi Kristina, Dolores O'Riordan, Jim Morrison.**) This was at the Los Angeles house of a "friend" who wasn't identified in any of the news reports.

The official verdict was that he had died from an "accidental overdose of fentanyl, heroin, and methamphetamine, with cardiomyopathy, chronic asthma, and cigarette smoking having played a role in his death." (Fentanyl is not one to be recommended, considering it is also said to have played a part in the deaths of **Prince** and **Michael Jackson**.) Coolio had been complaining of having been watched and been sent threats prior to his death. (**Wu Tang Clan** rapper **Ol' Dirty Bastard** had made similar claims shortly before he died in 2004, including the line "FBI, don't you be watching me" in his song '*Got Your Money.*')

Skulls & Bones

It's no secret that most of the recognisable names in classical music were freemasons, and my visit to the Zentralfriedhof cemetery in Vienna confirmed that most of the well-known Austrian composers were interred there. More surprising is to find among them the pop singer **Falco**, best-known for drawing attention to the fact that Mozart was indeed a mason in his 1985 hit '*Rock Me Amadeus*,' and who died at the age of 40 in a road accident in the Dominican Republic.

That cemetery wouldn't accept any old riff-raff, so Falco, real name Johann Hölzel, must have been "somebody" in that regard, though we're told his parents were working-class. He had been one of triplets and the only survivor after his mother miscarried his siblings.

"Died Suddenly"

2016 came to be known colloquially as the Year of the Celebrity Death Cull, but it has nothing on the years 2020 and 2021, where the music world's reaper was certainly putting in the overtime.

Naturally, theories emerged that so many "sudden deaths" at a rate never seen before may have been linked to certain forced medical interventions arising as a result of the Co(n)vid scamdemic. Certainly, many artists are known to have been mandated to receive what the Sheep Farm lads refer to as an "arm-spear" before being allowed to continue earning a living by touring. The same requirement was then passed on to many of their fans who were told they would have to do the same before being able to attend their live shows.

It was both encouraging and unfathomably frustrating in equal measure to see mainstream "news" finally playing catch-up in early 2025, with the UK's *'Daily Mail'* running a story titled 'Scientists call for more research into Covid vaccine side effects after unexplained spike in heart conditions.' The words no, shit and Sherlock spring to mind.

Immeasurable numbers of real investigative journalists, authors, film-makers, public speakers, doctors and other medical industry professionals have been presenting verifiable evidence linking the Co(n)vid "vaccines" with the otherwise inexplicable rise in "sudden deaths," yet we have been cancelled, de-platformed, de-monetised and defamed as "conspiracy theorists" (usually "far-right,") "Covid deniers" and "anti-vaxxers" for our efforts. We're probably "anti-semitic, homophobic Holocaust deniers too, while we're about it.

Thousands have had their livelihoods, relationships and families destroyed through having taken such a stance — usually coming from a place of care and concern... only for the mainstream media to now latch on to what so many of us have been saying for years. Will the *'Daily Mail'* now be branded a "far-right, anti-vaxxer. Covid-denying, conspiracy theorist" paper? It's a rhetorical question.

The 2020/ 21 body count included, but was by no means limited to, **Neil Peart**, the drummer with **Rush**, **Kenny Rogers**, **Alan Merrill** of the **Arrows**, **Bill Withers**, **Millie Small**, **Brian Howe** of **Bad Company**, **Betty Wright**, **Mory Kante**, **Bonnie Pointer**, **Charlie Daniels**, **Peter Green** of **Fleetwood Mac**, **Wayne Fontana**, DJ **Erick Morillo**, **Eddie Van Halen, Johnny Nash, Spencer Davis, Gerry Marsden, Phil Spector, Bunny Wailer, DMX, Nick Kamen, Dusty Hill** of **ZZ Top**, **Ian Carey, Charlie Watts** of the **Rolling Stones**, **Sarah Harding** of **Girls Aloud**, **Alan Lancaster** of **Status Quo**, **Barry Ryan**, and **Moody Blues** drummer **Graeme Edge**. **UB40** were particularly unlucky in losing three members — **Brian Travers, Astro** and **Duncan Campbell** all in 2021 — as were **Uriah Heap** in losing **Lee Kerslake** and **John Lawton**, (with **Alex Napier** following in 2023,) **Primal Scream** in **Andrew Weatherall** and **Denise Johnson**, (with **Martin Duffy** following in 2022,) the **Bay City Rollers** in losing **Les McKeown** and **Ian Mitchell**, **Kool & The Gang** in losing **Dennis Thomas** and **Ronald Bell**, (with **George "Funky" Brown** following in 2023,) and the **Supremes** in losing **Mary Wilson** and **Barbara Martin**. Admittedly, many of these were very old, but several were in their 50s or 60s — way too young to die.

Also too young to "die suddenly in his sleep" at his Spanish villa aged 48, as the media reported he did, was **Matthew Ward**, better known as the British DJ **Mighty Mouse**. The cause of death was given as an "aortic aneurysm." He died in October 2022. Six months previous he had Tweeted:

> *"Just had my booster jab. Definitely does not come with a boost of energy."*

One of his followers messaged back, with unintended irony: *"It's a killer. Hope you're OK soon, mate."*

Sinead O'Connor checked out in 2023 aged 56 a year after the documentary film '*Nothing Compares,*' with her participation, had detailed aspects of her troubled life. It didn't cover any hints of satanic ritual abuse or MK-ULTRA-style mind-control, but as I noted in '*Volume 3*,' she sadly ticks many of the boxes for these, and it would explain so many of her "erratic" and "unpredictable" behaviours, plus her desire to adopt alter-egos in her latter years and to distance herself from her past by effectively putting her own music career on self-destruct. (Like **Adam Ant**, her behaviours have been chalked up as her suffering from bi-polar disorder. **Mariah Carey** has also been claimed to be a bi-polar sufferer. Her output has been laden with MK-ULTRA/ Monarch-related symbolism, strongly suggesting that this is another cover story.)

Her official cause of death was given as "chronic obstructive pulmonary disease and bronchial asthma," though many suspected she had taken her own life. For me — though like anyone else I can only guess — this does seem plausible rather than any foul play being involved. It seems she was never able to recover from the suicide of her

17-year-old son Shane in a hospital in January 2022. Shortly before her death, in her final Twitter post she described herself as "an undead night creature" since Shane's passing, and that "there was no point living without him." As far back as 2017 she posted a Facebook video stating that she was staying alive only for the sake of others and if it were up to her she'd be "gone."

A surprising element of the story came from former **Smiths** frontman **Morrissey**. He was back in "controversial" territory when he slammed other celebrities for their tributes to Sinead. In a post on his website titled 'You Know I Couldn't Last' he wrote:

> 'Why is ANYBODY surprised that Sinead O'Connor is dead? Who cared enough to save **Judy Garland**, **Whitney Houston**, **Amy Winehouse**, **Marilyn Monroe**, **Billie Holiday**? Where do you go when death can be the best outcome? Was this music madness worth Sinead's life?
>
> 'She had proud vulnerability... and there is a certain music industry hatred for singers who don't "fit in" (this I know only too well), and they are never praised until death — when, finally, they can't answer back.
>
> "You praise her now ONLY because it is too late. You hadn't the guts to support her when she was alive and she was looking for you."

Speaking of Whitney Houston, it's now well-known that Clive Davis, the veteran music industry executive who is credited with having "discovered" her and signing her to the Arista record label, hosted the "celebratory" party at the time of the 2012 Grammys when news of Whitney's death had broken, in the very hotel in which she had died. Many, including singer **Chaka Khan**, commented on how inappropriate and in poor taste this was.

Davis has held influential positions in the business since the 1960s; among other dubious actions he set up **Sean 'P Diddy' Combs** with his Bad Boy Records imprint through which he was able to gain so much manipulation and exploitation of the many artists he signed, and to become a "celebrity" himself. The rest regarding Diddy and his activities, so they say, is history.

In 2024 a video emerged on the Trap Pulse YouTube channel which told of how Soul singer **Barry White** had tried to warn his friend, fellow singer **Luther Vandross**, about Davis' predilection for men, and to be wary of any moves he may try to make. Barry and Luther both died relatively young — aged 58 and 54 respectively.

Artists endorsed by Clive Davis don't always have the best luck. The first act he signed to Arista Records was the Southern rock band The Outlaws. We are told that Davis was in the audience when the band was the opening act for **Lynyrd Skynyrd**, and the latter's **Ronnie Van Zant** told him "If you don't sign Outlaws, you're the dumbest music person I've ever met — and I know you're not."

The group's **Billy Jones** and **Frank O'Keefe** both died in 1995, of suicide and apparent drug and alcohol abuse respectively, **Hughie Thomasson** of a heart attack in 2007, **Ean Evans** of cancer in 2009, **Herb Pino** (who served in the US Navy for 13 years) in 2014, both **Buzzy Meekins** and **Billy Davis** in 2015, **Jeff Howell** of health complications in 2022, and **Freddie Salem** of cancer in 2024.

Lynyrd Skynyrd didn't fare much luckier, either. Frontman and founder Ronnie Van Zant, **Steve Gaines**, his singer sister **Cassie Gaines**, their assistant road manager and the pilot and co-pilot were killed when a charter plane transporting them to a gig crashed in Mississippi on 20th October 1977. Several other band members and personnel sustained serious injuries.

It seems, when it comes to musicians, that if "Death by Bathtub" doesn't get you a plane crash just might, as the list of other performers who have departed this way includes: **Aaliyah**, (rumours persist that music director Hype Williams was due to travel in the plane that crashed while leaving the Bahamas, and that he switched planes at the last moment;) **Jim Croce**; **John Denver**; **Otis Redding** and four members of the **Bar-Kays**; four members of **Chase**; **Glenn Miller**; members of the **Nelons**, **Passion Fruit**, **Mamonas Assassinas** and **The Blackwood Brothers**, **Keith Green**, and **Stevie Ray Vaughan** in a helicopter which **Eric Clapton** narrowly escaped being aboard.

There was also the tragedy of **Buddy Holly**, **Richie Valens** and the **Big Bopper**, (real name Jiles Perry Richardson Jr.) in the early hours of 3rd February 1959 when the aircraft Holly had chartered to take them to the location of their next gig went down in Iowa. The three musicians and the pilot were killed in the crash. Valens and Richardson were not initially supposed to have been on the plane; Holly's guitarist Tommy Allsup had flipped a coin with Valens for a seat. When Valens won, he reportedly said, "that's the first time I've ever won anything in my life."

Richardson's seat should have gone to **Waylon Jennings**, but Jennings offered to give it up as Richardson was suffering from flu and was not feeling up to slogging it out on the tour bus.

Despite the apparent random-ness of the crash, suspicious researchers have wondered if it could have constituted one of the ritual sacrifices that the industry's occult practitioners seem to like to conduct.

In this regard we should consider the lyrics to **Don McLean**'s 1971 song *'American Pie,'* which is officially acknowledged as being about the tragedy. There are multiple lines with religious overtones, some of which, with some imagination, may hint at deals being made with "the devil," and the debt being called in:

> *"Now do you believe in rock and roll?*
> *Can music save your mortal soul?"*
> *"When the jester sang for the king and queen*
> *... Oh, and while the king was looking down*
> *The jester stole his thorny crown."*
> *"Eight miles high and falling fast,*
> *It landed foul on the grass.*
> *The players tried for a forward pass,*
> *With the jester on the sidelines in a cast."*
> *"Oh, and as I watched him on the stage,*
> *My hands were clenched in fists of rage.*
> *No angel born in Hell,*
> *Could break that Satan's spell.*

And as the flames climbed high into the night,
To light the sacrificial rite,
I saw Satan laughing with delight,
The day the music died."

In 2015 came the revelation that there had been a "lost' verse to the song which had never made the final recording. This formed part of 18 pages of original manuscript written in hand by McLean, then typed up, which was sold at auction in New York. The verse went:

"And there I stood alone and afraid.
I dropped to my knees and there I prayed,
And I promised him everything I could give,
If only he would make the music live.
And he promised it would live once more,
But this time one would equal four.
And in five years four had come to mourn,
and the music was reborn."

Could the "this time one would equal four" line be a reference to the "British Invasion" of America spearheaded by our old friends the **Beatles**, who had been chosen to be "the next big thing" following Buddy Holly, (or even **Elvis Presley**?)

The song speaks of the music being reborn in five years time. Five years on from the crash in February 1959 brings us to February 1964, when the Beatles were catapulted to mass fame following their first appearance on the '*Ed Sullivan Show.*'

Could there be more to know about this terrible event beyond it being down to random chance and extreme bad luck?

This sort of thing never seems to happen to plumbers on their way to fix a sink.

Resources:

Isaac Weishaupt's Substack: Liam Payne: Death Conspiracies, Symbolism & the Occult Music Industry:

- https://illuminatiwatcher.substack.com/p/liam-payne-death-conspiracies-symbolism

Liam Payne's Last Words Hauntingly Predicted His Tragic Demise: 'I'm Going to Die':

- https://stylecaster.com/entertainment/celebrity-news/1234722942/liam-payne-last-words/

The Internet Is Dead podcast: Maya Henry on Liam Payne's Abuse & The One Direction Fandom:

- https://www.youtube.com/watch?v=MP4qIFdfgPM&embeds_referring_euri=https%3A%2F%2Fstylecaster.com%2F&source_ve_path=MjM4NTE

Reuters: One Direction singer Liam Payne dead after falling from Buenos Aires hotel balcony:

- https://www.reuters.com/world/one-direction-singer-liam-payne-found-dead-buenos-aires-local-media-reports-2024-10-16/

Today: Liam Payne's cause of death confirmed in autopsy report: What is polytrauma?:

- https://www.today.com/health/news/liam-payne-autopsy-report-cause-of-death-rcna175959

Joseph Morris: "Struggle" before Liam Payne fall?:

- https://www.youtube.com/watch?v=P5Gh5lhRHt0

Staggering sum George Michael earned each day from beyond the grave last year revealed:

- https://www.thesun.co.uk/tvandshowbiz/25314967/george-michael-earnings-2023/

Daily Mail: George Michael will return to the stage as a hologram as early as next year after huge success of ABBA Voyage:

- https://www.dailymail.co.uk/tvshowbiz/article-12951059/george-michael-return-hologram-stage-estate.html

On This Day: 1984: Michael Jackson burned in Pepsi ad:

- http://news.bbc.co.uk/onthisday/hi/dates/stories/january/27/newsid_4046000/4046605.stm

Jennifer Hudson performs "Will You Be There" at Michael Jackson's funeral:

- https://www.youtube.com/watch?v=vwaOFP6vprk

The Michael Jackson Rebuttal (Part 1):

- https://www.youtube.com/watch?app=desktop&v=6pnoQqlygQs&t=681s

Mark Devlin "God" talks YouTube channel:

- https://www.youtube.com/@MarkDevlinGodTalks

Boss Hunting: THE PETTY REASON MICHAEL JACKSON BOUGHT THE RIGHTS TO EMINEM'S MUSIC FOR $515 MILLION:

- https://www.bosshunting.com.au/hustle/michael-jackson-eminem-music-rights-515-million/

Celeb Live: Before His Death Coolio REVEALED Industry's Plot to Turn Rappers Gay:

- https://www.youtube.com/watch?v=kCQ6zWHH3Zw

NBC News: Coolio, 'Gangsta's Paradise' rapper, dies at 59:

- https://www.nbcnews.com/news/obituaries/rapper-coolio-dead-59-rcna49916

TMZ: Coolio's Son Sentenced For Robbery:

- https://www.tmz.com/2012/09/13/coolio-grtis-ivey-sentenced-prison-robbery-vegas-10-years/

The musicians who died in 2020/ 21:

- https://www.bitchute.com/video/xU6b7bf2G5ku/

Daily Mail: Scientists call for more research into Covid vaccine side effects after unexplained spike in heart conditions:

- https://www.dailymail.co.uk/health/article-14329779/covid-vaccine-research-heart-effects-new-study.html

Morrissey SLAMS celebrity tributes to Sinead O'Connor following her death aged 56: 'You hadn't the guts to support her when she was alive':

- https://www.dailymail.co.uk/tvshowbiz/article-12343331/Morrissey-SLAMS-celebrity-tributes-Sinead-OConnor-following-death-aged-56-hadnt-guts-support-alive.html

Scott Hutchison, Frightened Rabbit Singer, Dies at 36 | Billboard News Flash:

- https://www.youtube.com/watch?v=U_UC7bdbQpI

Rich Planet TV: The Tragic Street Preachers:

- https://www.imdb.com/title/tt11058848/plotsummary/?ref_=tt_ov_pl

Mighty Mouse death: House and disco DJ dies 'suddenly' from aortic aneurysm, aged 48:

- https://www.independent.co.uk/arts-entertainment/music/news/mighty-mouse-death-cause-dj-house-music-b2210949.html

People: Did This French Aristocrat Have a Hand in the Deaths of Jim Morrison, Janis Joplin and Other '60s Icons?:

- https://people.com/music/did-french-aristocrat-jean-de-breteuil-have-hand-in-jim-morrison-janis-joplin-deaths/

Daily Mail: Is this new evidence the ultimate proof that Jim Morrison DID fake his own death?:

- https://www.dailymail.co.uk/tvshowbiz/article-14444483/new-proof-Jim-Morrison-DID-fake-death.html

Rolling Stone: Bobby Womack Obituary:

- https://www.rollingstone.com/music/music-news/bobby-womack-1944-2014-246105/

The Telegraph: American Pie's lost verse:

- https://www.telegraph.co.uk/news/worldnews/northamerica/usa/11518736/American-Pies-lost-verse.html

CHAPTER 12

I PREDICT A SYMBOL

The occult symbolism and Predictive Programming elements of popular culture show no signs of abating. Indeed, they're getting ramped up all the more.

Why?

> *"Why don't we see what's so obvious?*
> *Run from apparent claims.*
> *Recognise the time to open your eyes."*
> Teramaze: 'Esoteric Symbolism'

> *"Mundus vult decipi, ergo decipiatur"*
> *("The world wants to be deceived, so let it be deceived.")*
> Ancient Latin phrase.

If I asked readers to pick a three-figure number that has appeared in popular culture more than any other, I'd wager that most would suggest our old pal 666.

Its very mention can be triggering — particularly to those of a Christian persuasion. But it's worth remembering that numbers, just like symbols, are neutral in their base state, and are neither "good" nor "evil." We are reminded of this from 666's most notorious rendering in the Bible's *'Book of Revelation,'* verse 13:18, where it is stated:

> *"If one is wise and has an understanding to count the number of the beast, which is also the number of a man, the number comes to 666.*

In other words, as with all things in this reality, it's a choice. The number *can* be that of "the beast". But it's also the number of "a man." What can this mean?

Carbon-12, one of five elements in human DNA, is acknowledged as consisting of six protons, six neutrons and six electrons. In this regard, 666 could be said to be describing... *us*. Furthermore, it is said that, on the Fahrenheit scale, normal average human body temperature is 98.6F, 66.6 degrees above the freezing point of 32F. So this number *could* be regarded as being sacred to human existence.

Nevertheless, the occultists who control Organised Society have clearly adopted this number as one of their own, imbuing it with their dark energy and intent, and have twisted its meaning so that it has become one of their major symbolic calling cards. This is why we see so many famous figures, from politicians to music stars, flashing up the "666" hand sign with their fingers. It *doesn't* mean "everything's OK" when seen in these contexts, as per the mainstream cover story.

It's also why 666 is endlessly encoded into mainstream measurements and dates related to the cosmology of Earth, and its relationship to the sun and moon. Just a small handful of the claims made, (and there are *so* many more,) include:

The Earth's Axis: its Orbital Inclination around the Sun is 66.6 Degrees.

The Earth Orbits the Sun at 66,600 Miles Per Hour.

The Earth's Circumference is 600 x 6 x 6 Nautical Miles.

The Speed of Sound is 666 Knots Per Second.

The Force of Gravity on Earth is 666 Newtons.

The Arctic & Antarctic Circles are at exactly 66.6.°

The Distance to the Moon is 6 x 60 x 666 Miles.

The Diameter of the Moon is 6 x 6 x 60 Miles.

North America is 66.66° Wide on a Globe — from the furthest tip to the other (Key Largo, Florida, to Yesterday Island, Alaska.)

You get the idea.

What — honestly — are the mathematical odds of any other number cropping up so regularly in a study field?

When **Dave Grohl** and the rest of the **Foo Fighters** put out their movie '*Studio 666*,' it appeared to amount to mockery of the idea that rock bands such as theirs swear allegiance to the dark forces represented by the number. In it, the band hole themselves up in a haunted house to record an album, and end up getting picked off one by one after Grohl gets possessed by a dark spirit. Drummer **Taylor Hawkins** is depicted as being decapitated by a cymbal.

Just over a month after the film's release in 2022, Hawkins turned up dead for real in Bogota, Colombia. It was implied that his death had been caused by a cocktail of pharmaceutical and recreational drugs, even though he was reported as having been clean for some time.

Did his death in the movie act as a morbid pre-cursor to some kind of sacrifice? We have to consider the question, as it wouldn't be the first time.

The registration plate on the mini in which rock legend **Marc Bolan** died in 1977, driven by his singer girlfriend **Gloria Jones**, bore the number plate FOX661L. The word "fox" is the only one in English which equates to 666 in simple Gematria, F being the 6th letter of the alphabet, O the 15th (1+5 = 6) and X the 24th (2+4=6.) Coincidence?

The '666' sign is just one of a number of hand signals and visual motifs routinely employed by music-makers. Though each can be intricately deciphered on its own, ultimately they are all about the individual in question announcing their membership of "the club," and letting it be known that they are an owned and controlled asset of the industry machine.

Eye, Eye, Captain

Another extremely popular one is the "one-eye" sign. Various interpretations have been put on this. Many were detailed in '*Volume 1*,' but another take observes (forgive the pun) that the sixteenth letter of the Hebrew alphabet is "Ayin" which is derived from an Egyptian hieroglyph of an eye. If we cross-correlate that with the Tarot, the card known as "the Devil" (XV) corresponds to the Hebrew letter "Ayin." Could this partly explain why all these stars flash up the eye sign?

Another interpretation is that, when assets are pictured covering their right eye, they are symbolising their having chosen the "left-hand path." Various groups engaged with occult ceremonial magic view the left, (as in the individual has "left" the righteous path behind,) as representing malicious black magic(k), and the right, (as in it's the "right" way to go,) as embodying benevolent white magic on the right. Confusion arises from many artists being pictured covering their left eye, but we must bear in mind that many images on the internet get flipped around when published.

Sometimes it's difficult to imagine the signalling getting any more blatant. The electronic dance music DJ **Paul Van Dyk**, chronicled at length in '*Volume 3*,' announced his new album of 2018 as being titled '*Symbols*,' with promo artwork showing the largest array of "illuminati" symbology imaginable... before the title was then changed to '*Music Rescues Me*' without the visuals. This seemed like blatant mockery of his obsessive fanbase in the sure knowledge that most would neither notice nor care... as they didn't.

Then there's former **One Direction** singer **Louis Tomlinson** announcing his North American solo tour with merchandise showing a giant one eye above a black and white checkerboard floor. *HELLO???!!!* (That's a thought — the two parts of that word reversed come out as "o hell." I know — I really should get out more.)

There's **Annie Lennox** releasing a 2019 download-only album titled '*Lepidoptera*' featuring an array of butterflies on the artwork. These — particularly the Monarch species — are symbolically associated with the dissociative states brought on by mind-control programming, suggesting that Annie is part of that club. (Like artists such as **Bono**, **Bob Geldof**, **Sting** and **Peter Gabriel**, Annie is seen as something of a social justice warrior outside music, with her Annie Lennox Foundation said to "support social justice work around the issue of global feminism." See the separate chapter on "Extra Curricular Activities" for more on this dynamic.)

An entire compendium of images of "rebellious" **Oasis** brothers **Noel** and **Liam Gallagher** can be found on-line, with them flashing everything from the "666" and "devil's horn" signs, (Liam flashes this to the camera in a photo in which he is sitting next to Jimmy Savile,) to the "one eye" and Masonic "shhhh" signals.

Just as the band were used as assets during the 1990s Britpop era to help make psychopath Tony Blair and his New Labour party look "cool," and driving a pop-culture revolution, (with Noel famously pictured sipping champagne with Blair at a Downing Street reception,) so the group were wheeled out decades later for, seemingly, similar purposes. As Keir Starmer's Labour party were setting about their systematic fomenting of social chaos and destruction of the UK's national culture, the public were diverted by the news that Oasis were re-forming, the brothers having put aside their long-standing feud, and with the media full of stories of concert tickets exchanging hands for ridiculous prices.

Even as late as 2024, "anti-establishment" Noel was proclaiming "I'd still vote for Tony Blair in the morning if he was back in the game" ... in spite of Blair, by that point, having been labelled a war criminal, with millions of deaths resulting from the invasions of Iraq and Afghanistan that he facilitated.

It's clear that Oasis had modelled themselves, to a very large extent, on the Beatles, even down to Liam naming his son 'Lennon,' and that group fulfilling the Northern part of the Britpop dialectic as the Beatles had in the 60s, **Blur** and the **Rolling Stones** providing their Southern counterparts respectively.

Here's a real mindblower further connecting the two groups, however. It's *possible* that this could be the result of some intricate human planning, of course, but to my mind, is more likely another example of the mathematically-coded nature of this reality giving us a little reminder of its existence. The Beatles' final live concert was at San Francisco's Candlestick Park on 29th August 1966. Possibly in homage, Oasis' landmark '*Definitely Maybe*' album was released on 29th August 1994. Oasis split just shy of 15 years later, on 28th August 2009, prior to a scheduled gig in Paris. These dates are 5,479 days apart.

Another 5,479 days later — just shy of 15 years later — came the news of Oasis' reunion, on 27th August 2024.

I Predict a Riot

A cousin of occult signalling is the phenomenon known as Predictive Programming. This is a term popularised by the late Scottish researcher Alan Watt, referring to depictions of a real-world event which is known to be coming, in works of popular culture. The events are referenced in cryptic, coded form, aimed straight at the subliminal minds of the viewing masses. When the real-world event then happens, a familiarity with it has already been embedded, but without the conscious realisation of the subjects.

More pervasive than this element, however, is the notion that the controllers, through employing these methods, are deliberately exposing their own actions, (albeit in veiled, symbolic form,) as a way of fulfilling some kind of "karmic" law within their own twisted, religious belief system. As an article on veteran author G. Edward Griffin's '*Need To Know*' website puts it:

> *"(Occult researcher) Michael Hoffman suggests that the ruling elite are giving notice of their supremacy by telling people that they are without recourse, events are beyond their control, and it is destiny. Eventually a sense of apathy demoralizes to the point of conceding defeat to a system we are powerless to change.*
>
> *"But buried deep within the controllers' rules is a hidden version of contract law that allows them to perpetrate their crimes once the truth is hidden in plain sight, and it is assumed that you have agreed to it."*

The classic example of this factor came from the events of September 11th 2001. *Hundreds* of examples of 9/11 programming placed into movies, TV shows, music videos, ads and beyond have been identified. Most of these occurred years, or even decades prior to 9/11, indicating that this was an event planned long in advance.

Inevitably, it also demonstrates that those forces which were behind that terrible event, were working in collusion with those which control entertainment. Ultimately they are one and the same. This was further reinforced with the '*Illuminati: New World Order*' card game published in 1994 by Steve Jackson Games, in which players represent different secret-societies trying to take over the world. The game is said to have been inspired by the '*Illuminatus Trilogy*' novels by Robert Anton Wilson and Robert Shea, though Steve Jackson himself has said, rather predictably, that the game was meant to be a tongue-in-cheek gag and "not to be taken seriously."

Rather like '*The Simpsons*' cartoons, the cards displayed an uncanny talent for "predicting" coming events, such as the assassination of Princess Diana, the election of Donald Trump, the January 6th "insurrection" at the Capitol Building, 2020s "wokeness," the Co(n)vid scamdemic, and of course, 9/11.

(This phenomenon will also explain why, using the UK as an example, newsreaders are often elevated to celebrity status in their own right. Many will remember Angela Ripon doing a dance routine with Morecambe and Wise, Trevor McDonald horsing around with Lenny Henry on '*Tiswas*' and many BBC newsreaders taking part in comedy and dance routines on BBC1's '*Children In Need.*' This makes them seem less faceless and more "human" so that when they read the lies their teleprompter tells them to in the bulletins, viewers will be more inclined to trust them because they feel like they've got to know them. The dynamic will be just the same, though magnified many times, in America and beyond.)

If we accept that the real culprits behind such stunts are thorough enough to leave no stone unturned in their actions, there's no reason they would have left video games out of their arsenal, given the huge swathes of the population that are into them, some to an addictive degree.

Much subtle pushing of social-engineering agendas appears to have been achieved by these in recent times. The Polish '*Cyberpunk 2077*' presents a future society in which there is no gender and everyone has microchips inserted into their brains, (Elon Musk's Neuralink, anyone?)

The main character has a used chip and shares memories with the chip's previous host, a rock star and terrorist named Johnny Silverhand. A plot similar to this was featured in an episode of Charlie Brooker's terrifyingly dystopian '*Black Mirror*' TV series. It's no secret that human society is getting systematically nudged towards a Transhumanist society in which factors like brain chips will be the norm by the day.

I documented many music business examples of PP in '*Volume 1*' but we can throw in a couple which slipped through the net here. In the 1985 video to **AC/DC**'s '*Shake Your Foundations*,' the group perform, for no ostensible reason, in front of the Manhattan skyline, the WTC towers highly prominent as the lyrics go "shake it to the floor."

A year later came the video to **Genesis** spin-off group **Mike & The Mechanics**' '*Silent Running.*' A distinctive striped pattern appears overlaid on Mike's face. This bears a distinct resemblance to the pattern on the side of the towers which would come down 15 years later.

Though not the WTC towers themselves, John Lydon performed in front of two strikingly similar buildings in the video to **Public Image Ltd.**'s '*This Is Not A Love Song*' in 1983.

As indicated in the previous books, **Prince** was a deeply complex and self-contradictory character, (rather like **John Lennon** before him,) and it becomes difficult to second-guess his motives in some of his activities.

Why, for example, did he and his band appear to have foreknowledge of Osama Bin Laden being blamed for the 9/11 attacks three years into the future when, at a December 1998 concert in the Netherlands, he announced: "I got to get back to America. Osama Bin Laden gettin' ready to bomb," before one of his band chipped in with "2001 — hit me!"

Did this constitute Prince, in some way, trying to warn of what was to come? Or was he fulfilling some kind of obligation to his handlers through "revealing" it?

More ambiguity comes from his song '*New World*' on 1996's '*Emancipation*' album, where Prince clearly displays knowledge of "Illuminati" agendas, and gets uncannily accurate in some of what he "predicts" for the future. Examples include:

> "When the lines blur every boy and girl,
> How we gonna make it in this brave new world?"
> "When you wanna find some isolation,
> But the tracker you got from vaccination (keeps playing,)
> Keeps playing 'You'll Never Walk Alone' (over and over,)
> They're always listening, especially on the phone."
> "A pill that will stop the wrinkles, a pill that will stop the pain
> A pill that will make a baby never seek political gain
> What's it all for when you can alter biology?
> Who or what, then my friend, will you and I be?"

We might conclude that Prince was schooled in similar knowledge to hip-hop cultural pioneer **Afrika Bambaataa**, (real name Lance Taylor.) Bam's much-revered image was tarnished in 2016 when two men went public with accusations that he had sexually molested them when they were minors, and a part of his cult-like Universal Zulu Nation.

A 1996 track on *'Warlocks And Witches, Computer Chips, Microchips And You',* credited to Bambaataa's **Timezone** project, addressed just about every New World Order "conspiracy theory" going, a decade or two before ideas such as mind-control frequencies, implants and A.I. would become widespread tropes.

How did *they* know about such stuff so early on?

We might also ask ourselves what inside knowledge the makers of the song and video *'Cathy Don't Go To The Supermarket'* had in 1985. This cautionary tale displayed detailed knowledge of the New World Order agenda linking Chinese communist-style computerised social credit systems with the "mark of the beast" foretelling of the Book of Revelation, as it depicted a dystopian trip to the local store, the opening radio announcement stating:

> *"Hey guys and gals, get hip with the new craze. Register today for your very own personal '666' barcode implant. No more need to carry cash or credit cards. The price of the goods you buy is now automatically subtracted from your bank account by the computer at the checkout stand."*

The song turns out to be credited to The Family International, which is a modern name for the religious cult originally known as the Children of God, (which has faced multiple accusations of sexual impropriety within its ranks.) The song was arranged by former **Fleetwood Mac** musician **Jeremy Spencer**, who quit the group suddenly in 1971 to join The Family. It certainly had a strong heads-up on future world plans, however it gained them.

The song ultimately offers a hopeful message with its line:

> *"Honey don't worry just take my hand, we can make it even if we have to live off of the land."*

You've been Watching too Many Films, Mate!

It seems the same amazing prescient knowledge of future events was shared by film directors, and it goes back a long way. '*Metropolis*,' the 1927 German expressionist masterpiece from freemason and occultist Fritz Lang, depicted a dystopian society 100 years into the future, (so right around now,) which was amazingly accurate in its imagining of futuristic cityscapes, and a society where the downtrodden masses work in servitude for the privileged "elites." A lucky guess... or inside knowledge of the plan?

The Transhumanist robot in '*Metropolis*' has had a huge influence on many contemporary singers, becoming inducted into the performances of the likes of **Beyoncé** and **Lady Gaga**, while the band **Queen** based the video to their '*Radio Gaga*' entirely around scenes from the movie, with which they were said to be fascinated. A new soundtrack was created for a restored version of the film by Italian producer **Giorgio Moroder**... in 1984!

Some decades later came '*Soylent Green*,' a 1973 Richard Fleischer-directed adaptation of a novel by Harry Harrison. It is set in New York City at a time where over-population (!) has caused massive food shortages, and the state's solution is to provide a synthetic food named Soylent Green (soy/ lentils/ greens?) said to be derived from ocean plankton, but in reality, found to be made of dead bodies.

These are contributed to by the state benevolently offering "suicide pods" where those tired of life in such terrible conditions can opt to peacefully remove themselves from it.

The year in which the film's plot is set? 2022.

In 2024, the first "suicide pods" aimed at releasing the terminally ill, were made available.

Irony strikes again in that "Fleischer" is the German word for "butcher." Wryly amusing, given the film's over-riding theme.

2027 was also the envisioned year of the 2006 Alfonso Cuarón-directed '*Children of Men*.' This one depicts a... you got it, dystopian futuristic society, (note to all film-makers — other types of society are available,) in which humanity is facing extinction due to women having somehow become infertile. (I can't *think* what might have caused that?!)

Refugees seek sanctuary in the United Kingdom which has become a totalitarian police state.

No. I'm sorry. that one's a stretch too far. That could never happen.

I detailed many examples of the Co(n)vid agenda of 2020/ 2021 being portentously "predicted" in endless music videos, TV shows and movies in '*Volume 3.*' One that I missed was the 1979 German film '*The Hamburg Syndrome.*' So much of what we all went through in those years was right there in the script — the sudden outbreak of a deadly disease; quarantine; face masks; protective suits; travel restrictions; military intervention... and the sudden disappearance of the "disease."

The New World Order/ Agenda 2030 plan towards which the "elites" have long been working so feverishly, was also presented in 1976's '*Logan's Run,*' based on a 1967 novel. Here, the futuristic society is Utopian, (don't get too excited, though — this is just on the surface,) the community living under a huge dome.

Humans are not allowed to reproduce sexually, (just as in Aldous Huxley's '*Brave New World,*') and everything is controlled by an A.I. computer grid. Society is full of young and beautiful people, just as in the vision of the maniacal Hugo Drax in the James Bond film '*Moonraker*'

But there's a catch. No-one is allowed to live beyond the age of 30. All are implanted with a crystal chip which begins blinking when it is time for them to be "terminated" by a group of police enforcers known as "sandmen." (In the 1950s song '*Mr. Sandman,*' this character is assumed to be some kind of supernatural entity.)

In Season 1, Episode 4 of the 2009 American TV series '*V,*' we are shown how "the Visitors," (an alien race,) had added micro-trackers to the "vitamin/ flu jabs" that they were administering to humans in their worldwide "healing" centres.

The audience is also told about the secret healing technology that is being systematically hidden from the masses. I'm sure none of that could ever really happen, though.

More prescience was on display with the '*Lifehouse*' concept devised by **Pete Townshend** which he evidently tried to sell to the rest of the

Who. Townshend had in mind another multi-media rock-opera along the lines of '*Tommy.*' His bandmates weren't impressed, and many of the ideas ended up getting reworked into the group's 1971 album '*Who's Next.*' Townshend's initial vision, however, had been to explore a "dystopian" (yawn) future, where, according to notes on the project from his own official website:

> "... the population lived in environmental life suits to protect them from extreme pollution following an ecological disaster. The suits were all hooked up to a universal grid, and they were force-fed entertainment and life experiences from a huge media conglomerate controlled by the government."

There was also talk of people saving energy by not travelling too far from their homes and staying at home and putting on a suit.

Was Pete coming from a well-meaning place, and *just happened* to pinpoint, way back in the early '70s, ways in which human society would have changed by the 2020s?

Or, were we witnessing some calculated foreshadowing of 15-minute cities, pollution through geo-engineering, and the futuristic "climate change" scam from one in a position to know?

Resources:

The Hebrew letter Ayin comes from an Egyptian hieroglyph for an eye:

- https://en.wikipedia.org/wiki/Ayin

The Tarot card "the Devil" corresponds to the Hebrew letter "Ayin":

- https://www.llewellyn.com/encyclopedia/article_print.php?article=25354

Who Got at Marc Bolan's Millions?:

- https://www.youtube.com/watch?v=f9QiMbL9t38

G. Edward Griffin's Need To Know: Revelation of the Method: Why Do Elites Tell Us What They Are Going to Do?:

- https://needtoknow.news/2022/05/revelation-of-the-method-why-do-elites-tell-us-what-they-are-going-to-do/

The Independent: The 1990s card game that 'predicted' 9/11, Donald Trump, Covid and the Capitol riot:

- https://www.independent.co.uk/news/world/americas/us-politics/illuminati-card-game-trump-covid-b1839470.html

Prince: 'New World Order' lyrics:

- https://genius.com/Prince-new-world-lyrics

Afrika Bambaataa Presents Timezone: 'Warlocks And Witches; Computer Chips; Microchips And You' (1996):

- https://www.youtube.com/watch?v=K-RJ4Dj_KaA

'Metropolis' and its influences:

- https://metropolisfilm.fandom.com/wiki/Metropolis_film

Logan's Run: People Not Allowed To Live Past 30 Years Old:

- https://www.youtube.com/watch?v=h-ksRooSLs0

IMDB: 'Children of Men':

- https://www.imdb.com/title/tt0206634/

The Family International: Cathy Don't Go To The Supermarket music video (1985):

- https://www.youtube.com/watch?v=47TZ9MHI1qg

Pete Townshend: The Lifehouse Project:

- https://petetownshend.net/musicals/lifehouse

Louder Sound: How the Lifehouse album was almost the death of The Who:

- https://www.loudersound.com/features/how-the-lifehouse-album-was-almost-the-death-of-the-who

Guitar World: Pete Townshend on Who's Next, Lifehouse, and fun times with Superstrats:

- https://www.guitarworld.com/features/pete-townshend-the-who-whos-next-lifehouse

CHAPTER 13

SONICS – FROM DEMONIC TO HARMONIC

"Music and vibration are at the basis of all. They pervade everything; even human consciousness is reflected by music."
   Pete Townshend of The Who,"Melody Maker,' February 1971.

"There's a reason you can't get certain song lyrics or hooks out your head all day — they're curses & incantations. The truth is stranger than fiction. Idol worship leaves the eye dull."
   Electric Being in an Instagram post, 2024.

The consensus between both mainstream/ Establishment and alternative scholars, is that everything we experience in this apparently "physical" realm is made up of sound and light energy vibrating at an endless array of different frequencies. Sound, then, can be said to be at the very core of ourselves, all other living things, and the realm that we all inhabit.

Suspend all disbelief for a moment and just imagine — you know, for the sake of argument — that you were part of a sick, satanic, psychopathic control system which wished to dominate, enslave and control the rest of humanity. Would manipulating sound — particularly that which is offered up under the guise of "entertainment" — not be an *essential* tool in your toolkit?

From the mid-1950s, when the rock 'n' roll revolution paved the way for the contemporary popular music scene, all the major record labels had their roots in military activity — from RCA, the Radio Corporation of America, developed out of the U.S. Navy, to Electrical & Musical Industries, (EMI) in the UK, with its connections to military intelligence and, reportedly, Tavistock. These corporations were engaged in experimentation with sound and its various deployments.

Former Stone Roses singer **Ian Brown** had evidently done his homework when he Tweeted in 2023:

> *"As you know the music industry is an arm of the military. Roses worked with a great engineer, the latse (sic) Bill Price who told me himself in the early 50s he was a white coat working on the military potential of sound with Thorn EMI. Then came the record industry and mass mind-control."*

Cliff Richard's father, Rodger Webb, was a one-time employee of Thorn Electrical Industries, and Cliff began recording for the EMI record label in the 1970s prior to its merging with Thorn in 1979. (Purely as a matter of curiosity, Thorn Industries is the name of the business empire that Damien, the "anti-christ" uses to facilitate his rise to dominance in the '*Omen*' stories.)

A stepping-stone from analogue to digital music formats was provided by the advent of synthesisers, which played a major role in the Acid House/ Rave scene and the electronic dance music genre it led to. Some early models were reportedly recalled by manufacturers because they were capable of creating the very low frequency of 7 hertz, just slightly below Earth's natural frequency, called the Schumann Resonance, at 7.83 hertz.

7 hertz, (what's in a name?) is said to create an intense, low-down rumble as it pulsates to the point that it is said to be physically "felt" by the human body, rather than "heard" through the ears. It is described as "infrasound." We appear to be getting close to the perfect sound weapon here if this technology were allowed to fall into the wrong hands, (see **Kate Bush**'s song and video '*Experiment IV*' for more on this.)

Does anyone believe it hasn't?! Indeed, low-frequency sound weapons already exist for dispersing large crowds by inducing feelings of physical sickness.

British researcher and film-maker Chris Everard had been down this road by the time he released his documentary film '*The Empire Strikes Black*' for the Enigma channel in 2024. The promotional blurb stated:

> *"Infrasound has been investigated as a weapon by the Pentagon. But there are other frequencies too which have an almost immediate effect*

> *on the human brain.... We explore the sci-fi psychedelic multi-frequency phenomenon of free-form Jazz, which contains multi-layered harmonics, dissonance, cross-modulated frequencies, super bass, SHF (super high frequencies,) melodies, counter-melodies and all kinds of audio waves which can — and do — have a palpable effect on the brain, heart and other organs."*

Seemingly, it was not by accident that the revolution speeds of old vinyl record players were set to 16, 33 (sounds familiar!), 45 and 78rpm respectively. According to some musicologists, playing music at 33.3rpm, (leaving 66.6 recurring to complete the 100 per cent!) creates a frequency, (or "groove") that is in alignment with humans' physical and metaphysical forms, and result in a playback tuned to 432 hertz.

So albums would always be pressed to 33.3, bringing the listener a full, immersive experience. Singles were usually set to the faster 45rpm, with just one or two songs per side, still creating a harmonising frequency.

This would go some way to explaining why the controllers would have wanted to remove any such beneficial effects as part of the universal shift away from analogue sonic formats, to digital. The word vinyl enthusiasts use so often to describe the aspect of sound that was removed when vinyl was replaced by digital was the "warmth."

I was surprised — though probably shouldn't have been — to have heard from a listener who had happened across the ritual drumming rhythms associated with the occult art of voodoo, and its similarities to modern salsa. As he wrote:

> *"Because I'm a Salsa dancer, I immediately recognised that rhythm. In Salsa there is a so-called clave — two hard wooden sticks which make a pattern. There is a so-called 2-3 clave and a so-called 3-2 clave. In this voodoo-rhythm I immediately recognised a 3-2 clave, but ... played with a cow bell."*

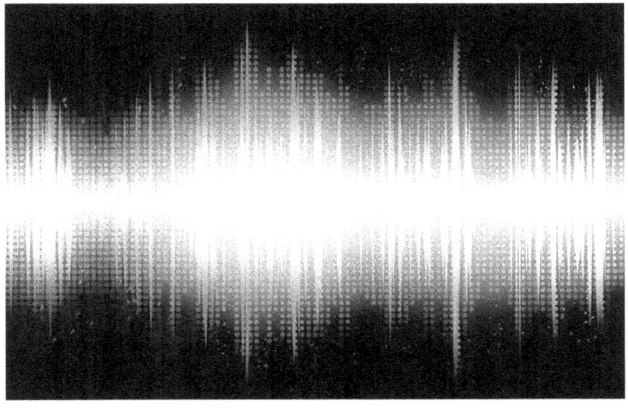

Sound under the 'scope.
https://picryl.com/media/sound-audio-waves-music-084515

Has some of the sonic power of ancient voodoo rhythms been systematically incorporated into a much more benign-seeming genre, therefore, but with some of the same effects still occurring on an unseen level?

Good Vibrations

OK, that's the bad stuff. Lest I be accused of being negative, (*me??!*) let's now flip the script to consider some ways in which sonics and intonation can be used for healing and upliftment.

I mentioned the good work done by the Nordoff-Robbins Musical Therapy Centre in London in '*Volume 2.*' Musical therapy is a recognised method within psychology for the treatment of physical and mental health disorders.

The World Federation of Music Therapy was founded in 1985 in Genoa, Italy, now based in North Carolina, and there are over 9,000 certified music therapists around the world.

Music — if pitched to a beneficial frequency — is thought to reduce levels of the stress hormone cortisol, and increase the body's production of the antibody immunoglobulin A. Even low-intensity vibration is reckoned to bring established benefits for those diagnosed with osteoporosis, with 40 hertz appearing to help work against other diseases.

Music lights up neurons between the right and left hemispheres of the brain, thus providing a total brain workout.

In 2024, British Professor Gloria Moss delivered a thought-provoking presentation at the Questioning Science conference in Nottingham. In it, she questioned whether churches and cathedrals were *really* intended as places of worship, or rather, as places of healing through sound.

The design and construction could have facilitated acoustic effects, she suggested, which would have brought beneficial results to the congregation — like a giant communal sound bath. She noted how the extremely long pipes of the oldest organs produce overtones, harmonics and fine, low healing frequencies.

Furthermore, the sonics from bells are on the ultrasound frequency. There are claims that the bells increase immunity and shorten the recovery time from infectious diseases. The unique spiral path of the sound wave is said to destroy cell structures of micro-organisms, including hepatitis, typhus, influenza and cholera.

During many centuries of epidemics in Europe, the bells from churches rang all day. Bells are also thought to operate at a psychological level, relieving stress and various autonomic dysfunctions associated with fear, anxiety, sleep disorders and depression.

As with all things in this realm, seemingly, duality is at play when it comes to sound. It can be a hugely effective weapon... or a wonderful asset for human health and wellbeing.

The outcome, as ever, is entirely dependent on the consciousness and intent of the user.

Resources:

'The Second Summer of Love' 4-part podcast series, including Matt Sergiou's info on the military connections of the major record labels and their sonic research:

- https://www.spreaker.com/episode/good-vibrations-second-summer-of-love-full-4-part-series--56411376

Electric Being on Instagram: Music is Magick..Hip Hop is Hypnosis:

- https://www.instagram.com/reel/C7ceB4yuMu6/?igsh=MX-I2bmc0MHYzbjE3MQ%3D%3D&fbclid=IwZXh0b-gNhZW0CMTAAAR2U2foUJRLgmDiipVrO6g-tr5Ow-HK-RYYbEJbnbIM9XijLspHxptYw66Ao_aem_AVg4T-Ku802r6ftGoq2hFOQHQkfBnSItZ6hXD0MwH_f-IV6ucSnp-1dKLrDedzT5RSkxaH-Z47ipqLbrEBf-aG5SZ-

Voodoo rhythms similar to salsa:

- https://www.youtube.com/watch?v=cL4YYCv7nSs

The Gatekeepers

I'm conscious that, with the following section largely covering the purveyors of electronic dance music and its derivatives, there might be a temptation among those who don't care for these styles of music, or were never caught up in the culture, to switch off and give this one a swerve.

I would urge such readers to, in the words of that classic piece of British arthouse cinema, "Carry on Regardless" as I feel such perseverance will pay dividends. Ultimately, these chapters are less about the music and more about the dynamics of Culture Creation and Lifetime Actors, and the way the leaders of certain fads/ trends/ movements/ scenes are chosen over and above all others.

I have opted to hone in on these characters since I have a lot of personal familiarity with them and the scenes they represent, but could just have easily have used influencers from, say, the New Wave, Heavy Rock or Bubblegum Pop scenes to make the points.

That being said, let's proceed with a deep dive into the world of the specially selected industry "Gatekeeper."

CHAPTER 14

THE GATEKEEPERS: CARL COX

For those who may not be "fortunate" enough to come from the "right" bloodline family, there is another way to get to the very top ranks of the music industry. Provision is made for those with pure, natural talent to be elevated to household-name status.

There is, however, a heavy price to be paid for the wealth, privilege and exposure that such characters are afforded, and so only those prepared to sacrifice their sovereignty and personal integrity, and content to take direction from other forces, get to thrive and survive in this way.

Such owned assets always show their true colours in the end, though, sometimes after years of flying under the radar without any particular red flags. But when you know what you're looking for, the success stories become easy to take apart.

There is no disputing that **Carl Cox** is immensely talented within his field. Often described as "the DJ's DJ" due to the huge influence he has had over others in his field, he has been cited as a mentor to countless other creators within electronic dance music. Even when cutting his teeth in his early days he picked up the nickname "The People's Choice."

There is no suggestion that Cox came from any important bloodline, and he appears to be the first within his family to have achieved any notable influence. He was born on 30th July 1962 in Oldham, Greater Manchester. His father, Henry Carlisle Cox, and mother Patricia, hailed from Barbados and had moved to England in 1958, in Carl's own words "with the idea that they would earn a lot of money and go back to Barbados one day." Henry became a bus driver and Patricia a midwife. Carl had two sisters, Angela and Pamela.

Shortly after Carl's birth, the family moved to South London — first to Tooting until 1967, then to Carshalton, a town which had also served as home to a young **Cliff Richard** when his family relocated to Britain from India. Carl evidently had his natural propensity towards music ignited very early on. He says he bought his first record at the age of six, and was turned on to an eclectic variety of sounds due to the house parties that his parents would regularly host for their friends.

His earliest sessions behind a turntable involved him selecting 7-inch singles from his father's collection and playing them on the single gramophone deck. This experience, he has said in many interviews, taught him much about the DJ's artform of choosing the right records to play at the right time in order to generate the best dancefloor reaction, and to build mood and atmosphere. As Cox related in an interview with '*DMC World*' in 2012:

> "*My family had all of the finest records back then, and when I was about 8 my mum used to let me play all of the vinyl just to keep me quiet. So I'd play these tunes, artists like Aretha Franklin, Booker T and the M.G.'s and Elvis Presley, and off it went with my mum, dad, family and friends all dancing around the living room with me sitting on the floor choosing the next record. And I caught the bug.*"

As his reputation grew, he began playing at weddings, bar mitzvahs and other private functions. He was inspired by a mobile disco playing at a function in his school, and tried to emulate it by building his own sound system. He began clubbing aged 14, and developed an insatiable appetite for buying new music, spending all his disposable income on records.

He certainly seems to have been a hard worker in his formative years, developing a work ethic early on which has stayed with him throughout his career. In his autobiography '*Oh Yes, Oh Yes*' published in 2021, he opens with a tale of having trimmed a neighbour's hedge for pocket money, only for the man to refuse to pay him the agreed fee because he was not satisfied with the result. When Carl protested he was told, "save it for your book, sonny." He did just that.

Entering the world of work, like his father, Cox took on many working-class labouring jobs, further reinforcing the idea that he did emerge from a regular walk of life, with no privileges afforded by his genealogy. Having studied electrical engineering, he spent time variously as a supermarket shelf stacker, a mechanic, a painter and decorator, a scaffolder, and with an undisclosed job "at Peugeot."

His day job wages continued to be used to fund his DJing ambitions. By 1979 he was earning just £12 a night DJing in a wine bar in Kingston-on-Thames. His appetite for entertaining crowds kept him pressing on with gigs at bars, smaller clubs and private parties around South London and beyond, however, playing a varied mix of Soul, Funk, Disco and early Hip-hop.

Accounts of this period have him rubbing shoulders with other young DJs and promoters who would go on to become well-known figures within the Acid House and dance music revolution that would explode at the end of the 80s, including **Paul Oakenfold, Pete Tong, Terry Farley, Gilles Peterson, Norman Jay, Fabio** and **Trevor Fung**.

By the mid-80s, at which point he had moved to Brighton after his parents had returned to Barbados, leaving him and his sisters to fend for themselves, he had mastered the art of turntablism, and had become a regular entrant in the DMC Mixing Championships staged by the Disco Mix Club.

These had become the industry-standard gauge of the best DJing talent on the scene. Despite entering many heats and becoming a finalist twice, however, being described by iconic music journalist **James Hamilton** as "messily enthusiastic" at one, Cox never came first to emulate the likes of **Cutmaster Swift, Chad Jackson, DJ Cheese** or **DJ Cash Money**. Another string to his bow, however, came from his having become a proficient disco and breakbeat dancer, also entering competitions recognising this skill.

1987 has been immortalised in legend as the year that the genesis of Acid House culture was sown on British shores, the fabled trip to Ibiza made by four young London DJs having been covered at length in '*Musical Truth Volume 2*.' (And see the coming section on Paul Oakenfold for more.)

Though claiming to have been too broke to have joined the four lads on their overseas jaunt, fortuitously, Cox was present at the opening night of **Danny Rampling**'s '*Shoom*' event in Southwark in November 1987, having been hired by Rampling to provide the sound system. In his book, a disgruntled Cox talks of Rampling having subsequently axed him from the '*Shoom*' roster for no good reason.

With the events of Rampling, **Paul Oakenfold** and **Nicky Holloway** lighting the touchpaper for the Balearic Beat, and later Acid House scene in the UK, however, it wasn't long before what even the mainstream media dubbed "The Second Summer of Love," (actually two summers — 1988 and 1989,) was underway, and Cox found himself in just the right place to get booked for many of the largest open-air raves that were appearing.

The most infamous of these was the Sunrise event held just after the summer solstice in June 1989 at White Waltham Aircraft Hangar, and promoted by public schoolboy-turned convicted fraudster **Tony Colston-Hayter.** It was here, as he played his set at daybreak in front of thousands of ravers, that Carl first picked up the moniker of "the three-deck wizard." He related this experience in his *'Oh Yes, Oh Yes'* biography:

> *"I was rocking it. I could feel the energy back from the crowd and I felt like I had more to say, a lot more. Every top DJ was there and I was still quite unknown, but felt I was ready to step up. There were over 15,000 people still there and Maxine, my girlfriend and manager at the time, looked at me and said, 'There are three decks there, you know you can do it.' Caught up in the moment, I stuck a record on the spare deck and mixed it in.*
>
> *"... I had two copies of 'French Kiss' by Lil Louis and I mixed in the accapella of Doug Lazy's 'Let It Roll.' The crowd had been winding down, ready for the journey home, when the music hit them. It was as if I had just re-energised them with this magical sound as 15,000 people found the hidden reserves to get back on the dancefloor."*

Carl Cox. When it's claimed he was once a "soul boy" it may mean he no longer has one left to sell.
Carl Cox in Argentina, 2016
www.entradarecital.com.ar/carl-cox-en-argentina-2016/
https://creativecommons.org/publicdomain/mark/1.0/

Cox's reputation as a top-league DJ on the UK's dance music scene had been firmly cemented as the 1980s gave way to the '90s. He went on to play at many other high-profile raves, and later, key nightclubs, both throughout Britain and abroad. This was a scene which revolutionised youth culture in the same way the music, fashions and drugs of the late 1960s had, and I shared my suspicions and evidence that it, at least to some significant degree, represented a military-grade social-engineering psy-op in '*Musical Truth Volume 2.*'

As the '90s dawned, the sounds began to change. The genres known as "hardcore," "jungle" and simply "rave" emerged, and Cox was at the forefront of all of them, going on to create his own record, regarded as a staple rave anthem, '*I Want You Forever.*' The record was released on Paul Oakenfold's Perfecto label, and led to Cox performing it on BBC1's '*Top Of The Pops.*' Having always been something of a musical chameleon, however, he went on to embrace the styles of Hard House and Techno later in the decade, the latter remaining the genre for which he came to be recognised as a worldwide pioneer.

Like a handful of his contemporaries, Cox has no children. He did marry, briefly. In an interview with the '*Sydney Morning Herald*', he commented:

> "*I got married in 1993 to Rachel Turner. She was 22 and I was 32. We were married for three years, but she felt I was wrong for her and I felt the same. It was difficult to split because when I went to the altar I meant marriage for life. It was horrible to go through that.*"

Turner went on to become an entrepreneur, first in the music industry, then in psychology and personal development.

Cox went on to travel internationally, at one point providing a set for BBC Radio 1's **Pete Tong**-hosted '*Essential Mix*' from a different country each month. He appears to have always had a strong affinity with Australia, performing there many times, and going on to make it his second home, buying a house in Frankston on Melbourne's Mornington Peninsula in 2004.

On New Years' Eve 1999, he gained an experience that no other human ever had, or could have done, by seeing in the new millennium twice, first playing in Sydney, then jumping on a private jet, (as you do,) to go "back in time" by crossing the international date line and playing a second set as midnight dawned in Hawaii.

As well as producing records under pseudonyms such as Stone Circle and Conqueror, he also got into running his own record labels, starting with the small MMR (Most Music Records,) then Worldwide Ultimatum Records, Ultimatum Trax and Ultimatum Breaks, and latterly, Intec (International Techno,) which has become one of the key outlets for that genre.

It's difficult to pinpoint a time in his career when elevation to the very top ranks would have taken place, but by this point, Cox's talent and drive would have been noticed by the industry's spotters, whose job it is to keep an eye on which bands, musicians, or in this case DJs, have built up major fanbases largely off their own backs, and can therefore be utilised as assets to push certain agendas and steer attitudes within youth culture in certain desired directions ... provided they're prepared to do what's required of them and take the deal.

At this stage it would take an individual with high moral standards, or lacking the street savvy to understand the true nature of the industry and its objectives, (an ability which would have been very much lacking in the pre-internet era,) to turn down a highly attractive offer.

Carl has talked of getting locked up on a couple of occasions in his youth — once for three months in 1980 around the time of his 18th birthday, where he was incarcerated at Ballantyne House in Kent for joyriding, and again for a weekend following a raid on a party elsewhere in Kent, where his equipment was seized. (He also complained of being routinely followed by police when he was driving to "illegal" raves, the coppers having decided this was their most reliable way of discovering the remote locations at which these parties would be taking place.)

I feel it worth pointing out — just for the record — that when youngsters get into trouble with the police, deals are often known to be made, where leniency is offered in exchange for co-operation in one area or another.

Just as an aside, I have a personal suspicion that many so-called YouTube "influencers" who apparently revel in great wealth, are paid by the intel services to produce their content, presumably as part of some social-engineering agenda to make viewers feel hard done by and insignificant in comparison to the lifestyles flaunted in their faces. Demoralisation is one of the psychological specialities of the type of behavioural scientists employed by the likes of Tavistock. By way of example, besides such "influencers" as the Ingham Family, the Fizz Family and the Norris Nuts, all of whom seem to have expensive houses and endless foreign holidays with first-class travel coming out of every orifice, the large size of their families seemingly presenting no financial obstacle, there is also the Wilson family out of Nottingham.

In 2015, Nigel Wilson was fined £1,800 at Westminster Magistrates Court for "illegally" flying drones over professional football matches and tourist landmarks in breach of the Air Navigation Order. (It's a shame the courts don't show the same strict attitude towards "illegal" chemtrail planes.)

This represented the first case in England of a person being prosecuted by the CPS for using drones after a police-led operation. Not long afterwards Wilson, who had previously been listed as a security guard, had started his own YouTube channel, plus one in the name of his daughter, Tiana, where he and his family were seen goofing around in a hugely extravagant mansion complete with private swimming pool, which is presented as their home.

Can such riches really be accumulated from YouTube ad revenue alone? If they could, wouldn't every family in the land be doing it?

Anyway, back to Carl, and perhaps one of the earliest red flags suggesting something had changed was the appearance of his official logo, which bore some resemblance to the winged sun disk of Egyptian legend. The controllers of the music industry are, at their core, occultists and sorcerers. They had already shown their hand during the Rave era with the naming of many of the key events, alongside the graphics on the accompanying flyers, many of them embracing mystical, spiritual, religious and metaphysical themes.

Carl's vector logo, which has accompanied his name on festival flyers for years, joins those of other league-one DJs which bear elements of occult or 'Illuminati" symbolism. (An earlier logo had depicted Carl's head with two lions emerging on either side as a kind of coat-of-arms, though this would doubtless be explained away by his zodiac sign being that of Leo the lion, just as his initials, CC, representing a Freemasonic 33 within gematria, are written off as a meaningless coincidence given he couldn't have chosen his birth name.)

Given the nature of electronic music, it has always been the ideal vehicle through which to push, popularise and normalise ideas of Transhumanism. Cox would appear to have been way ahead of his time when, in 1995, React Records released his now fabled *'F.A.C.T'* compilation mix album, the title standing for *'Future Alliance of Communication and Technology.'* His face appears in holographic form on the sleeve.

Years later he released an artist album titled *'Electronic Generations,'* the sleeve design featuring audio device robots in various stages of evolution, culminating in a contemporary-era cyborg. A record release, *'Welcome To My World,'* featured the same cyborg circumnavigating a globe earth. (Cox further pushed the spinning ball earth nonsense through his long-running syndicated radio show simply titled *'Global.'*)

In the years to follow, many of the large-scale festivals and club nights at which Cox would perform, would begin to embrace the notion of humanity merging with technology. This was evident in their naming, ('*Digital Dreams*,' '*Electric Daisy*,' '*Electric Bay*,' '*Electro Magnetic*,' '*Eastern Electrics*,' '*Glitch*,' '*Timewarp*,' '*Hypnotic*,' '*Secret Projects*,' '*Ultra* (as in MK?) *Music Festival*,') plus in their decor and symbolism.

These events, and the DJs headlining them, would appear to have been playing their part in conditioning fans to accept that electronic and digital ways of doing things really are the only viable future for human society. These ideas are implanted with stealth into the collective subconscious mind, so that when such changes gradually creep into everyday society — cash becoming replaced by digital "money," human operators in shops becoming replaced by machines, standalone electronic devices becoming replaced by radiation-emitting "smart grids" and the "internet of things" — they are much more readily accepted, because a familiarity with, and an acceptance of them, has already been slyly implanted through methods such as these.

Carl has been an enthusiastic pusher of virtual reality games, and has crowed proudly of having holograms of himself created for such applications, at one point posting on his Facebook: "*my 'Intermundium' show has arrived in the virtual world featuring my avatar, 'Coxy 2.0,' performing in Sensorium Galaxy.*" At least one commenter was on-the-ball, observing: "*amazing but scary. A.I. is closer than we think.*" Another, *hopefully* sarcastically, commented, "*nice to know that when we connect to the metaverse Carl will be there for everybody.*"

Further reinforcement of this dystopian, not-too-distant-future society, came from the Resistance club night which Cox helmed at Privilege in Ibiza in the 2010s. The related artwork featured a cyborg-type figure with three lines, resembling a barcode, covering the eyes, and the same three lines comprising the capital E at the end of the brand name.

A separate Cox brand, Resistance, featured a fist as its logo, implying opposition to authority. The trouble is, this fist design is the same as that which has been used to symbolise communism, which represents anything *but* resistance to authority. It's a shame the spirit of resistance was markedly absent during the highly communistic times of the Co(n)vid-19 lockdowns. But more of that shortly.

A flyer advertising a Carl Cox Space Ibiza special in London featured a pyramid next to Cox's head for no good reason. Many flyers of recent times have seen him bathed in blood red with black in the background, the colours of Saturn and those who venerate it. One design had part of his head glowing an ominous red, suggesting his brain being radiated from the inside out.

Alone, any of these could be written off as meaningless or circumstantial. But, when all placed together, a pattern starts to form. The controllers of Organised Society do offer us clues as to which groups or individuals are now "in the club" and are doing their bidding. The signs are always there for those with the eyes to see. But they will always be dismissed as "conspiracy" by those who will perform any kind of mental gymnastics necessary to avoid having to hear it about "their" personal hero.

There is much to be gleaned from Cox's participation at another, even more dubious festival.

Every August/ September, over the U.S Labor Day weekend, tens of thousands flock to a remote location known as Black Rock City, way out in the Nevada Desert, on land we are told was formerly, (or is that "formerly,") owned by the United States military. There, after several days of "performance art," they gather to witness the burning of a human figure in a scene reminiscent of the pagan human sacrifice depicted in the 1973 film '*The Wicker Man.*'

As such, the Burning Man event is steeped in occult symbolism and ritual. This would be one thing if all attendees were there entirely of their own volition, yet this appears not to be the case. New Zealand entrepreneur-turned alternative researcher Steve Outtrim, worked for many years in the I.T. industry based in California's Silicon Valley. There, he states, it is almost obligatory for those who reach a certain rank to attend Burning Man as a condition of their employment. The coercion runs strong. As he mentioned in comments I included in '*Musical Truth Volume 2*':

> "*I was in a meeting in Sydney in about 1997, with quite a high-level executive from SUN Micro Systems, a big computer company spun out of the Stanford University Network, just like Google. And back in the day they were a major military and defence contractor, and this guy, the chief science officer, said, 'hey, do you go to Burning Man?'*

He was a guy in his 60s, highly respected, a guy that's met presidents and prime ministers all over the world, and I'm like, 'wow, he knows about Burning Man? What's going on with this thing? I have to go!'

"I first went in 1998. Once you've been there more than ten times, you start to look at things a little differently as the initial novelty starts to wear off. I started my blog as a huge Burning Man enthusiast, but as I did more and more research about what's really going on there — the organisation behind it, the occult elements, the military/ government elements — I became a little bit more cynical."

Though the musical element of Burning Man has mainly involved bands, electronic music has slowly crept in over the years, and some time in the 2010s Carl Cox began making annual pilgrimages to the site to perform.

At first, these visits would be unannounced; he would simply take a week off from his weekly residency at Space in Ibiza to travel to the States. A few years later, however, he became more transparent, speaking publicly of the wonderful experiences he had had there, and staging fundraiser club events, usually in San Francisco. Evidently, those attending Burning Man do so on their own dime, and these events were to help cover the cost of Cox curating his own stage there. Although he was claimed to be worth around $16 million in 2024, apparently he still can't afford such an outlay, and it's only right to let others to pay for it.

Could attendance of Burning Man now be an obligatory rite of passage for certain carefully selected names in the electronic music field, therefore, in the same way it has for those in I.T. and other professions, given that DJs/ producers **Diplo, Skrillex, Lee Burridge, Damian Lazarus, Above & Beyond** and **The Crystal Method** are among those who have made the pilgrimage?

Burning Man turned to disaster in 2023 when the site was engulfed in rain storms almost unheard of in that desert area, but attributed to "Tropical Storm Hillary," entirely consistent with the government-sponsored weather manipulation now proven to be occurring on a mass scale.

Black Rock City is built on the remnants of Pleistocene Lake Lahontan, and the Biblical floods turned the desert's sandy surface into clay-like thick, grey sludge. All vehicles were banned from entering or leaving the site, leaving attendees stranded for several days with food and water conservation becoming of major concern, not to mention toilet facilities. The comedian/ actor **Chris Rock** and DJ Diplo, who had been in attendance, were reported to have trudged through six miles of mud before eventually gaining a lift away from the site in a passing truck.

Could Burning Man 2023 have been used as a government/ military weather experimentation testbed? And could there have been advance knowledge of this in some quarters? San Francisco's SFist website reported that tickets, normally sought after and in short supply, were abundantly available that particular year, stating: "For whatever reason, lots of people have had second thoughts and decided they don't want tickets they already bought."

Cox, like most others, was caught up in the deluge and stranded for several days. In spite of the disaster, however, he put on a brave face, stating on his Facebook page that he was simply having fun and getting though it. He was back for more the following year, too — complete with the obligatory crowdfunder event in San Francisco, naturally.

In 2024, Cox posted a picture of himself to his social media in which he was wearing a jacket embroidered with a pyramid design, with an eye in the centre.

Given that the occult controllers of society, (and their minions,) feel duty-bound to announce the truth of what they are really all about, is it too much of a surprise that Cox himself, in a comment given to 'Channel 4 News,' commented: "I feel like the Gatekeeper of the scene"?

With specific reference to dance and club music, it seems each genre does have its allotted Gatekeeper in the UK — a figure in place to help steer the scene and its fans in certain desired directions, and to ensure that only others who have been "approved" achieve prominence and success. While Pete Tong, **Tim Westwood** and **David Rodigan** can be seen to have fulfilled this role within electronic music, Hip-hop and Reggae respectively, there is much to support the notion that Cox has long been the "chosen one" to lead *his* particular genre.

(In the same interview, Cox revealed that it was funding from King/ Prince Charles' Prince's Trust platform which first allowed his mobile DJing activities to get off the ground ... but there may not be anything too nefarious about this link, given that the Prince's Trust was a major source of funding for many sole traders and small businesses looking to get off the ground in the 1980s.)

Cox has also been fortunate enough to indulge his love of motorsports alongside his music activities, ever since his days of drag racing on Chelsea Bridge and that arrest for joyriding. He went on to set up his own operation, CC Motorsports, running his own team and competing himself in motor races around the world.

How much good fortune can one man have, really, all off the back of learning to play records as a kid?

The trouble with a Gatekeeper's role would appear to be that it's never complete. While it clearly comes with many a perk, it also carries a price, that being that the individual concerned is always going to be beholden to the forces which have either allowed them to attain the fame, influence and success that they have, or have simply handed it to them on a plate in the case of performers less naturally talented than Cox.

Gatekeepers may be permitted to go their own way and please themselves for months, or even years at a time without any interference from their higher-ups. But when an agenda comes along that needs pushing among certain demographics, they will know that to decline the instruction is not a move that will be in their best interests.

Assets always show their true colours in the end, and, as *'Musical Truth Volume 3'* amply demonstrated, so many of them were smoked out from their lairs by Co(n)vid-19 and associated agendas.

In Cox's case, as the worldwide lockdowns of March 2020 hit, he was midway through a North American tour which he was forced to cut short. Despite then being stuck in Australia and unable to play live for well over a year, there was no hint of any discord from Carl. Why would there be when none of his peers were exhibiting the slightest dissatisfaction with having their livelihoods severely disrupted either?

Strange, though, that Carl had felt sufficiently motivated to attend protests in Trafalgar Square in the early '90s against government threats to shut down illegal raves and place restrictions on licenced club events. But no such opposition to the *far* greater threats to *everyone's* rights and freedoms, and not just when it comes to parties.

Instead, he lauded the benefits of house arrest on Facebook, posting himself making banana bread and growing vegetables in his garden, and musically, producing plenty of tracks and beginning a weekly livestream *'Cabin Fever'* show where he took viewers through his record collection. In one episode he was joined by fellow DJ **Christopher Coe**. Naturally, the pair appeared in facemasks, playing their part in enforcing that aspect of the agenda.

The real clincher came, however, in 2021 when the world started to re-open — albeit slowly, and with all manner of restrictions in place. Carl *appeared* to be up for speeding the process along when he recorded an info-mercial with an NHS doctor, Kishnan Bodalia, stating... as the late **Rolf Harris** might have said, can you tell what it is yet?... that the *only* way the event world could ever get back to normal is if all club and festival goers take an untested experimental gene therapy, (commonly known as a Co(n)vid-19 vaccine,) in exchange for the return of their freedom. As he stated in the ad:

> *"My whole life existence over the last 30 years has been entertaining people in small clubs, in bars and wine bars, and big clubs and festivals alike. What I do, it creates a gathering of people. So that's what I'd like to see happen more than anything, that we can basically all be safe in knowing that we're going out to party safe and enjoy ourselves.*
>
> *"We are in a pandemic. This is something that we are all trying to deal with and all trying to work on, and what we don't want is the clubs to not work. At the end of the day, we are all on the frontline now. So, it's the only thing we can do to protect ourselves, to be able to enjoy our moments."*

He added at the end:

> *"My first jab was nice and easy, no problem. My second one was a bit bruisy, felt a bit woozy for about a day or so, and I'm absolutely fine talking to you now here today."*

I wonder how many of those he coerced into taking the "arm-spears" or "the three-dart finish," in order that he could get back into increasing his millions, are lucky enough to be able to say the same?

Resources:

Mixmag: 60 Reasons to Celebrate the Legendary Carl Cox:

- https://mixmag.net/feature/carl-cox-60-birthday-dj-legend

DMC World Magazine: Carl Cox interview, February 2012:

- http://www.dmcworld.net/uncategorized/carl-cox-2/

World-famous DJ Carl Cox: 'I want to find love and stability in my life':

- https://www.smh.com.au/culture/music/world-famous-dj-carl-cox-i-want-to-find-love-and-stability-in-my-life-20220323-p5a79d.html

Carl Cox Tops the List of Highest-Paid Techno DJs in the World with a Whopping $16 Million Net Worth!:

- https://www.exitfest.org/en/carl-cox-tops-the-list-of-highest-paid-techno-djs-in-the-world-with-a-whopping-16-million-net-worth

Carl Cox charges £50,000 per DJ set:

- https://storm-djs.com/how-much-does-a-dj-cost/

Carl Cox in conversation: the late 80s and the thrill of vinyl | Mixmag x Ballantines True Music:

- https://www.facebook.com/carlcox247/videos/823075015198514/

Carl Cox interview with The Edge Video Magazine, June 1992:

- https://youtu.be/SPCTfHeDZfU

DJ Magazine: How Carl Cox became known as the 'Three-Deck Wizard' :

- https://djmag.com/longreads/how-carl-cox-became-known-three-deck-wizard

CNN: Tens of thousands at Burning Man told to conserve water and food after heavy rains leave attendees stranded in Nevada desert:

- https://edition.cnn.com/2023/09/02/us/burning-man-storms-shelter-black-rock-city/index.html

Channel 4 News: Superstar DJ Carl Cox says Prince Charles' charity kick-started career

- https://www.channel4.com/news/supestar-dj-carl-cox

Carl Cox Crosses the International Time Zone to See in the Millennium Twice:

- https://www.youtube.com/watch?v=7jk3R7NGfRc

Mixmag: Carl Cox teams up with the NHS to encourage people to get vaccinated:

- https://mixmag.net/read/carl-cox-nhs-vaccinations-jabs-nightclubs-reopening-news

Dr. Bodalia discusses the vaccine and the safe reopening of nightclubs with Carl Cox:

- https://x.com/NHSuk/status/1423606129758810115

Cral Cox & Christopher Coe DJ back-to-back . . . in masks:

- https://www.facebook.com/watch/?v=937975790025597

How She Got There: Rachel Turner, the founder whisperer:

- https://march8.com/articles/how-she-got-there-rachel-turner-the-founder-whisperer

Man fined after flying drones over Premier League stadiums:

- https://www.bbc.co.uk/news/uk-england-nottinghamshire-34256680

Who is Chris Ingham? YouTube star revealed after he denied paedophile claims:

- https://www.dailymail.co.uk/news/article-6095153/Who-Chris-Ingham-YouTube-star-revealed-denied-paedophile-claims.html

CHAPTER 15

THE GATEKEEPERS: PETE TONG

In the second volume of '*Musical Truth*' I drew attention to the well-worn radio ID recorded by rappers **Salt 'N' Pepa** proclaiming, "Pete Tong got power!" (Tong had just signed them to his record label, FFRR.)

It's a statement which has only grown truer with time, and whereas back then I applied some rudimentary questioning, it's now time for a deeper dive into, arguably, the most influential figure within electronic dance music in the genre's history. A Gatekeeper, by any other name.

At a cursory glance, Tong appears to have middle-class origins. His biography tells us he was born on 30th July 1960, in Dartford, Kent. This turns out to have been at the same hospital as **Mick Jagger**, a fact Tong himself revealed some years ago when posting a picture of himself together with the grizzled old rocker.

Tong was raised in the villages of Longfield and Hartley, near Gravesend, living in, as he describes it "quite a big house." He attended the "elite" Kings School in Rochester, which describes itself as the second-oldest school in the world, with mentions in the pages of Dickens. Others educated there include the author Clive King, the cricketer Geoffrey Lees, the Royal navy officer Desmond Hoare, and assorted priests and bishops. His father was a turf accountant with a chain of bookmakers' shops. In interviews, Tong has stated that his father was an alcoholic, a trait which Pete himself has admitted to adopting for a period.

We may have the first of a series of red flags very early on in Tong's life story, so in the interests of chronology I'll insert it here. The insufferable loudmouthed BBC Radio 2 host Vanessa Feltz, has stated that her first kiss was with Pete Tong in Majorca, during a chance encounter when both their families were holidaying at the same time. What *are* the mathematical odds of two children who would both go on to become prominent BBC radio hosts, just happening to meet in this way by pure chance?

We'll return to this line of thinking later.

Young Pete's love of music was first sparked through a fascination with rock bands like **Led Zeppelin** and **Deep Purple**, and his parents bought him a drum kit when he was 12.

Everything changed, he has stated, when he witnessed a DJ at a school disco and thought it looked much more fun than being in a band. He played his first gig at the local village hall, before the entrepreneurial spirit which appears to have driven his entire career began to appear, and he invented himself as a mobile DJ, buying a transit van and travelling around to play at weddings, private functions and pubs.

After falling in with a crowd who would regularly travel to many of the cooler clubs in London, the young Pete discovered the world of Soul, Jazz, Funk and Rare Groove, and fine-tuned his output to become a specialist in these areas. He comments in his website's biography:

> *"Gravesend was an unusual town because at that time, in the 1970s, it had quite a big West Indian community and quite a big Indian community. So I had different flavours. A lot of Soul music and Reggae ... I was also getting turned on to American imports for the first time, and understanding that there was like a secret society of record collectors. You had to be in the know. Then I would go up to London and go to shops like All Ears in Harlesden. My reputation grew. I also worked for a bit in a record store in Gravesend."*

In March 1978, still only 17, he won the London regional final of the Tea Council's Young DJ competition. This earned him his first column inches from **James Hamilton** in '*Record Mirror*', who would promote Tong enthusiastically for the next several years:

> *"Peter Tong of Dartford won the London regional final of the Tea Council's Young DJ competition at Southgate's Royalty last Friday, establishing a good rapport with the audience and playing some funky goodies in the three minutes allowed him."*

From here, the young Pete finished second at the final at The Empire in Leicester Square. This one got him noticed by the highly-respected

'*Blues & Soul*' magazine, which took him on the following year for his first proper day job.

Initially, his role was loosely defined, he says, but he was expected to sell advertising space. He ended up becoming a staff writer. (I myself scored a writing job on the same magazine until its demise in 2007 after 40 years in the business, and worked out of the same offices in Paddington's Praed Street as Tong had. Veteran editor Bob Killbourn regaled me with stories of how he had written a letter to confirm Tong's salary when he was applying for his first mortgage, and of how the magazine had also counted DJs **Graham Gold**, **Paul Oakenfold** and **Tim Westwood** among its columnists.)

By the early 1980s, Tong had become a part of the South East's "Soul Mafia." This was a tight-knit collective of DJs who would play at each other's gigs, and would collaborate at Soul alldayers and events such as the Caister Soul Weekender. Others in the collective included **Robbie Vincent**, who had a highly influential show on BBC Radio London, and later BBC Radio 1, **Chris Hill**, **Jeff Young, Sean French, Tom Holland** and **Steve Howlett**, (better known as **Froggy** due to his propensity for jumping wildly around while playing tunes, and supplier of the most sought-after sound system on the scene.)

Tong was by far the youngest member of the clique, barely out of his teens by the time he had fortuitously made their ranks. Among his early gigs was a night he ran in London's Baker Street titled '*Family Function*', which coincidentally would become the name of the warehouse party sound system that fellow BBC Radio 1 DJ **Judge Jules** would begin a few years later.

Pete Tong. The turf-accountant's boy done good.
https://upload.wikimedia.org/wikipedia/commons/e/e5/Pete_Tong_%28crop%29.jpg

Andrii Khliakin from Kyiv, Ukraine, CC BY-SA 2.0 <https://creativecommons.org/licenses/by-sa/2.0>, via Wikimedia Commons

Radio-wise, Tong's association with the BBC also began at a ridiculously young age when, around 1981, he scored a spot, alongside some of his Soul mafia buddies, on **Peter Powell**'s Radio 1 drivetime show, reviewing the latest Soul and Funk releases and giving news about the scene. He also appeared alongside Powell and Froggy on an episode of '*Oxford Road Show*,' a BBC2 programme named not after the city of Oxford, but rather Oxford Road in Manchester, from where it was broadcast.

His website biography mentions that he participated in pirate broadcasts as well as his local BBC Radio Medway, before landing a weekly Sunday show on Kent's Invicta Radio, (a legal operation not to be confused with the pirate station of the same name.) From there he became part of BBC Radio London's '*Nite FM*' roster alongside the likes of **Dave Pearce** in 1987, before being recruited later that year by Capital Radio to replace **Greg Edwards**, who was departing after more than a decade of presenting his '*Soul Spectrum*' show on Saturday evenings.

This gave Tong a highly influential radio platform ready for the emerging Acid House scene and the revolution in dance music culture which was to begin right at that time. The fabled trip of the four young DJs to Ibiza took place in August 1987, (see the chapter on Paul Oakenfold for more on this,) Tong's Capital gig began in September, and his old mate Jeff Young got hired by BBC Radio 1 to present '*The Big Beat*' show in October, which similarly would chronicle the emerging scene.

Slowly, DJs such as Tong, Oakenfold, **Danny Rampling**, Judge Jules, Graham Gold, Carl Cox and Dave Pearce, who had all been known for playing "black" forms of music like Soul, Funk, Rare Groove and Hip-hop, were all embracing the new House sounds beginning to trickle out of cities like Chicago, New York and Detroit. Jeff Young seemed to resist the shift, staying truer to his soulful music roots.

As his DJing profile grew, by 1983 Tong had departed '*Blues & Soul*' for his next day job, a position at London Records where he was placed in charge of managing acts such as **Bananarama**. Four years later, he was gifted his own imprint at London, a revamped version of a much older label called FFRR — Full Frequency Range Recordings. This became London Records' platform for the rapidly emerging dance music genres, and Tong was in the right place at the right time, as head of A&R, to begin signing prominent acts of the day, ranging from Salt 'N' Pepa to early House music pioneers like **Joe Smooth, Sterling Void, Frankie Knuckles, Satoshie Tomiee** and **Lil' Louis**.

This meant that, by what the mainstream media dubbed "The Second Summer of Love" of 1988, (a nod to the many cultural similarities between this scene and the hippie/ flower power one which had emerged out of California in 1967,) Tong had influential positions as both a radio and club DJ, and a record industry executive. In his '*Encyclopaedia of Popular Music*,' Colin Larkin writes of this period:

> "*This gives him tremendous influence in determining which tracks transfer from the club scene to the national charts, and often international success.*"

The influence would go much, much further when Tong cemented his relationship with the BBC even further.

When Jeff Young left his Friday evening dance show in late 1990, Tong was poached by Radio 1 to replace him, and so began his '*Essential Selection.*' Acid House culture had given way to a much more expansive dance scene by this point, with many British productions joining the American releases.

In 1993, apparently inspired by the uninterrupted mix shows broadcast by New York stations like Kiss FM and WBLS, Tong and his manager/ producer **Eddie Gordon**, hit upon the idea of the '*Essential Mix,*' late on Saturday nights, to complement the Friday show. Running for the next three decades-plus, this would at some point feature pretty much every world-class DJ in the mix for two hours straight.

There seems to have been some animosity in the relationship between Eddie Gordon and Tong in the intervening years, however, with Gordon accusing Tong of claiming credit where it was not due. In his own on-line biography, Gordon mentions:

> "*On Wikipedia, though, he keeps deleting 'his' history, embellishing it with lies. For example, Steve Wolfe came up with the now infamous phrase 'It's all gone Pete Tong' one Sunday night at Invicta Radio during Tong's weekly Soul show, when the studio phones all rang at the same time for tickets to a weekender competition. But on Tong's history, it was Mark & Lard on Radio 1. Total rubbish!*
>
> "*. . . My very important chat with my main client Jeff Young, the departing BBC Radio 1 DJ, about passing the baton on to Pete to protect the ground-breaking work he had established on the national radio station, was indeed an essential bit of work for Mr. Tong's career!*"

Though Tong has recalled his early Friday nights at Radio 1 as being lonely affairs, where he was pretty much left alone to do as he pleased, by the mid-90s he had become a much more valued asset, as new controller Matthew Bannister consulted him on how to consolidate Radio 1's championing of all forms of dance and club music yet further. Tong is said to have facilitated the recruiting of Danny Rampling, Tim Westwood, Judge Jules and **Fabio & Grooverider** as a result.

(No need for Tim Westwood to be chronicled in this book's section, as I exposed the reasons to consider him an appointed Gatekeeper in the last volume. Now, in the wake of the allegations levelled at **Diddy**, **R. Kelly**, **Afrika Bambaataa** and **Drake**—all of whom Westwood has counted as friends—he has found himself embroiled in his own accusations of sexual abuse. Reportedly, investigations by both the BBC and London's Metropolitan Police are ongoing... though at time of writing the latter has been underway for three years, Westwood in the meantime freely travelling back and forth between the UK and Lagos, Nigeria.)

Though all of the above names were eventually axed, Tong has survived every single cull of specialist DJs. When **Annie Nightingale** (CBE) died, he became the longest-serving and oldest DJ remaining on Radio 1, more than three decades on from when he was first hired. *Something* has kept him in good favour in a fast-moving and cut-throat industry where most of his fellow presenters are of an age to be his grandchildren.

A word which gets used more than any other in media articles profiling Tong is "ambassador." Or, as his own website puts it:

> *"In fact, throughout his varied and astonishing career, he's been a catalyst, a genuine agent for change."*

As if these achievements weren't enough, in 2013 he moved to Los Angeles, by this point the epicentre of the explosion in EDM, as it was known in the United States. (He had moved there with his second wife. Here he shares a factor with fellow DJ **Paul Van Dyk**. Both had previous marriages—to Debbie and Natasha respectively, but went on to marry Latino wives—in Van Dyk's case a Colombian, Margarita Moreno and in Tong's, a Brazilian, Carolina Acosta.)

After a good couple of decades of being popular in Europe, but being largely sidelined in America, where styles such as Hip-hop, Grunge and Rock had prevailed, dance music had suddenly burst through to the mainstream, aided by collaborations between R&B artists like **Kelly Rowland, Usher, Ne-Yo** and **Chris Brown**, and producers like **David Guetta, Afrojack, Will.i.am** and **Benny Benassi**. Its coinciding with large quantities of "Molly," the new slang name for MDMA or ecstasy, in scenes reminiscent of all the LSD which was arriving in California to complement the hippie scene, didn't do any harm to the music's popularity either.

All eyes were on LA, and in addition to his already prolific activities, Tong became Director of the Electronic Department of William Morris Entertainment. This he co-founded with **Joel Zimmerman**, better known as the Canadian DJ and producer **Deadmau5**. Zimmerman is an obvious candidate for having undergone MK-ULTRA-style mind-control, his gimmick being performances wearing a giant mouse's head. (See '*Musical Truth Volume 1*'s information on the symbolism behind Disney's Mickey Mouse.)

According to a 2020 '*Variety*' magazine article:

> *"Arriving from his own company, Division One, Zimmerman brought with him an impressive stable of artists, and built the division as EDM was exploding as a genre. The popularity of dance music led to astronomical fees for top acts throughout the world, but especially in Las Vegas, where seven-figure nightly pay-outs were not atypical for residency runs. Speaking at a conference in 2012, Joel Zimmerman famously declared: 'If there was a movie about bidding wars in EDM, I'd probably be Darth Vader'."*

The long and short of this is that both Zimmerman and Tong would have added considerably to their personal riches through their WME division, capitalising on an industry that had become worth billions. Tong had indeed moved to LA at just the right time to benefit from it all, having also become an A&R Consultant for the Warner Music Group, and, like his pal Paul Oakenfold from the old days, executive producer on an assortment of film soundtracks.

In 2015, yet another string was added to his bow when he was asked to curate a showcase of new interpretations of dance music anthems for The Proms classical music concert, alongside conductor **Jules Buckley**. This led to the '*Ibiza Classics*' series of concerts which he has been touring ever since to sold-out audiences at venues like the 02 in London.

The extent to which he had endeared himself to the Establishment was indelibly confirmed when, in March 2014, he collected an MBE, (Member of the Order of the British Empire,) from Prince William at Buckingham Palace, placing him in the company of other DJs who have been knighted, including the late Annie Nightingale and **John Peel**, **Norman Jay**, David Rodigan, **Trevor Nelson, Jazzie B** and **Goldie** (whose debut artist album Tong had signed to his label.)

And so, all of the above inevitably leads any intrepid researcher to ask one over-arching question. Is it actually even *possible* for an individual — in this case a regular middle-class lad from Kent — to achieve *this* much reach and sway an an industry worth billions, and with a fanbase measurable in millions, *without* having been specially chosen for the role by those who wield the real power in this scene?

His very name has even entered the lexicon of cockney rhyming slang, "Pete Tong" meaning "wrong," and inspired the title of the '*It's All Gone Pete Tong*' movie starring Paul Kaye, and including a cameo from Tong. Who *gets* that?

In considering the question, perhaps the time has come to consider another assortment of red flag warning signs from over the years.

Very early in his career, Tong was mixing with many of the pop stars of the time; he reportedly booked **Culture Club** for one of their earliest gigs, and **Spandau Ballet** are said to have hung out at his regular DJing spot at West Kingsdown Hilltop.

By the mid 90s, he was taking midnight dinners and flying around on private jets with **U2**, and warming up on-stage at the Phoenix Festival for **David Bowie**. It's not that I envy him in being in such close proximity to Bono — at least without a sick bag. It's more a case of wondering how anyone gets into such a position through pure chance or good (?) luck.

Decades later, he became the opening DJ for **Duran Duran** in Ibiza. When **Quincy Jones** passed away in 2024, Tong shared a story on his Instagram of how Bono had summoned him to a late-night dinner in Las Vegas after one of his DJ shows in LA. The young lad from Kent with a box full of Jazz Funk records had come a long way.

By 2001, Tong had mentioned that he must have visited New York City "at least 50 times." He speaks of early trips made to buy records and to visit seminal clubs like the Paradise Garage, the Palladium and the Danceteria. (Judge Jules and the previously-profiled Tim Westwood talk of similar experiences.)

No-One's Dad's a Plumber

Even though Laker Airways was offering cheap flights from London to NYC in the early 1980s, we must still ask ourselves how a young lad on meagre earnings was able to fund so many trips all by himself?

An early DJing photo of Tong shows him in a black-and-white checker shirt. This design has symbolic ties to Freemasonry, and while it may simply be an innocent choice of fashion, equally, it may not. Decades later, in 2024, Tong posted a promotional picture of himself holding both index fingers to his lips—a rendering of the Masonic "sshhhhh" sign denoting the telling of no secrets. His '*10 Years of Ibiza Classics*' tour in 2025 was promoted with an image of him doing the usual, tired "one eye" hand signal.

Like fellow pioneers Danny Rampling and Paul Oakenfold, Tong received many of his bookings as UK club culture was first beginning to kick off, from promoter **Nicky Holloway**, one of the four DJs present on *that* iconic trip to Ibiza. Holloway's parties went under the name '*Special Branch*,' the title of an intelligence-gathering division of the police and military intelligence. Somehow, Holloway and his mates, all in their early 20s, were able to gain access to such iconic landmarks as Regents Park Zoo, Jubilee Gardens, the Natural History Museum and Lords Cricket Ground.

Like almost all of his peers, Tong helped to publicly push the official line on the Co(n)vid-19 scamdemic, obediently staying at home and producing DJ mixes from his LA "bunker." In one livestream, he appeared wearing a cloth facemask throughout as as he taught his wife, who *was* not wearing a mask, how to DJ!

Tong is close personal friends with actor and sometime DJ **Idris Elba**, (OBE,) who was one of the very earliest celebrity pushers of Co(n)vid propaganda in the UK. In an interview with '*Mixmag*' dated 22nd November (22+11=33) 2021, Tong added legitimacy to the idea of vaccines being the only way back to social normality by commenting:

> "*We'll see how the winter goes. But hopefully it's just the case of the vaccination levels getting up to the same standard all across Europe.*"

Tong was a co-founder of the International Music Summit, which takes place annually in Ibiza, (though didn't in 2020 or 2021, for obvious reasons!) By its return in 2022, besides considering how the dance music industry should move forward "post-pandemic," and with talk of "co-existing with Covid," it had quite obviously begun promoting an assortment of "globalist" agendas, with titles like *'Environment:* **Brian Eno** *on the impact of the music industry on the world's climate,' 'Sustainability At The Heart of The Music Industry,'* (presented by Marina Ponti of the United Nations,) *'Humanity: Ukraine — Emergency Discussion,'* and *'Diversity & Inclusion.'* (How could it be any other way?)

The following years boasted among their features, *'Planet in Progress... a workshop to teach key skills... for women, queer and non-binary folk,'* and, *'How the industry can positively address the climate crisis.'* (I can offer a revelation in that regard; there isn't one.)

By this point, Tong had started espousing spiritual views, commenting on how yoga and meditation had helped him cope with his busy schedule, and publicly endorsing Jagadish Vasudev, aka Sadhguru, and his Soil Foundation project.

Though masquerading as an Indian Yogi and "philanthropist," (note for context: Bill Gates, Bill Clinton and Barack Obama are also described as "philanthropists,") who cares deeply about the environment, Sadhguru is an associate of an organisation which seeks to take the world down a very dangerous road — *without* anyone's approval or consent — the World Economic Forum. (The WEF has another "ambassador" from the electronic music world in the form of **will.i.am**, who, after years of flaunting ideas of Transhumanism and digital futurism through his group **Black Eyed Peas**, became named an "Ambassador For A.I." to the WEF!)

Sadhguru was an attendee at the WEF's 2020 meeting in Davos following a personal invitation from its founder and James Bond/ *'Allo Allo'* pantomime villain Klaus Schwab. Sadhguru's was one of 50 inputs from "global thought leaders" included in *'The Great Narrative,'* a book by Schwab and Thierry Malleret that describes "how we can create a more resilient, inclusive and sustainable future post-COVID-19." (Orwellian Translation Unit: How we can take away more and more rights and resources from everyone under the guise of 'saving the planet,' which was only ever in peril because of the greed and psychopathy of the likes of us anyway.)

Sadhguru described himself as a "worm on the planet." He ought to be careful given that Schwab has advocated the eating of bugs and such as part of "The New Normal."

Sadhguru had been at Davos the year before, also. (He sure covers a lot of air miles for someone concerned about "human-caused climate change".) In a conversation filmed there, he commented: "All the religious groups are against me because I'm talking about population. They want more souls, I want less on the planet," before collapsing into maniacal laughter.

So to summarise: Pete Tong publicly endorses a eugenicist.

For his part, Tong hosted an Isha Foundation conversation between Sadhguru and Brian Eno on "saving the planet," in line with such "globalist" agendas.

Could Tong himself have been mind-controlled into conformity with these agendas, therefore? Direct proof of this is never going to be made publicly available, of course, but perhaps there are some clues.

Prior to his relocating from London to Los Angeles, he had headlined his own night at Eden in Ibiza, with a primary launch at Ministry (as in government department?) of Sound in London, titled '*Wonderland.*'

Besides Wonderland Avenue being one of the main thoroughfares through the fabled Laurel Canyon district in which many of the 1960s "counter-culture" bands congregated, and in the vicinity of the Lookout Mountain Air Force base chronicled in the brilliant work of the late Dave McGowan, the name also has connotations of '*Alice in Wonderland*' by the author (and alleged paedophile,) the Reverend Charles Dodgson, better known as Lewis Carroll. The Alice stories and their hallucinatory symbolism — not least the white rabbit — have been endlessly linked with research into MK-ULTRA, and have been identified as triggers frequently used to send subjects into dissociative states.

'*Wonderland*' seems to have become a catchy name in the wider EDM field, too. Aside from the Ibiza sessions, Tong has also performed at '*White Wonderland*' in Anaheim, and '*Beyond Wonderland*' in San Bernardino, (both hotbeds of activity during the 2000s EDM explosion, as ever in the experimental testbed of "SoCal,") '*Wonderland*' in both Manila and Cebu in the Philippines, '*Electric Wonderland*' in Hong Kong, and '*Serbia Wonderland*' in Belgrade.

A compilation CD accompanying Tong's Ibiza residency pictures him holding up his hand, as if casting a spell upon the viewer/ listener. Another CD sleeve has him in another black-and-white sweatshirt looking upwards as if in a dazed state. The main '*Wonderland*' poster sees Tong clutching a giant letter W. This equates to the letter "waw," the sixth in the Arabic/ Hebrew alphabets. "Waw" appears similar to a figure 9 when written in Arabic, or an inverted 6. This is why "www" was selected as the prefix for internet addresses, because it equates numerically to 666, a favoured number of the dark occultists who control Organised Society, (and who like to invert everything, so that a 9 becomes a 6.)

These are all minor things which the average person would write off as insignificant or "coincidental." When all stacked on top of each other though, for those who have become symbol-literate and streetwise to the way popular culture has been weaponised, patterns form, and meaning starts to emerge.

As an aside, while many of his peers have found themselves embroiled in accusations of sexual harassment or molestation, Tong's name has never come up in such discussions. In fact, he himself appears to have been a victim, if a truly strange story involving **Massive Attack** singer **Shara Nelson** is accurate. In 2011, Tong told a magistrate's court that the vocalist had been plaguing him with nuisance calls, and had been telling others that she was his manager, his wife and the mother of his child. Nelson even gave her last name as "Tong" at the hearing! She was issued with a restraining order.

In conclusion then, Pete Tong appears to have worked very hard in his early career, but equally, has enjoyed a plethora of "lucky breaks" right from the start. Without doubt, he has become a "chosen one," and an allotted Gatekeeper in his particular scene, and circumstantial evidence suggests he was being "kept an eye on" right from the start.

He has been well-rewarded, (for those who place value on such things,) for his decades of faithful service to the BBC, and through pushing assorted "globalist" agendas, by way of both his MBE gong and his financial remuneration.

According to Celebrity Net Worth, Tong was worth £33 million (neat figure!) in 2024, placing him ahead of Carl Cox ($16 million) but, apparently behind Judge Jules ($42 million.) His has been a jet-set lifestyle of first-class travel, world-class cuisine, and extravagant homes and cars.

The same question which always emerges when one appears to have sold their soul for all of the above—whether literally or metaphorically—has to be asked:

Can it *ever, really*, be worth it?

Resources:

Pete Tong's official website biography:

- https://www.petetong.com/contact/

Pete Tong Early Interview on Oxford Road Show, Feb 11 1983:

- https://www.youtube.com/watch?v=lnez6KO4i9M

The generation game: Pete Tong and Daisy Lowe on who parties better:

- https://www.thetimes.com/culture/music/article/the-generation-game-pete-tong-and-daisy-lowe-on-who-parties-better-w50slsxjs

Vanessa Feltz sends This Morning viewers wild as she reveals her first kiss was with DJ Pete Tong:

- https://www.dailymail.co.uk/tvshowbiz/article-5917441/Vanessa-Feltz-reveals-kiss-DJ-Pete-Tong-hilarious-travel-segment.html

"Hopefully it's just the case of the vaccination levels getting up to the same standard all across Europe."

Mixmag; November 2021 interview with Pete Tong:

- https://mixmag.net/feature/pete-tong-ibiza-classics-interview

Watch "Co-Existing with Covid"— Carl Cox in Conversation With Yousef (hosted by Pete Tong):

- https://www.thedjrevolution.com/co-existing-with-covid-hosted-by-pete-tong/

Ibiza: International Music Summit 2022 programme:

- https://www.tudobeats.com.br/home/international-music-summit-2022-confirmed-get-to-know-more-here/

World Economic Forum: Yogi Sadhguru reflects on depleting resources in a future world:

- https://www.weforum.org/agenda/2022/01/yogi-sadghuru-reflects-on-depleting-resources-in-a-future-world/

Sadhguru joins a meeting with civil society leaders upon an invitation from Klaus Schwab:

- https://www.facebook.com/sadhguru/photos/sadhguru-joins-a-meeting-with-civil-society-leaders-upon-an-invitation-from-klau/10157957466639146/?_rdr

How Musicians Can Help Protect the Planet | Brian Eno & Pete Tong with Sadhguru:

- https://www.youtube.com/watch?v=bH2jCXhbIm0

Pete Tong sits with Sadhguru:

- https://www.instagram.com/p/CbSxlDtMGTC/?hl=en&img_index=1

Variety Magazine: Joel Zimmerman, WME's Former Global Head of Electronic Music, Exits Agency Amid Cutbacks (EXCLUSIVE) :

- https://variety.com/2020/music/news/joel-zimmerman-wme-electronic-music-exit-cutbacks-1234608374/

Pete Tong's Net Worth:

- https://www.celebritynetworth.com/richest-celebrities/richest-djs/pete-tong-net-worth/

NME: Pete Tong granted restraining order against former Massive Attack singer:

- https://www.nme.com/news/music/massive-attack-2-21-1272963

CHAPTER 16

THE GATEKEEPERS: NORMAN COOK/ FATBOY SLIM

There's absolutely nothing unusual about a mind-altering drug-endorsing pusher of Rave culture, a pioneer of the superclub era, and a flag-waver for a whole genre within Dance music, having attended a posh and exclusive public school alongside a future primetime BBC comedian and ITV '*X Factor*' judge, and a future British Prime Minister. No, really — there isn't! There *should* be. But there isn't.

This factor provides us with a good insight into a by-now familiar dynamic, as it turns out that **Norman Cook**, better known in the Dance music world by his alias **Fatboy Slim**, attended the same exclusive school in Surrey as David Walliams (OBE) and Sir Keir Starmer. Reigate Grammar School, which, despite its name has been an independent fee-paying establishment since 1976, also turned out further celebrities in the form of comedian Romesh Ranganathan, and bushcraft survivalist and TV presenter Ray Mears. By 2024 the school, whose roots go back to 1675, was reported to be charging just under £7,000 a term.

Cynics will say that, being an "elite" school, RGS was bound to turn out many who would become successful in the public eye. This may be the case. But it also reinforces the notion that certain establishments — the BRIT School in Croydon as covered in '*Musical Truth Volume 2*' being another example — seem to be set up for grooming those who will go on to become hugely influential in their respective fields.

It's never left to chance as to which names will occupy the most prominent positions in Organised Society. Those who control it with military precision, and an obsessive compulsion, would never allow such randomness to occur.

Cook and Starmer both attended the school from 1974 to 1979, Starmer going on to complete another two years. In a narrative which reads like something out of a work of fiction, the pair studied violin together, and Cook, in comments given to the '*Daily Star*,' stated that there was a point where he thought that Starmer would go on to a career in music, rather than in politics:

> *"He was in my class for five years. We used to have violin lessons together. He was probably more interested in music than politics in those days. We weren't close mates, but we knew each other very well.*
>
> *"Funnily enough there was another kid called Andrew Sullivan who was the genius and brilliant at everything academic. He used to say his ambition was to be Prime Minister of England. Keir never said a word. He was playing the long game."*

Cook's comments are telling, since it seems the exact fates of many of the kids getting their system indoctrination at such schools may not be decided upon for many years. All that is certain is that they will be influential in society in *some* way, and will be used to push *some* agenda or other which suits the system, and the fine detail can be worked out later. In a different scenario, Cook may well have been inserted into the world of business, law or politics, and Starmer may well have been a musician. (I shudder at the thought.)

The former Pfizer pharmaceutical executive Mike Yeadon, who became a whistleblower during the Co(n)vid era by speaking out about the severe dangers of the related so-called "vaccines," has said that he attended university with Sir (there's another one) Patrick Vallance, one of the key figures to push the UK's Co(n)vid narrative.

Yeadon recalls some shock on the part of himself and some friends, at how quickly the wheels seemed to get greased for Vallance's meteoric rise to the top of his particular field, as if he had been hand-picked for the role by certain parties.

The writer and broadcaster James Delingpole has said much the same of his time at Malvern College, Worcestershire, spent alongside future Co(n)vid propaganda scaremonger Chris (not so) Whitty, and at Oxford University alongside Boris Johnson, (known among his peers as "the shagger" — it seems wealth as well as beer is known to lead to "goggles" when it comes to the "attractiveness" of a a sexual partner.)

As it goes, though Starmer's official biography will proudly crow of his becoming UK Prime Minister in 2024 — despite less than 20 per cent of the population actually voting for him due to the flawed nature of the country's electoral system, (ain't "democracy" great?) — those who seek their information from sources *other* than the mainstream will remember him most for his role as the Director of Public Prosecutions, who had the allegations of child sex abuse against fellow 'Sir' Jimmy Savile brought before him while Savile was still alive, and therefore had the chance to bring him to justice.

Despite this, Starmer threw the case out and allowed Savile to remain free for the rest of his days. Boris Johnson brought this very accusation against Starmer when he himself was Prime Minister, but — predictably — to no avail. It all rather makes a mockery of Starmer's status as a "human rights" lawyer. Apparently the "rights" of Savile's multiple victims don't count.

It seems Cook's own position as a Dance music Pied Piper had not been decided upon by the time he left RGS. After attending Brighton Polytechnic to study English, politics, and sociology, he found himself utilising his musical grooming when he became a member of the Hull-based "indie" band **The Housemartins**.

Perhaps "leftist' politics was a standard part of the agenda at Reigate, with Starmer emerging as a rabid communist and earning himself the nickname "Keir Stalin" in the process, (as Prime Minister of "Great" Britain, what could possibly go wrong, right, folks?)

The Housemartins also espoused socialist ideals in their early days, though most of this seemed to come from lead singer **Paul Heaton**. A clue as to the group's mindset came from a note on the back cover of their debut album '*London 0 Hull 4*,' which read:

"Take Jesus — Take Marx — Take Hope."

We're told that Heaton and Cook had earlier known each other as teenagers when they were together in Heaton's band the **Stomping Pond Frogs**, based in Reigate. This positioned Cook as an obvious replacement when original bassist **Ted Keys** left Heaton's first full Housemartins line-up. Cook relocated to Hull in 1985 as a result. The band had hits in '86 with '*Happy Hour,*' and their accapella cover of **Isley-Jasper-Isley**'s '*Caravan of Love.*'

When the group disbanded in 1988, Paul Heaton and **Dave Hemingway** went on to form the **Beautiful South**. This was the year marked out by the mainstream media as containing the "Second Summer of Love," and Cook's career as a hero of the Dance music world was just about to begin.

Norman Cook/ Fatboy Slim. Violin lessons with Keir Starmer put to good use.

https://commons.wikimedia.org/wiki/File:Fatboy_Slim_in_2004.jpg

Description: Fatboy Slim in 2004

Author: Shokophoto

Permission

(Reusing this file) CC-B

Before we get into that, let's return to Cook's beginnings. Though known publicly by the more proletariat-sounding "Norman," his actual birth name was Quentin Leo Cook. He was born and raised in the affluent London suburb of Bromley. (Isn't it interesting that three of the Dance music titans covered in these chapters have their birthdays on consecutive dates? **Carl Cox** on 29th July, **Pete Tong** on 30th July and Norman Cook on 31st July?)

It seems a decision was taken to drop the Quentin once he had become famous, possibly as a way of sounding less posh, though he did DJ for a period on the Brighton club scene under the name **DJ Quentox**. In a 1999 interview with *'The Independent,'* Cook commented;

> *"Two years after I was born, Quentin Crisp became the most famous homosexual in the world, and people at school seemed to think that was really funny."*

In the same interview he added how much he detested Reigate, and how he desperately wished he had been born working-class.

We're told that Cook inherited a passion for music in his teenage years, gravitating towards Punk and New Wave. He played drums, and then became a vocalist in the group **Disque Attack**.

Once the Housemartins had broken up and Cook had returned to Brighton, he reportedly immersed himself in Hip-hop and Dance culture, said to be his real musical passion rather than Indie or Punk. His first solo hit, credited to **Norman Cook Featuring MC Wildski**, was 1989's *'Blame It On The Bassline.'*

By early the following year, he had formed the first of many acts through which he would achieve future hits in the form of **Beats International**. Fusing Hip-hop and Reggae-style dub influences, the band, with **Lindy Layton** on vocals, achieved a UK number one hit with a cover of the **SOS Band**'s Soul/ Funk anthem *'Just Be Good To Me.'* This was Cook's second number one hit following *'Caravan of Love.'*

Further aliases in the Dance music field followed — **Freak Power**, with which he scored a hit with *'Turn On, Tune In, Cop Out,'* **Pizzaman**, (an unfortunate moniker in the wake of the "Pizzagate" revelations and the *real* meanings of food-related terms a couple of decades later,) which brought three top 40 hits, and the **Mighty Dub Katz**. In fact, Cook earned himself a Guinness World Record for the most top 40 hits under different names.

It was in 1996, however, that the moniker through which he would receive his most high-profile status was launched, with the unveiling of Fatboy Slim.

By this point, Cook had established a nightclub in Brighton alongside his former flatmate **Gareth Hansome**, known as The Big Beat Boutique, its name coming from a style of Dance music which Cook was credited with having helped invent. "Big Beat" eschewed the regular 4/4 beats of House music for a more "broken" style, heavy on the samples, and this became the signature sound of Fatboy Slim.

Of the origin of the seemingly self-contradictory moniker, Cook stated in 2017:

> *"It doesn't mean anything. I've told so many different lies over the years about it I can't actually remember the truth. It's just an oxymoron — a word that can't exist. It kind of suits me — it's kind of goofy and ironic."*

By the time Fatboy was launched, the Electronic Dance Music revolution had been firmly embedded within UK youth culture, and the superclub era was in full force. As Fatboy, Cook released three studio albums and scored major crossover club hits with the singles '*The Rockafeller Skank*', (interesting choice of family name,) '*Praise You*', '*Right Here, Right Now*,' '*Weapon of Choice*,' and '*Wonderful Night*.' The filmmaker Spike Jonze and actor Christopher Walken appeared in the videos to two of his songs.

Cook also became a major fixture on the DJing circuit, playing all over the UK and internationally under the Fatboy Slim name. His trademark garb became loud Hawaiian-style shirts. He also became strongly associated with the smiley yellow face motif.

The smiley had been a symbol of the Dance music scene since the very early Acid House days, when it came to adorn T-shirts, banners and flyers for the early parties, not least **Danny Rampling**'s pioneering Shoom events. One of the most highly-circulated pictures of Norman/Fatboy has him with a yellow bingo-style ball stuffed into his mouth, '*Pulp Fiction*'-style, with a smiley adorning it.

As I detailed in this series' second volume, however, there is a dark side to the smileys which is at odds with its status as an icon of peace, love and togetherness. Not least the sinister overtones with which it appears in occultist Alan Moore's '*Watchmen*' graphic novel series and its resulting film, and the disturbing phenomenon of the so-called "smiley face killings." This is a series of disappearances of young men in both America and Britain whose bodies are later discovered in water, a smiley face daubed in graffiti somewhere in the vicinity.

Alongside the likes of **Brandon Block** and **Alex P**, Fatboy picked up something of a reputation for being a "caner." The dance music press of the '90s was laden with stories of his hedonistic antics, the implication being that these were chemically-fuelled. Indeed, a none-too-subtle clue came from the title of his 1996 album, '*Better Living Through Chemistry.*'

In an interview given to squaremile.com during the Co(n)vid era of 2020, when asked how "Fatboy Slim," (rather than Cook himself,) would cope during a "pandemic," he replied, perhaps tellingly:

> *"He'd be a nightmare. Fatboy Slim's an irresponsible fucking lunatic. You can't be him during the week, and definitely not as a father."*

When the interviewer asked just where Norman Cook ends and Fatboy Slim begins, he responded:

> *"Nowadays I don't really let Fatboy Slim out of the box apart from when I'm on stage. As soon as I come off stage, he goes back in the box. He comes out every now and then if I have to get into character for a Q&A, or if I'm making an online video or something. But that's the only time he ever really comes out — he's useless for pretty much anything else apart from showing off and playing records.*
>
> *"... To be honest, neither of them can really get it together. Norman's far too frail of ego to put something out under his own name — he would worry about what people thought of him, whether he's too old.*
>
> *"... So, originally, it was self preservation — I didn't wanna take the irresponsible hedonist home with me. And now, it's more I have to make an effort to get into character, to be that person. It doesn't take much, though."*

Though such a comment will be written off by fans as merely conversational, there is a sense in which it fits the scenario of invented personas within institutionalised mind-control, and the Dissociative Identity Disorder with which it's affiliated.

Cook's party-guy lifestyle resulted in him checking himself into "rehab" for alcohol addiction for a period in 2009. Though there is of course no proof that this is what took place with Cook, as previously noted, "rehab" within the entertainment industry is often synonymous with mind-control programming facilities.

At this point, we might pause and re-consider some pertinent questions in the sincere pursuit of truth. Did Cook's time at Reigate Grammar School, which seems to be an important breeding ground, mark him out for prominence in some future role? Did his years working on various productions prior to Fatboy Slim constitute him cutting his teeth as a producer and DJ? And was his *real* role within these guises to help push the culture along in the right direction — in particular the drug-fuelled debaucherous aspects of it? This is, after all, what London School of Economics graduate **Mick Jagger** was doing through Rock music.

In seeking to answer the questions, we must factor into the mix a number of Establishment connections, and Norman/ Fatboy's pushing of various social-engineering agendas which suit its goals.

Could things ever really be any other way?

Would it surprise anyone to learn that Norman's father, Ronald Cook, was awarded an MBE in 1982 for services to the environment, and was one of the pioneers of the glass recycling bottle banks of the 1970s? In his latter years, Ron proposed imposing a "Brown Tax" to encourage food and drinks firms to switch from using brown bottles and jars to green glass. Norman's mother was reportedly a teacher in a hospital school.

Cook became an affiliate-by-proxy of the BBC, when he married Radio 2 presenter **Zoe Ball** in August 1999. Her father, Johnny, had previously been a presenter of BBC childrens' television programmes. (Fellow "big beat" DJ **Jon Carter** married another future Radio 2 breakfast show host, **Sara Cox**, two years later.)

Cook and Ball's wedding was one of many to have taken place at Babington House, a private members' club in Somerset of which BBC Radio 1 DJ **Tim Westwood** had once boasted of being a member. They separated 17 years later. By this point they had a daughter, **Nelly**, and a son, (whose name **Woody Cook** is just one letter away from being a really great porn star handle,) both of whom followed their dad into the DJ game, just as **Judge Jules**' and **David Rodigan**'s sons and **Pete Tong**'s daughter have. Woody had also appeared on the TV shows '*The Circle*,' '*Gogglebox*' and '*Cooking With The Stars.*'

Like many of his contemporaries, Fatboy played gigs at several notable and unusual sites, in his case, at the House of Commons in 2013, as well as at the closing ceremony of the London 2012 Olympics, and several times at the symbolism-laden Glastonbury Festival. In 2019, he used Lifetime Actor Greta Thunberg's "how dare you?" United Nations speech as the basis of a mash-up track performed live at a venue in Gateshead, thus helping her system-serving message to reach a wider audience.

In 2002, Cook joined the dubious likes of the **Rolling Stones**, the **Who**, **Pearl Jam** and **Travis Scott**, when attendees of one of his concerts died. The second of his free Big Beach Boutique gigs had been staged on Brighton Beach, where an estimated 250,000 people — four times the expected amount — had turned out. A 25-year-old woman fell 20 feet over railings, later dying in hospital, and a 45-year-old man died from a heart attack, with coastguards rescuing several people from the sea.

In spite of this misfortune, Cook was awarded a star on Brighton's "Walk of Fame" for his contributions to the city's culture, appearing right next to that of Winston Churchill.

One agenda that tends to stand as a tell-tale sign of an owned asset, is the systematic pushing of LGBTQ themes. It's hardly a cause that's running short of mainstream airtime, and the number of celebrities publicly endorsing it is *way* out of proportion to the percentage of society whom it affects.

Not to disappoint, the Cook family are right on board when it comes to this one. Woody has publicly stated that he is bisexual, and had known it from the age of 15. Perhaps he was taking a leaf out of his old man's book, as Norman had earlier commented that he had experimented with men sexually. He is himself described as "a staunch LGBTQ advocate" and regular Pride attendee. (Living in Brighton he certainly finds himself in an appropriate setting.)

It was what Lance and the *'Rise Above Live'* crew call the Coviet era, however, which stood as the *real* acid test of where any celebrity's loyalties lay. In the aforementioned Squaremile 2020 interview, Cook gave mixed messages — rather similar to those that were offered by the Gallagher brothers of **Oasis** — at times reverting to his socialist stance through being critical of the Conservative government for "fucking shit up," and pouring scorn on their lack of support for the creative arts... but always stopping short of being openly critical of lockdown measures, much less exposing the "pandemic" for the monumental scam it was. At times, he entirely endorses "official" narratives, such as when criticising the raves — ironically, a concept he had helped to popularise — that had sprung up "illegally" in 2020:

> *"Someone asked me recently: 'Oh isn't it great that illegal raves are happening again?' and I said: 'I'm gonna have to play a dad here and say no, actually, that is irresponsible right now — it's dangerous. I never thought I would hear that coming out of my mouth, and if it is, you know it must really be bad."*

There's only one thing that would have been more nightmarish than living through Coviet under Boris Johnson's Conservative government, and that's the communistic dystopian hellworld that would have been the UK under Fatboy's old violining pal Keir Starmer.

In bleak times, small mercies can be in short supply. But this, surely, was one.

Resources:

Pressreader: Fatboy's pal Keir A Shock:

- https://www.pressreader.com/uk/daily-star/20220713/281994676206941

Independent Surrey school where Fatboy Slim, Sir Keir Starmer and David Walliams were students:

- https://www.getsurrey.co.uk/whats-on/film-news/independent-surrey-school-fatboy-slim-19880997

Origin of the name Fatboy Slim:

- https://web.archive.org/web/20171201081243/https://www.npr.org/programs/watc/features/2001/fatboyslim/010908.fatboyslim.html

Ronald Cook, MBE, Norman's father, pioneer of the glass recycling bottle bank:

- https://www.letsrecycle.com/news/uk-glass-recycling-tragically-off-course-minister-warned/

The independent: Norman Cook/Fatboy Slim — You've come a long way, Quentin:

- https://www.independent.co.uk/arts-entertainment/interview-norman-cook-fatboy-slim-you-ve-come-a-long-way-quentin-1107292.html

Squaremile: Fatboy Slim: "I was a drugged-up lunatic in the 1990s":

- https://squaremile.com/culture/music/fatboy-slim-interview-back-mine/

Gayagenda.com: "One of Us?" Not As Much ... On Fatboy Slim's Queer Behavior:

- https://gayagenda.com/one-of-us-not-as-much-on-fatboy-slims-queer-behavior/

The Guardian 2002: Nurse dies after fall at Brighton beach party:

- https://www.theguardian.com/uk/2002/jul/17/stevenmorris

The Independent: Brighton restricts beach parties after Fatboy Slim concert chaos:

- https://www.independent.co.uk/arts-entertainment/music/news/brighton-restricts-beach-parties-after-fatboy-slim-concert-chaos-136932.html

Arlington Talent: Woody Cook:

- https://www.arlingtontalent.com/portfolio-item/woody-cook-2/

Contact Music: Fatboy Slim's Gay Revelations:

- https://www.contactmusic.com/fatboy-slim/news/fatboy-slim.s-gay-revelations

CHAPTER 17

THE GATEKEEPERS: JUDGE JULES

"It has been noted that people who aspire to the highest office in the land often have experience of trauma or tragedy which perhaps drives them on to succeed.
   Article on the lordashcroftpolls.com website.

"All lawyers must be BAR members to work in the JUdiciary and courtroom. JUdge JUles is a Lawyer. All BAR Members on Earth say this as part of the BAR Cult Oath: "No law or fact shall be tried in court." If their mouths are moving they are lying. They all write/ speak using fraudulent conveyance of language."
   Correspondence from a 'Musical Truth' reader.

The London School of Economics is regarded as one of the finest "elite" educational establishments in the UK. Its Latin motto, *"Rerum Cognoscere Causas"* translates as "knowing the cause of things." It describes itself as "a world-leading international social science specialist university."

This is a public relations way of saying that the LSE concerns itself with social engineering—the slow and methodical shaping and moulding of public perceptions through its comprehension of how the human psyche works and how, therefore, it can be manipulated. It was founded in 1895 by Fabian Society members Sidney Webb, Beatrice Webb, Graham Wallas, and George Bernard Shaw. Given the objectives of these individuals, it's clear that the LSE's roots are in Fabian/ Marxist socialism. This, inevitably, will have always coloured the type of "education" its students receive.

Most graduates go on to careers within these fields, as well as in the areas of finance, big business and law. Occasionally, however, the LSE throws a curveball.

One was **Mick Jagger**. Grizzled, drug-addled, debaucherous old rock stars aren't necessarily the calibre one might expect from an institution as celebrated as the LSE. Nevertheless, the Rolling Stones Data website tells us that Jagger had considered becoming "either a lawyer, journalist or politician" when he enrolled at the LSE in 1962, studying finance and accounting on a government grant. But no, he became a rock star instead.

Another curveball was the club and radio DJ and music producer known as Judge Jules. Rather like Jagger, Jules embarked on a course studying law at the LSE straight after leaving school, yet, though achieving his degree, embarked not on a career in law but as a DJ — serendipitously at just the right time to play a major role in shaping and moulding the emerging house/ dance music scene within the UK. (See the separate chapter on **Paul Oakenfold** for more on this phenomenon.)

Jules' own website biography describes him as follows:

> *"One DJ that has been there, done that and done it all again. A career that has successfully spanned three decades, been littered with awards, accolades and praise from his peers, making it very easy to say why this Judge won't budge."*

And they're not kidding. Jules has occupied just about every job title available within the dance music industry — internationally touring club DJ, radio DJ with a 15-year stint on BBC Radio 1, record company A&R executive, label proprietor, artist producer, remixer and artist manager. He has also guested on multiple TV shows such as *'Kilroy,' 'The Chase,' 'Celebrity Top Gear'* and *'Celebrity Masterchef.'*

So the question which always emerges at this point has to be asked by any genuine seeker of the truth. Is it even *possible* to achieve this level of influence and success entirely through hard work and a generous dose of good fortune? Or would a random individual operating under their own steam *never* be allowed to reach such lofty heights *unless* their career were "approved" by the controllers of Organised Society?

While some DJs — **Carl Cox**, for example — do seem have climbed the first rungs of the ladder themselves, their talent then getting noted by interested parties, Jules ticks all the boxes for his success having come largely as a result of his bloodline family connections. I know. Here we go *again*!

Judge Jules. NOT a real judge … but the very real nephew of a BBC celebrity chef and a transhumanism-pushing Oxford lecturer.
https://upload.wikimedia.org/wikipedia/commons/e/ee/DJ_JudgeJules.JPG
Mr Jolly, CC BY-SA 4.0 <https://creativecommons.org/licenses/by-sa/4.0>, via Wikimedia Commons

Jules himself actually gave a clue when he appeared on BBC1's '*Celebrity Masterchef*' in 2019. In the show it was revealed that Jules' uncle was the celebrity chef Rick Stein, who had himself enjoyed many years of primetime shows on the BBC. This was not the first time this fact had been publicly shared, however; Jules had been peppering interviews with this tidbit of information for years by that point.

Another fact Jules had shared widely in comments over the years was that his father had been a radio and TV actor, and later producer. His old man turns out to have been Shaun O'Riordan — or to give him his full name, Shaun Stuart Henry Daniel O'Connell O'Riordan. (D'you think he might have been Irish?)

Though he was indeed of Celtic stock, Shaun was actually born on 19th February 1927 in Kandy, Sri Lanka, a province at the time under British colonial rule and still known as Ceylon. The O'Riordans were a family of tea planters. Shaun's father, Donal Stuart Champion d'Espinassy O'Connell O'Riordan, (imagine the size of his business card,) had moved from Dublin to Ceylon. Later the family became brokers. Donal had served as a 2nd Lieutenant in the King's Liverpool Regiment during the Great War.

Donal's full name suggests some French lineage, and sure enough the d'Espinassy Dynasty figures in the mix. One of Donal's ancestors, Lucy Stuart (Bland,) married Alfred David Augustus d'Espinassy de Fontanelle, the fifth Marquis of Fontanelle. This family is descended directly from the King of France, Louis IX.

One of Shaun's 18th century ancestors, meanwhile, was Sir (Francis) Christopher Bland, whose family owned Derryquinn Castle (now demolished) in County Kerry. His descendent, also named Christopher Bland, as well as writing the novel '*Ashes To The Wind*' in which Derryquinn Castle is one of the settings, had also been a chair of the BBC board of governors, as well as serving as chairman of London Weekend Television, British Telecom and the Royal Shakespeare Company. "The Establishment" in short. Bland would have been a distant cousin of Judge Jules.

The name O'Riordan translates as "royal poet." (Though it would be tantalising to think that Jules may be related to the ill-fated **Cranberries** singer **Dolores O'Riordan** I've not been able to establish any such links.) In Irish tradition the poet was highly regarded in any royal household as he acted as scholar, historian and adviser to the king.

From his Ceylon beginnings Shaun moved to England where he found work as an actor, his biggest coup being his role as the troublesome son Eddie in the ITV sitcom '*The Larkins*,' which aired between 1958 and 1960. Eddie is revealed as having "a government job abroad somewhere in one of them far-flung outposts." Shaun had also appeared in a few episodes of '*The Adventures of Robin Hood*,' as had a childhood

Jane and Peter Asher, later McCartney/ Beatles affiliates. The theme tune was produced by **George Martin** and sung by Dick James, who would later become a music publisher to Lennon and McCartney.

Shaun moved into TV production, where one of his key roles was as producer/ director on the ITV science-fiction drama '*Sapphire & Steel*' starring Joanna Lumley and David McCallum which aired from 1979 to 1982. I recall this show well, particularly the second series which featured the ghost of a World War 1 soldier which haunts a derelict railway station, and which scared me to death when watching as a kid. The writing of this story by creator Peter J. Hammond, who had worked on many BBC and ITV shows, was quite skillful, and of much interest to me now that I've started asking big questions about the true nature of this realm, what force could have created it, and to what end.

The episodes concerned a malevolent force which Sapphire & Steel, as visitors from another dimension, must combat. It feeds off of the negative energy of resentment, which it uses as sustenance to empower itself. The WW1 Tommy was unjustly killed after the armistice; a pilot was killed when he took on "one last mission" to make up his flying hours; a crew of submarine engineers were killed when the craft they were working on ran out of air. The spirits of all feel they were unfairly taken before their time. These narratives appear to demonstrate knowledge on Hammond's part of ideas coming from the Gnostic tradition — how this realm was created by some kind of 'Demiurge," a lesser "God" being, and was specially constructed to cultivate fear-based negative energy as what the researcher and broadcaster Robert Monroe described as "loosh' energy for the Demiurge and its "archon" subordinates, existing outside of human sight.

Though Jules has freely mentioned that his dad was a TV actor and producer and later taught acting at RADA (the Royal Academy of Drama & Art,) he has never specifically referenced either '*The Larkins*' or '*Sapphire & Steel.*' Shaun died in Holmfirth where he had lived for many years, and, appropriately, the setting for the BBC sitcom '*Last of the Summer Wine*', on 9/9 2018 (2 + 1 + 8 = 11) at the ripe old age of 91. (Nines and ones all round.)

Let's move on to Jules' mother, since it is so often through the mother's bloodline that we find the most interesting links. This brings us back around to Rick Stein since, though this link is never mentioned by either Jules or Rick, Jules' mother, Priscilla 'Janey' Stein, was one of Rick's older sisters.

Priscilla is completely missing from some of Rick's biographies, which mention only that he had an older brother, John, and an older sister named Henrietta, (who seems to have been sometimes known as Zoe,) born in 1950. Jules has mentioned in several interviews that his mother died when he was 18 and just about to embark on his time at the LSE, though in other accounts he has mentioned that he was 19. Either way, this tallies with the date of 29th November 1984, when Priscilla died of cancer in London. She had married Shaun in 1958. Jules, whose birth name was Julius, (taking his first name from that of his maternal grandfather, Julius Wilhelm Stein) was their firstborn, arriving on 26th October 1965. They had a second son, Samuel, born in 1968.

It's fair to say that the Stein family has not been a lucky one. Sure enough, Rick himself commented in a 2019 interview with the 'Daily Mail,' in this case in reference to his divorce, that:

> *"Many people go through some serious trauma in their lives but never have to have it brought out in public. It's a particular cruelty, really, but that's the price you pay, I guess."*

In another interview, though describing his one-time propensity towards depression, ("I became obsessed with the meaninglessness of life. I could see nothing but death everywhere,") he still neglects to mention the death of his sister Priscilla at the relatively young age of 47. In many biographies, strangely, she has been all but scrubbed from the public record.

Rick, Priscilla and Henrietta's father, Eric Stein, died in 1965, aged 67, when he committed suicide by jumping from a cliff near the family's holiday home in Cornwall.

In a 'Daily Mail' article in 2013, Rick recounted:

> *"They left Redland, our holiday home on the Cornish coast, and walked up the small road towards the lighthouse on Trevose Head.*

> *Three-quarters of the way up, they turned right to cut across to the cliff path. Just beyond a herring-bone slate wall with a tamarisk growing out of it, where the track runs very close to the cliff edge, my father turned to (his sister) Zoe.*
>
> *'I told you I'd do it,' he said. Then he dived on to the rocks beneath.*
>
> *I was just 17 at the time — too young to realise it would take years to work through the repercussions of his violent death".*

There's a morbid irony in that 'Stein,' when translated from the German, means "stone," 'rock or "rocky outcrop. Ancestry.com documents the name as follows:

> *"Someone who lived on stony ground, or for someone who lived by a notable outcrop of rock, or by a stone boundary marker or monument. It could also be a metonymic occupational name for a mason or stonecutter or among Jews an artificial name."*

(Rick's family is consistently acknowledged as having hailed from Germany, though 'Stein' is a name more commonly associated with those Europeans who identify as "Jewish." The reference to a "mason" is interesting.)

Rick dropped a further bombshell in that 2013 interview, however, revealing that his father, whose profession was listed as a "chemical manufacturer," had been the managing director of the Distillers Company, the organisation involved in the marketing of Thalidomide. This was a drug prescribed to pregnant women suffering from morning sickness, but gained notoriety when it was linked to hideous birth deformities occurring in many resulting children.

Wikipedia states:

> *"The total number of infants severely harmed by Thalidomide use during pregnancy is estimated at over 10,000, possibly 20,000, of whom about 40% died around the time of birth. Those who survived had limb, eye, urinary tract, and heart problems."*

Even in spite of these acknowledged horrors, it goes on to tell us all we need to know about the Big Pharma Industrial Complex by adding:

> *"It was approved in the United States in 1998 for use as a treatment for cancer. It is on the World Health Organization's List of Essential Medicines."*

("Children of Thalidomide" made the lyrics of Billy Joel's song '*We Didn't Start The Fire,*' documenting the world-changing events of the 20th century.)

In that '*Mail*' interview Rick added of his father:

> *"Did he kill himself because of the shame and horror attached to the scandal? I'll never know. What I do know is that he retired — or was forced to retire — at the relatively young age of 58, and committed suicide shortly afterwards."*

By 2024, however, Rick himself was promoting a product which had also been identified as harmful to human health when he announced that he was now cooking with MSG — MonoSodium Glutemate. "It's not dangerous!" insisted Rick, perhaps protesting too much. This in spite of accounts even in the mainstream linking MSG to high blood sugar levels, and diabetes.

Back to Eric, and it turns out that he and his wife Dorothy were sharing a house with the Chairman of the Distillers company, Sir (what else?) Cecil George Graham Hayman in 1939.

Young Rick's luck appeared to turn around in the early 1970s. In a BBC2 show titled '*Rick Stein's German Bite*' aired in 2022, Rick recounts having received £10,000 from a great uncle whom he had never known, which enabled him to kick-start his chain of seafood restaurants. I'm sure many of us would love to receive such a generous grant from a previously-unknown benefactor, yet how many of us do?

His businesses have since come to dominate the Cornish town of Padstow, much to the chagrin of many locals, and causing it to be nicknamed 'Padstein.' As his business empire grew, so Rick's good fortunes continued as he landed a series of programmes on BBC television lasting decades, and picked up a CBE (Commander of the British Empire) "for Services to the Economy" from Prince Charles at Buckingham Palace in 2018.

What of Rick's remaining siblings, I hear you ask? Well, brother John has done well for himself too, earning the alphabet soup 'FRCPath FMedSci' after his name, and having attained strong ties to Oxford University. He is a fellow of Magdalen College there, having become a prolific physiologist. His forays into the field of neurology have seen him working on the development of a "deep brain stimulation" programme involving the implanting of chips and electrodes to the human brain, ostensibly to seek a cure for Parkinsons Disease. His co-partner in this endeavour is Kevin Warwick, one of the most outspoken advocates of Transhumanism — the "augmentation" of humans by linking their nervous systems with computer systems.

John Stein is an outspoken advocate of vivisection. When added to his brother Rick's enthusiasm for killing and eating untold amounts of sea creatures, it could be claimed that the Steins have little regard for the value of non-human life.

John's daughter Lucy — Jules' cousin — born in 1979, has also carved out a name for herself in a different career area. She is a renowned painter who has had her work exhibited at galleries around Europe. In a self-penned article appearing on the frieze.com website, Lucy hinted at an interest in Pagan occult traditions when she wrote of the traditional May Day (Beltane) celebrations in Padstow as follows:

> *"With skipping acolytes known as 'Teasers' drawing them through the streets, provoking them into endless whirling dervishes, each 'Oss (hobby horse) sweeps bystanders under its robes like the Madonna della Misericordia. They say that if a lady gets caught under them then she will bear a child within a year. I am proud to be a product of such an encounter."*

Adding also:

> *"I have been going into the fogous in Cornwall lately, ancient underground structures that are like granite-clad birth canals leading to serene deprivation chambers."*

And:

> *In 2010, when I lived in the Burren in County Clare, Ireland, I had an epiphany that reactivated in me some magical knowledge that had lain latent since my early twenties."*

This latter statement remains ambiguous. But perhaps some clues lie in her paintings themselves, many of which are decidedly disturbing in tone, and hint at themes of trauma-based mind-control. (Well, as someone who has studied the subject for many years they do to me, anyway!) Several appear to depict frightened and traumatised children, (one has a child having apparently been cut on her legs and covered in blood,) with a few also hinting at the presence of non-human entities. We must ask the question — is it possible this could constitute Lucy channelling deeply-buried subconscious memories of her own?

In the frieze.com piece she adds:

> *"I found I could process complex feelings or reconfigure my relations to and within patriarchal society by way of the painting canon. Within my expanded painting process these relational strategies often lead me to collaborate with family and close friends in the spirit of positive nepotism."*

It's intriguing that she raises the concept of nepotism since, all these family links having been established, they lead us all the way back around to Judge Jules, (at last!) Are we to believe that his own meteoric career took off purely as a result of hard work and good luck, (what researcher Mike Williams, aka Sage of Quay refers to as "the Cinderella Fairy Story")?

Or, is a mature mind with no ulterior motives or belief systems to defend more likely to conclude that it comes as a direct result of who his other family members are, and the bloodlines from which they emanate?

Is it possible that through his public school education, then his time at the LSE, the young Julius was being groomed for *something*, but at the time it had not yet been decided by whoever was directing his future path just *what* that something would be? When the Acid House/ Rave scene got going in the late 1980s, therefore, (which I personally see as bearing many hallmarks of military-intelligence-grade social engineering infiltration,) did the natural enthusiasm he appeared to have towards music and partying mark him out as someone who could be usefully deployed as an influential leader of that scene?

The controllers of Organised Society don't seem to mind in which ways those from important families become influential — just as long as what they do ends up pushing one of the many society-changing agendas which suit them. With this in mind it's nothing unusual to find a prominent TV chef, a prominent pusher of Transhumanism, a prominent marketeer for a dangerous chemical drug, a prominent painter of dark art, and a prominent dance music DJ and producer, all emanating from the same long-running bloodline.

Even pre-fame, the young Julius was rubbing shoulders with other characters who would become well-known in the dance music realm. He attended Highgate Wood School in Crouch End with Sonia Clarke, who would go to become the singer **Sonique**. (Highgate Wood was also attended by the Scottish computer hacker Gary McKinnon, accused by a U.S. prosecutor of committing "the biggest military computer hack of all time")

From there he moved on to University College School in Hampstead, where he befriended, and promoted early parties with the future DJ and producer known as **Rollo**, (named after the Viking Warrior who became the first ruler of Normandy. Rick Stein has spoken of being descended from French nobility, possibly in Normandy, in his TV cooking shows.) Rollo's sister would go on to become the singer **Dido**.

Jules has recalled how he and a teenage Rollo would regularly travel to New York to buy records and hang out at clubs like the Paradise Garage. These accounts are entirely consistent with those of **Pete Tong**, **Tim Westwood** and **Paul Oakenfold**. How did such fresh-faced young lads, on meagre means, manage to fund so many expensive trips of this nature?

By the time he exited the LSE Jules was reportedly staging "illegal" warehouse parties around London under his brand name Family Funktion. At this point, like so many of his contemporaries, he was playing black soul, funk and rare groove sounds. He forged an alliance with the other other key warehouse party promoters of the time, **Norman Jay** (now an MBE) of Shake 'N' Fingerpop, and **Jazzie B** (now an OBE) of **Soul II Soul**.

It was during this period that Jules reportedly earned his "Judge" moniker from Jay. Owing to his law training he was often thrust out front when the police would arrive to try and shut down the illegal gatherings, at which the partygoers were technically trespassing. Jules would use legal jargon to convince the police that these were simply private parties for his university chums and that no law was being broken, evidently with much success.

Jules' first forays into radio involved a brief stint on the pirate station WBLS, formed by the now-deceased Derek Boland who would go on to a brief career as the rapper **Derek B**, and titled after the New York station of the same name. This station lasted barely a month and a few of the casualties, including Jules and Tim Westwood, got picked up by Kiss FM, another London pirate inspired by a New York station, at the start of 1987. A recording exists from New Year's Eve of that year where Jules, Norman Jay and Jazzie B reminisce on the fortunes their respective sound systems had enjoyed during '87. Jules predicts that house music will become the big trend for '88.

And it sure did. That year became what the mainstream media dubbed 'The Second Summer of Love,' (see '*Musical Truth Vol. 2*' for *way* more on the parallels this scene shared with its socially-engineered predecessor of 1967.) Jules took on a key residency at Club MFI at London's Legends, and by this point had completely ditched the soul and funk sounds to become an early purveyor of synth-driven 'Acid House' from both Britain and America. This placed him in a perfect position to get picked up for many of the open-air raves which would follow — colossally-sized dance events in fields where tens of thousands of young people — fuelled by seemingly endless supplies of ecstasy tablets which conveniently appeared out of nowhere — would dance until the sun rose and beyond.

In 1989 Jules guested on an episode of the ITV chat show '*Kilroy*' defending acid house culture. "Coincidentally," also appearing on the very same show, though not mentioned by name, is a young Keir Starmer who announces himself as being 'from the national Council of Civil Liberties." (Starmer, who went on to become the UK's worst ever prime minister (and just *think* of the competition!) is an avowed communist. I'm not quite sure how communism and civil liberties go together??)

The scene was a paradigm-shifting phenomenon on a scale not seen since that late 1960s movement, and it changed youth culture and social attitudes towards things like drugs, parties, music and sex forever. As previously observed, *no* scene of this magnitude is *ever* permitted to flourish on its own. It only *ever* occurs if it is "approved." And *only* "approved" gatekeepers get to flourish and thrive within it.

(Interestingly, when asked for '*The Big Questions*' feature in the UK's '*Mixmag*' in 1996 if he had ever done drugs, Jules replied: "put it this way — Timothy Leary was a close friend." Jules is known for his frivolous banter, so it's difficult to know whether this comment should be taken seriously or not. Leary died shortly after this interview would have taken place, on 31st May 1996.)

Jules remained on Kiss FM until 1997, by which point the "superclub" era had followed in the wake of the raves — the parties had been driven indoors into licenced venues which could be much more stringently controlled...and observed. That year the inevitable occurred when he was poached by BBC Radio 1 for primetime shows on both Friday and Saturday evenings.

During his 15-year stay at the corporation, alongside the likes of Pete Tong, **Danny Rampling**, **Dave Pearce**, **Fabio & Grooverider**, **Seb Fontaine** and **Fergie**, Jules would frequently find himself broadcasting to crowds hundreds of thousands strong at various Radio 1 events. This in the midst of a clubbing schedule which appears totally insane on paper, but which somehow got achieved. On New Year's Eve 2000, for example, he managed to DJ in Belfast, Sheffield, Manchester and Birmingham all on the same night. Such frantic UK motorway (and private plane) dashes would be sandwiched between regular DJing visits to every continent in the world (except Antarctica.)

For a time during this period his younger brother Sam briefly entered the picture when he headed up the Serious DJ agency, (of which Jules was, naturally a part,) with an accompanying club night under the same brand at London's The Cross nightclub. It was clear that Sam was always going to be in his elder brother's shadow, however, and little has been heard from him on the public front since.

There was no way Ibiza was going to be left out of the picture, either. It having become such an epicentre for dance music culture, any big-name DJ *not* playing a regular residency there would have been regarded as lacking in credibility. In 2000, by which point his style had evolved into what was loosely termed "trance," Jules began promoting his Judgement Sundays event at Eden nightclub, which ended up becoming the longest-running residency on the island. Intriguingly, for the opening night Jules appeared with a buzz cut and his hair dyed peroxide-blonde. It's intriguing, at least, for anyone who is familiar with bleached-blonde hair on celebrities being symbolic of their having undergone mind-control programming. (More on this in *'Musical Truth Volume 1.'*)

In March 1998 Jules married Amanda Jane Shaw in London. (The night before he had played in Bournemouth and London, and straight after the ceremony dashed off to play in Bristol, Wolverhampton and Birmingham!) There don't appear to be any important bloodline ties when it comes to Amanda, but interestingly her birthdate is 21st June, the summer solstice, and their son Jake ended up entering the world on the very same date in 1999. What were the odds?

Around the time of his leaving Radio 1, Jules re-trained to become a lawyer, attaining a new degree. This he put to use by eventually founding his own company, Sound Advice, where he specialises in handling the legal affairs of others in the music business. This, along with his unending DJ schedule, has made him one of the richest men in UK dance music, with some reports claiming his millions can be measured in tens rather than ones.

The family legacy appears to be continuing, meanwhile, with Jules' son Jake having followed him into the electronic scene as a DJ/ producer under the alias **Reiss Reuben**, and his daughter Phoebe having become a vocalist, launching with a pop-tinged D&B tune in 2024 titled *'Trust Issues.'*

Conclusion

Naysayers will doubtless pick up on Lucy Stein's earlier comment on nepotism, and claim that the success and prominence of this extended family is down solely to this factor. Though this certainly explains why some people are "fortunate" enough to gain some positions, given the huge number of people whose lives will have been affected majorly by O'Riordan, Stein and the others in this story... is it *really* plausible to write it all off so innocently?

Or, do things reach a point where an adult mind capable of critical thought has to draw the conclusion that culture-creation is manufactured by design, and *not* achieved by random happenstance?

Ever?

Resources:

(I'm hugely indebted to Dom of Sheep Farm Studios, (Chris remains head of wine,) and his vigilant assistant Lorraine, for their sterling work uncovering some of these amazing family connections. I have no idea how they find this stuff… but they find it!)

London School of Economics website:

- https://www.lse.ac.uk/

Rolling Stones Data: Mick Jagger & the LSE:

- https://rollingstonesdata.com/articles/mick-jagger-london-school-of-economics-1962/

Robert Monroe:

- https://en.wikipedia.org/wiki/Robert_Monroe

ITV The Chase: Judge Jules' life away from music from famous family including well-known actor dad:

- https://www.mylondon.news/news/tv/itv-chase-judge-jules-life-22612133

Sapphire & Steel complete second series: The Railway (1979):

- https://www.youtube.com/watch?v=0KrZaT2fnVk

The Guardian: Christopher Bland, tough and admired former chair of the BBC, dies at 78:

- https://www.theguardian.com/media/2017/jan/28/christopher-bland-dies-78-tough-admired-chair-bbc-bt-rsc

Shaun O'Riordan in The Adventures of Robin Hood:

- https://www.imdb.com/title/tt0047706/characters/nm0642517

Peter Asher, Jane Asher, and Arthur Skinner in The Adventures of Robin Hood (1955):

- https://m.imdb.com/title/tt0047706/mediaviewer/rm4218305024/

The Daily Mail: Rick Stein: 'Public trauma? It's the price of fame':

- https://www.dailymail.co.uk/home/you/article-7584505/Rick-Stein-Public-trauma-price-fame.html

Ancestry.com: Origin of the name 'Stein':

- https://www.ancestry.co.uk/name-origin?surname=stein&srsltid=AfmBOornz99rIJNv8B_fGMvmYFC-Y1DdnPTKuvc-1CQFKNIMxcr7V6Jj_

Rick Stein's German Bite:

- https://www.bbc.co.uk/programmes/b03864gh

Wikipedia: Thalidomide;

- https://en.wikipedia.org/wiki/Thalidomide

Wikipedia: John Stein:

- https://en.wikipedia.org/wiki/John_Stein_(physiologist)

Frieze.com: Portfolio: Lucy Stein :

- https://www.frieze.com/article/portfolio-lucy-stein

Mutual Art: Lucy Stein artworks:

- https://www.mutualart.com/Artist/Lucy-Stein/D0B70E623FCC4B70

Why I am cooking with monosodium glutamate: It's not dangerous, says Rick Stein:

- https://www.dailymail.co.uk/tv/article-13820623/Why-cooking-monosodium-glutamate-not-dangerous-says-RICK-STEIN-recipes-new-book-here.html

Mum of Crouch End UFO hacker Gary McKinnon tells of 'marathon' ordeal:

- https://www.hamhigh.co.uk/news/21383680.mum-crouch-end-ufo-hacker-gary-mckinnon-tells-marathon-ordeal/

Young Judge Jules and Keir Starmer appear on the same episode of ITV's 'Kilroy' in 1989:

- https://www.youtube.com/watch?v=3ihm3f1nOn8

Boston College on BAR admission: "No law or fact shall be tried in court."

- https://www.bc.edu › OPCA-Document-Bestiary

CHAPTER 18

THE GATEKEEPERS: PAUL OAKENFOLD

DJ/ producer turned podcast host Lenny Fontana nailed it in his 2023 interview with Paul Oakenfold for his *'True House Stories'* podcast. The phrase "in the wrong place at the wrong time" has entered common parlance, Fontana observed. When it comes to Oakenfold's career, however, the very opposite is true. Lenny was also more on-the-money than he probably realised when he observed that the successful trajectories of Oakenfold and so many of his contemporaries, such as Fatboy Slim, Goldie (MBE), the Chemical Brothers, Leftfield, the Prodigy, etc, happened to them "without even trying."

Serendipity indeed. If only it were that easy for everyone!

I used to have a favourite meme featuring Paul Oakenfold's face with the slogan: "Went on a lads' piss-up . . . Accidentally started a worldwide revolution in youth culture."

It refers to the story, endlessly circulated, of the mythical holiday to Ibiza which Oakenfold undertook in late August 1987 to mark his birthday. He was joined by fellow London DJs **Danny Rampling**, **Nicky Holloway** and **Johnny Walker**. **Trevor Fung**, who seems to have been an early mentor (handler?) for Oakenfold, was already established as a DJ on the island. The four, so the story perpetually re-asserts, danced open-air under the stars at Amnesia nightclub to sounds spun by **DJ Alfredo**, and tried the drug known as ecstasy for the first time. They are said to have undergone an epiphany where the spiritual freedom brought about by the music all suddenly made sense, and went on an evangelical mission upon their return to recreate their incredible experience within London clubland.

(Ibiza itself had already figured as a key location in the earlier "Summer of Love" in the 1960s, having become a haven for hippies and Bohemians, and a retreat for many figures on London's "counter culture" scene of those times. Drug experimentation was a big part of the "underground" culture there, just as it would be two decades on when what even the mainstream media referred to, possibly tellingly, as "the Second Summer of Love" got underway. It seems Ibiza had been a social experimentation hotspot long before it burst into prominence in the Acid House era.)

As serendipity would have it, this legendary pilgrimage *just happened* to coincide with an influx of 'house,' a new energetic form of electronic dance music being imported from Chicago and New York. These styles came to be pushed, along with an eclectic array of other sounds known as 'Balearic Beat,' by the intrepid pioneers.

Their fledgling club nights are said to have awakened a dormant creative spirit in thousands of DJs, music producers and party promoters in London and beyond. I covered this entire phenomenon at length in '*Musical Truth Volume 2*', but to summarise, within a very short space of time the musical landscape in UK clubland and radio had been transformed beyond recognition.

As Oakenfold himself put it in his 2022 autobiography:

> *"Suddenly, there was a moment where the youth of Britain could go to nightclubs, be euphoric, enjoy music, dance and have fun. Out of that shift came Britain's dance music culture that went around the world.*
>
> *"I never in a million years thought I'd end up in Hollywood, writing music for $100 million movies and going on world tours with Madonna. But it all came out of one moment in the '80s in the UK."*

The implication here, of course, is that if Oakenfold had decided to stay home in London and that mythical trip had never happened, the worldwide explosion in electronic dance music that occurred in its wake would never have happened, or if it *had* still occurred, would have involved very different circumstances. Phew! Good thing he got to the airport on time, eh?

Of the Ibiza Four, Holloway became a celebrated promoter on the party circuit, while Rampling and Oakenfold became the UK's first 'superstar DJs,' the latter off the back of his "seminal" club night known as Shoom, (the name said to embody the energy rush experienced by a user when an ecstasy tablet begins to stimulate the brain's chemistry,) plus his radio slot on Kiss FM. For his part, Oakenfold is said to have established the Spectrum club night, (staged at London's Heaven nightclub, owned at the time by Establishment stooge Sir Richard Branson) and Future.

One thing led to another, and as Oakenfold's influence began to expand he found himself in demand at many of the big house nights that cropped up all over the UK, paving the way for a residency at Liverpool superclub Cream in 1997, with a pay packet to rival that of a league-one footballer, as covered extensively by the dance music press of the time.

From there he cemented his place in history by becoming the first DJ to secure a long-running residency in Las Vegas, spearheading the trend of DJs replacing rock bands and singers as sell-out headliners at the city's biggest venues. By this time he had topped '*DJ Magazine*'s annual '*Top 100 DJs Poll*' twice, an accolade considered the ultimate arbiter of success in the field.

Paul Oakenfold. Thank god he went on a lads' piss-up to Ibiza in 1987, 'else club culture as we know it may never exist. Phew!

https://upload.wikimedia.org/wikipedia/commons/f/fa/Paul_Oakenfold_3_2009.jpg

Stuart Sevastos, CC BY 2.0 <https://creativecommons.org/licenses/by/2.0>, via Wikimedia Commons

All of these sound like the achievements of some energy-fuelled, razor sharp, business-savvy, visionary maverick. Oakenfold, however, has never come across as ... how can I put this kindly? ... the sharpest tool in the box. His lifelong dyslexia is well-known and doubtless accounts for his slow drawling speech in interviews, (and will be the reason he never achieved a radio show like most of his high-profile peers.) Nobody wishes to gloat about another's natural disability, of course, but even so, questions have to be asked about Oakenfold's ability to achieve all that he's been credited with. In the aforementioned Lenny Fontana interview, for example, he struggles majorly with the call connection. Isn't he supposed to be a technical whizz? (He has also said that his parents "brought someone in for about six months" to help with his dyslexia. That can't have been easy on a humble newspaper distributor man's salary.)

It's a matter of factual public record that many musicians do not actually perform on the records that are credited to them. **Phil Spector**'s **Wrecking Crew**, for example, provided the music for albums offered under the names of many famous bands, including **The Doors**, in the 1960s and '70s. And the researcher Mike Williams, known as Sage of Quay, has pretty much proven through his exhaustive canon of work on the Beatles, that it's *physically impossible* for **John Lennon** and **Paul McCartney** to have written the vast number of songs we're told they did in the extremely limited period in which they are said to have done so. And also that the band *cannot possibly* have performed all the tracks on their '*Rubber Soul*' album (and probably others,) because the timescale was too small. Others *had* to have laid down the music beforehand, with the band simply coming in to add their vocals, then soak up the glory for the resulting product.

If this dynamic can be shown to have routinely been the case with the corporate music industry's key bands ... why should we really expect it to have been any different with its key DJs and producers?

The question *must* therefore be asked by anyone seeking the truth of the matter ... did Paul Oakenfold *really* programme all the productions and remixes for which he has been given credit ... or was he merely selected as a publicly-acceptable figure through which to unleash the many sounds which carry his name, his legendary status having been been built up through the starry-eyed surprise which first put him in the spotlight? Certainly he dislikes being drawn on the subject as, by his own admission, in a 2013 article for vice.com titled '*The Worst Interview of All Time*' he comments: "I hate interviews. I'm sorry. But I do."

I have long asserted that the routes to household-name success are facilitated either by coming from the "right" family bloodline, or by becoming a "chosen one" deemed useful to the control system, and being prepared to do whatever is required of you in order to make it big. There is no evidence that Oakenfold ticks the first of these boxes, so we must assume that, in his case, it is the second.

Either way, there appear to have been attempts to fudge the data when it comes to his birthdate. His Wikipedia entry gives this as 30th August 1963. IMDB, however, the Internet Movie Database, lists it as the same date in 1961, and the England & Wales Births database lists a Paul M Oakenfold as having been born in Stepney in 1961. His father is said to have worked as a distributor for the London Evening Standard, and the family's move from Mile End to Croydon said to have occurred as a result of his work. Oakenfold senior is said to have been in a skiffle band, which ignited the young Paul's interest in music.

It's noticeable that all of the first-generation big-name DJs who helped house music gain a foothold within UK clubland had earlier gained themselves a following through playing soul, funk, hip-hop and other forms of black music. If we consider for a moment that the acid house/ rave revolution *was* a social-engineering psy-op, (and I outline my ideas for what the overall objective might have been in '*Musical Truth 2*',) then it makes sense that the orchestrators would have drawn from a pool of already-established names when seeking flag-bearers for these new styles. Far easier to have done this in the hope that they would have brought many of their existing followers along with them for the ride, than to have introduced entirely new names.

On this basis, Oakenfold certainly fits the bill. By the time of 'Holiday '87' he already had another feather to his cap which won't have done him any harm in making himself credible; he had become head of UK A&R for the Champion record label. At this time his name was most closely associated with the burgeoning hip-hop scene — a very far cry from the musical direction his career would later take. His time at Champion saw him sign **DJ Jazzy Jeff & The Fresh Prince** and **Salt 'N' Pepa** to the label. He later took up similar positions at the Profile and Def Jam labels, and became a promoter and UK agent for **Run-D.M.C.** and the **Beastie Boys**.

Prior to this, Oakenfold's biog tells us that he had spent some time living in New York with his friend Ian St. Paul, (Trevor Fung's cousin) and that the pair had used fake IDs to gain entry to many of the city's most celebrated nightspots such as Studio 54.

Oakenfold tells us himself in his 2022 autobiography *'Ready Steady Go: My Unstoppable Journey In Dance*' (if he really wrote it!) that he "blagged his way" into interviewing many big-name artists during his time in NYC, including **Frankie Beverley** of **Maze**, **Bobby Womack** and **Bob Marley**, by claiming to be a journalist from the *'NME'* or *'Melody Maker'*. An earlier biography written by **Richard Norris** of the group **The Grid**, *'Paul Oakenfold: The Authorised Biography,'* tells us the Marley interview occurred in 1981.

This is a curious claim as Marley died in May of that year and had been seriously ill for many months prior — hardly in a fit state to be interviewed, much less hanging out in nightclubs. *If* Oakenfold had really been born in August 1963 he could have been no more than 16 or 17 at a stretch when this event occurred. This adds some weight to the suggestion that he was really born in 1961.

We might also ask ourselves how a totally unknown random teen from England with fake credentials would have been allowed close access to Bob Marley, particularly given that Marley was almost certainly taken out by the CIA and so his associations would have been under close scrutiny, (see *'Musical Truth Volume 1*' for more on this story.)

Social-engineering ops are military-grade, and what I and many other researchers first look for is any ostensible connection between a name under scrutiny, and expressions of the military. Sure enough with Oakenfold we find it.

Prior to taking on DJing full-time he had qualified as a chef, and his biog informs us that one of his earliest placings was a stint "at the Royal Army and Navy Club in London." Ding, ding. Is it possible the young Paul could have made some useful contacts in this role, and, being a part-time DJ also, had placed himself on the radar of the industry's ever-watchful eye?

The CV certainly built up at a lightning pace once Balearic Beat/ Acid House culture had gained its initial foothold. The studio career was the next element to take off, one of his earliest assignments being to remix '*Step Off*' by the **Happy Mondays**. Coming out of **Tony Wilson**'s Factory Records stable in Manchester, an operation which had previously housed **Joy Division/ New Order** and the Hacienda nightclub, this was a band and a song considered to have bridged the gap between indie music and the exploding dance music culture. His studio partner in this venture was producer Steve Osborne.

Elsewhere in his autobiography, Oakenfold admits that he'd had no previous experience in remixing or production and had pretty much stumbled into the role, learning on the job as he went. He continued to "luck out," beating all other contenders to be the name picked to remix, usually alongside Osborne, for the likes of the **Rolling Stones**, **Michael Jackson**, **Britney Spears**, **Madonna**, **Duran Duran** and **Moby**. Some recordings were made at the Bunkka studio owned by **Peter Gabriel**. (See elsewhere in this book for more on him!)

By 1990 Oakenfold had a new record label to his name in the form of Perfecto Records. An early company emblem featured a thumb and fingers being arranged in the form of what, in occult circles, has come to be known as "the 666 sign" — though, given Oakenfold's past in kitchens, it will doubtless be written off simply as the sign chefs make to say "just right!" Among the label's early releases was '*I Want You Forever*' by **Carl Cox**. (Cox had earlier installed sound systems for Oakenfold at the Project Club in Streatham, we are told. It's amazing how often the paths of these gatekeeper names crossed in those early halcyon days.)

By 1994 Perfecto had undergone a logo change to suit the shift in musical style, this one more akin to a football club emblem, with the Perfecto Fluoro brand added to the mix. Oakenfold had been credited with having established an entire new genre within a dance scene which had lost much of the unity under which it first started. It had splintered into countless sub-divisions.

This particular one was known as Goa Trance, a distinctly electronic style delivered at frantic tempos and, according to many commentators, structured to accentuate the mind-altering effects of MDMA, or ecstasy, still the drug of choice. Ibiza had been joined by a new overseas haven in the form of the autonomous Portuguese colony of Goa in South West India. This area, as well as being known as a haven for backpackers, runaways and criminals from all over the world, was the site of free-spirited, open-air beach parties, often at the time of a full moon.

Oakenfold had been propelled to pioneering hero status within this field virtually overnight, and much of the credit is given to two Pete Tong-presented '*Essential Mix*' shows highlighting the Goa sound, which had been broadcast on BBC Radio 1 in 1994.

Goa Trance was about as far removed from the black music styles for which Oakenfold had been known in the 1980s as it's possible to get. Though a cynic might argue that he was simply chasing the fame and money wherever they happened to be, this shift is also consistent with an allotted gatekeeper fulfilling a role as a pied piper, shepherding entranced (excuse the pun) followers in certain pre-established directions.

Within a few years production and delivery methods would be completely revolutionised, with everything going digital at the expense of earlier analogue technologies. In '*Musical Truth Volume 2*' I also explored the possibilities that exist for those who may not have the upliftment and advancement of all humanity as their number one priority, to use sound frequencies and electronic production as ways of stripping unseen elements into recorded music as methods of potential mind-control, or of doing harm to the mental, emotional and physical states of listeners — especially when combined with the effects of mind-altering drugs and occult symbolism, all being absorbed within a communal setting. Could Goa trance have been playing *its* part in this overall process?

An enquiring mind might also elect to ask why it is that, by the 2000s, heritage sites of major cultural importance were serving as unlikely backdrops for some much-hyped sets by dance music's heavy hitters.

For his part, Oakenfold secured another place in the record books by not only becoming the first DJ to play on the main stage at the Glastonbury Festival, but also to perform a set on the Great Wall of China, at base camp at Mount Everest, (this one reportedly to raise money for Nepal earthquake victims) and among the monoliths at Stonehenge, (alongside old buddy Carl Cox.) Why? Was Ministry of Sound unavailable that weekend?

Is it possible that the intention was to somehow flood the energy fields at these sacred sites and key points on the Earth's energy grid system with sounds which were completely artificial and removed from nature, pitched to who knows what frequencies, and with who knows what lying unseen within the digital soundwaves?

Could this have been part of a wider agenda being routinely employed by the most prominent electronic dance music festivals around the world, all pushing esoteric symbolism, often hinting at MK-Ultra-style mind control and Agenda 2030-style AI Transhumanism? Was the long-term goal always to use dance music and club culture to normalise this kind of societal futurism? (Oakenfold and Carl Cox's participation in the intriguingly-named 'Cyberfest' as long ago as 2000 should perhaps have been telling us something.)

Can Oakenfold even be said to be an amazing DJ? This is subjective, of course, but the Reddit discussion thread linked to at the end has several users complaining of his sloppy sets, with others suspecting that many of the better ones may be pre-recorded.

Serendipity aplenty, Oakenfold continued blazing new trails by getting hired as the resident DJ on **U2**'s 'Zoo TV' world tour following the success of the Perfecto Remix of the group's song *'Even Better Than The Real Thing.'* He went on to get hired by (allotted to?) Madonna in a similar capacity for three of her world tours.

Few other major achievements remained for Oakenfold's name to be attached to. But he ticked one more box through his progression to producing full scores for Hollywood movies, the likes of *'Swordfish,' 'Planet of the Apes'* and *'The Bourne Identity'* among his output.

Oakenfold has become such a regular fixture on the American club circuit, the nation having been his main home for decades, that a novice might reasonably assume that he is indeed American. It would appear that his trailblazing as an overseas DJ making it big on the stateside circuit represented some metaphorical table-setting, some years in advance, for the huge explosion in Electronic Dance Music, or EDM, which would hit American shores around 2008. This movement saw the likes of **David Guetta, Calvin Harris, Afrojack, Steve Aoki** and

will.i.am blurring the lines between uptempo club music and what had previously been categorised "R&B" and "hip-hop," to make the new sounds appealing to as wide a demographic as possible.

Having been a tried and trusted asset for many years by this point, Paul had clearly ingratiated himself to the social-engineers to have earned such rewards. As if to reinforce the point, by this time his official vector logo had taken on the same "Illuminati" overtones as those of many of its peers, the A's in his names looking distinctly like pyramids.

And could another breadcrumb have been dropped through Oakenfold, over and above all competitors, being selected to produce, alongside **Andy Gray**, the theme music to Channel 4 TV's '*Big Brother*' at the turn of the millennium — a show later exported to other nations and indicating the direction that society was headed, with increased surveillance and monitoring all in line with the New World Order masterplan?

The '*Ready Steady Go*' book relates stories of Oakenfold partying with Hollywood and celebrity "elite" like Keanu Reeves, Johnny Depp, Jack Nicholson, Sean Penn, Paul McCartney, Naomi Campbell, Kate Moss and Julia Roberts. As fellow DJ **Fatboy Slim** might say of his progression from playing soul and funk in South London wine bars, "you've come a long way, baby." Even Oakenfold himself has expressed amazement at finding himself in such circles, commenting:

> "Of course, I'm wondering how the hell I'd got there. It doesn't happen often in my world."

Well, actually, as it turns out... it does.

Oakenfold opens up in '*Ready Steady Go*' about aspects of his personal life, including a failed marriage which he says suffered at the hands of his career. An on-line article for the '*Sun*' newspaper published in September 2022, discusses Paul's grief at the death of his father an hour before his 60th birthday, and also mentions his brother and sister both dying of heart attacks within three years of each other.

Other aspects of his personal life take things in a different direction, however.

Certain factors become tediously frequent when researching the A-list heavy hitters within any expression of popular culture, and there's a very unsavoury one which sits alongside the endless military connections, dodgy symbolism and bloodline family links.

In 2023, a short while before his own 60th birthday, Oakenfold was publicly accused of sexual harassment and workplace violations by a former female employee of his management company. The 24-year-old woman, identified only as 'Jane Roe,' filed a case at Los Angeles' Superior Court alleging that Oakenfold had masturbated in front of her on four occasions, one inside her own car, while she was employed as his personal assistant working out of his LA home.

The accuser said she was presented with a non-disclosure agreement after reporting the incident to management. She claims she was prevented from returning to work when she did not sign and was threatened with firing. Eventually she is said to have signed the NDA "under duress" and was allowed to return to work, but was not re-assigned to Oakenfold. She was eventually laid off in March 2023 for what court papers called "a lack of work."

The claims came amidst a slew of sexual misconduct accusations against prominent figures in the dance music field, including American DJ/ producer **Erick Morillo**, techno pioneer **Derrick May**, Israeli DJ/ producer **Guy Gerber**, (who has collaborated with **P Diddy** and has a studio in Laurel Canyon!) and EDM artists **Bassnectar** and **Diplo**.

It was all a far cry from the spirit of freedom, togetherness and fun that the early days of dance music symbolised. It wasn't just the music that had changed.

Resources:

The Independent: Passed/Failed: An education in the life of Paul Oakenfold, DJ and producer:

- https://www.independent.co.uk/news/people/profiles/passed-failed-an-education-in-the-life-of-paul-oakenfold-dj-and-producer-319036.html

The Guardian: DJ Paul Oakenfold accused of sexual harassment by former assistant:

- https://www.theguardian.com/music/2023/jun/05/dj-paul-oakenfold-accused-of-sexual-harassment-by-former-assistant

Deadline: Paul Oakenfold Faces Sexual Harassment Suit By Ex-Personal Assistant:

- https://deadline.com/2023/06/paul-oakenfold-sexual-harassment-allegations-grammy-nominated-dj-major-remixer-1235399650/

Ministry of Sound: Oakenfold — Blagging it at Studio 54:

- https://web.archive.org/web/20071112103400/http://www.ministryofsound.com/News/Features/20071108_oakenfold1.htm

The Sun: Paul Oakenfold interview, 2022:

- https://www.thesun.co.uk/tvandshowbiz/19684178/bez-turned-down-hollywood-megastar-paul-oakenfold/

The Times: Paul Oakenfold: How A Boy From Croydon Became The World's No.1 DJ:

- https://www.thetimes.com/culture/music/article/paul-oakenfold-how-a-boy-from-croydon-became-the-worlds-no-1-dj-d5x3wkr0r

Resident Advisor: Paul Oakenfold Biography:

- https://ra.co/dj/oakenfold/biography

Sacha Wall: The Light And Dark Side of DJ Club Culture:

- https://istreemradio.com/
the-light-and-dark-side-of-dj-club-culture-by-sacha-wall/

'True House Stories' — Lenny Fontana chats to Paul Oakenfold:

- https://www.youtube.com/watch?v=404oe09Z3Sw

Vice.com: The Worst Interview of All Time With Paul Oakenfold:

- https://www.vice.com/en/article/
the-worst-interview-of-all-time-with-paul-oakenfold/

Reddit: Paul Oakenfold DJ sets:

- https://www.reddit.com/r/trance/comments/1ar228j/
has_anyone_seen_paul_oakenfold_live_recently_how/

CHAPTER 19

THE GATEKEEPERS: JAMES HAMILTON

There is a different kind of Gatekeeper to join the DJs mentioned elsewhere in this tome.

Although having enjoyed a prolific DJing career himself, James Hamilton was always better known as a music journalist, faithfully documenting the evolution of black dance music from its more Soul-influenced roots, through the disco era of the 70s, and culminating in its evolution into the early stages of House.

Gatekeepers who document music are required just as much as those who play it, and it would appear to have been Hamilton's natural talent for descriptive writing and exhaustive completism — along with a truly remarkable work ethic — which marked him out for a role of this nature.

To an outsider, Hamilton was a most unlikely candidate for the line of work he would move into. Born on Christmas Day of 1942 into an aristocratic family with its ancestral links in Nottinghamshire, his plummy accent betrayed his public school education, and his stocky, imposing frame and height ensured his presence would be immediately noticed upon entering a room. As journalist Alan Jones wrote in his *'Music Week'* tribute piece *'Farewell Doctor Soul'* in 1996:

> *"I found his physical presence even more impressive and overwhelming than his telephone manner. James was 6'8" tall but no beanpole. He immediately made any room he entered seem a great deal smaller than it had before."*

With "eccentric" being a word which would have adequately described his mannerisms, he might have looked more at home as a stockbroker, lawyer, doctor, lecturer... or anything *but* the legendary black music tastemaker that he became. Selina Webb, Deputy Editor of *'Music Week'* magazine, which featured Hamilton's column in his latter years, remarked of him:

> "*RM's most enduring contributor was a formidable character, deep of voice, enormous in stature, and quite frankly, headmaster-ish in manner. I think it is true to say that everyone who worked at 'Music Week' and 'RM' was just a little bit scared of this big man with his fascination for BPMs and a style of reviewing records previously unknown to journalism'."*

According to friends and associates, he could be difficult, aloof and grumpy, yet balanced this out with a sardonic sense of humour and a warm geniality towards those he liked. On the JH tribute page on Facebook, former collaborator Mike Nicholls recalled:

> *"James used to bring his portable typewriter into the 'Record Mirror' office every Monday and bash out his column — complete with BPMs which he apparently invented — with one chunky finger on each hand. During this time he would be unfailingly rude about whatever was playing on the office stereo, ("turn off that catererwalling bitch!")"*

If we are to chalk all of Hamilton's achievements simply up to "serendipity," then he would appear to have been an extremely lucky young man. In 1963, barely out of his teens, and following a private education in France, we find the first of many eyebrow-raising connections when his apparently authentic enthusiasm for black dance music expressed itself through his becoming one of Britain's very earliest disc-jockeys. (The first is generally accepted to have been **Jimmy Savile** when, still based in his native West Yorkshire in the late 1940s, he hit upon the then-revolutionary idea of playing gramophone records in the dancehalls in which he worked, as an alternative to the entertainment coming solely from live bands.)

For his part, Hamilton struck "lucky" — if that's the right word — by becoming the resident DJ at Esmeralda's Barn in West Kensington, the discotheque owned by the notorious Kray Twins as they were consolidating their hold over London's criminal underworld.

As British researcher Matt Sergiou, proprietor of the *'Occult Beatles'* and *'Conspiro Media'* sites observes of this unlikely scenario:

> "The twins actually bought Esmerelda's from so-called "slum landlord" Peter Rachman, who was embroiled in the Profumo affair. He was friends with Stephen Ward, had slept with Christine Keeler and Mandy Rice-Davies, and his henchman was Michael de Freitas, later to be called Michael X, a friend of **John Lennon**'s and a key mover and shaker of the London Underground scene, and who was hung for murder in Trinidad in 1975.
>
> "I mention all this partly because one of the main partners in Seltaeb, Nicky Byrne, used to be manager of a nightclub owned by none other than Peter Rachman, and that was frequented by the Krays and Keeler and Rice-Davies. Small world, eh?"

By the following year, Hamilton had relocated to New York City. Where many a wide-eyed youth from Britain had arrived in the Big Apple before him seeking fame, fortune and adventure — and many since — young James appeared to have a very clear agenda, wasting little time in establishing himself as a plugger/ promoter for artists such as **James Brown**, befriending **Sam Cooke** (who would die in suspicious circumstances at the end of that year,) and as a talent scout for the music side of the aforementioned Seltaeb, the American company charged with pushing Beatles merchandise for the stateside market, (its name being 'Beatles' spelled backwards.)

He had brought his budding DJing experience to bear also, introducing New York clubbers to the European discotheque concept at a time when, he says, nightlife venues were still playing the likes of **Frank Sinatra** and **Andy Williams**. The young James had certainly landed on his exceedingly large feet.

Recalling this period himself in an edition of '*Record Mirror*' magazine, dated 18-31 May 1982, Hamilton wrote:

> "I was able to hold my own in, on reflection, a horribly precocious way with all the Soul stars, DJs and music business people I encountered.
>
> "In fact a party trick of Seltaeb's president was to trot me out as soon as we encountered anyone in the record business, snap his fingers, and

then let me deliver a short accurate spiel all about whoever it was we were facing. I cringe at the memory!

"*I also wish I had the same passionate interest now as I did then. It was reported back to me that I was evidently the talk of a black DJ convention in Miami that summer, ('Hey, who is this white English kid who spends all his time in Harlem and knows more about Soul than we do?'!).*

"*During this halcyon era I socialised with the likes of Sam Cooke, James Brown, the* **Miracles***,* **James Baldwin** *and so many more, caught all the shows at the Apollo in Harlem, and generally hung out around the black life. At the weekends I was DJing out on Long Island at a club called Mitty's General Store in Water Mill, near Southampton, introducing black American dance music to upper-crust white Americans.*"

Though he wrote with perhaps understandable pride of his achievements at this time, Hamilton neglected to expand on just *how* he had been able to build such key connections as a foreigner in an exceedingly competitive, cut-throat and volatile industry. Indeed, he became the first English writer to bag an interview with **Diana Ross**, his article securing his long-running relationship with '*Record Mirror*' back in London. In the same period he happened across a song by **Bessie Banks**, '*Go Now*', which he sent to the management of the **Moody Blues**, resulting in one of that group's earliest and most successful hit singles.

Upon returning to London, James maintained his hobnobbing expertise, landing work at a South West London venue run by Moody Blues co-manager Tony Secunda. One of the resident groups here was **The Cheynes** featuring a pre-Fleetwood Mac **Mick Fleetwood** and **Pete Bardens**.

Hamilton then admits to spending the rest of 1965 running a publishing company for Mike Jeffery, well-known at the time for being the manager of the Newcastle-based group the **Animals**, before going on to manage **Jimi Hendrix**, and according to many, arranging Hendrix's death.

As I wrote on this matter in '*Musical Truth Volume 2*':

"It's widely acknowledged among alternative researchers that Hendrix's death occurred at the hands of his manager, Michael Jeffery, who hired a gang to break into Hendrix's Notting Hill hotel room and murder him.

"Jeffery was born in London in 1932, and after a brief bout of military service, embarked on a career as an 'intelligence' agent. According to Hendrix biographers Harry Shapiro and Caesar Glebbeek, Jeffery often boasted of "undercover work against the Russians, of murder, mayhem and torture in foreign cities."

"Jeffery was also acknowledged to have ties with organised crime networks. Quite how these credentials qualified him as a rock musician's manager over all other contenders, therefore, remains unclear. It seems Jeffery was deliberately sent into Hendrix's inner circle by parties unknown. Jeffery reportedly exercised a manipulative hold over Hendrix, and, having come to realise his true nature, the musician became desperate to escape his binding contract with him.

"In May 1969, Jeffery reportedly planted heroin on Hendrix, leading to his subsequent arrest in Toronto, as an intimidating reminder of the control he could exert. Through his Mob connections, Jeffery is said to have embezzled and laundered large amounts of Hendrix's income."

With Jeffery having been an asset of British "military intelligence" (an oxymoron,) then, it's a fairly safe bet that close tabs would have been kept on anyone who he came into contact with — particularly on a business basis — so that only those of "approved" status would have been allowed near him. Hamilton, through whatever means, clearly passed the test.

Hamilton continued to reminisce on his connections of the 1960s in that 1982 '*Record Mirror*' article, as follows:

"**Jimmy James & The Vagabonds** and their late manager Peter Meaden, (fresh from letting the High Numbers become **The Who**,) introduced me to The Scene in Ham Yard, Soho, and it was at The Scene that I then did most of the all-nighter sessions every Friday/

> *Saturday, through the summer of 1965 until the club's closure in early '66. Jerry Wexler himself used to send me all the Atlantic-distributed promos every week from the States, the club had such a reputation. This was after Guy Stevens had left, but it was still one of the leading Mod venues."*

(The "Mods Vs. Rockers" fad bore all the hallmarks of being yet one more weapon in the arsenal of the social engineers — a dialectic aimed at creating division between two more manufactured "tribes" in society.)

It was in 1975 that the aspect of James' work for which he is best-remembered began. In June of that year, he began his weekly Disco column for '*Record Mirror*,' initially reviewing the latest American and British releases, and going on to pioneer the idea of a weekly club chart based on feedback from working DJs as to which records were generating the best reactions in their respective clubs.

Hamilton's talent for a unique style of writing became apparent from the start, as he would go to great pains to accurately describe any record. Many DJs would buy their week's tunes without hearing them, based entirely on his descriptions. His review of 1985's '*High Fashion*' album by **The Faily**, by way of example, read:

> "... this (0-)114¼-114¾-113¾-113¼-112¾-112¼ bpm lightly flowing lurcher, which bridges straight into the raunchier 112½-111¼-113¼-112-114bpm 'Mutiny,' the here intro-less chunkily-rolling duetted 104½bpm 'The Screams Of Passion' being also on 12in, while their ever important jazzy sax comes into its own on the choppily half-stepping 108¼-107¾-107¼-105¾-109-110-0bpm 'Susannah's Pajamas,' and even more angrily free-form 114¾-114½-114-113-111-112-0-112bpm 'Yes' instrumentals."

DJ-wise, James was an early champion of the New York City style of mixing — blending records together in long seamless sequences, rather than interjecting with microphone banter as was the British way. This technique became a cornerstone of the dance/ club culture which would eventually follow on from the waning disco genre.

Another string to his bow was his association with London's Capital Radio. As well as occasionally guesting on **Roger Scott**'s daytime show, from the late '70s to the early '90s, James put together the non-stop mix which was aired each New Year's Eve, (latterly alongside **Les Adams**, who produced a series of hit records under the pseudonym **LA. Mix**.)

For these, Hamilton drew on his long experience of playing multiple styles of music, synching together records with similar tempos, but wildly differing in style — so **Louis Prima** or **Elvis Presley** might suddenly get chopped into an offering by **Chic** or **Luther Vandross**. (A further pseudonym of his around this time was "The Mighty Chopper.")

The technique for which Hamilton has been most credited as a British pioneer, however, was his painstaking calculations of the BPMs — beats per minute — of all new records to cross his path. Such was his attention to detail that he would dutifully detect and report the slightest shift in tempo — perhaps from 118.5 to 118.3 and back to 118.5.

This unique aspect of writing ensured that his column became essential reading for DJs, music industry types, and fans of the music alike. (It certainly had a big influence on me when I was introduced to his work by a schoolfriend in the mid-'80s, and his BPMs helped me develop my own style of sequencing early DJ sets.)

James was a walking encyclopedia of black music, and he would frequently pepper his columns with examples of this knowledge. Commenting on the emerging hip-hop electro sound which was beginning to eclipse more soulful output — much to the chagrin of black music purists — he began a piece dated 3rd September 1983 as follows:

> *"Seems the moment to put recent developments into their historical perspective. Black American music began outside when Southern slaves relieved the tedium of picking cotton with rhythmic call-and-answer "field hollers" derived from dimly-remembered tribal chants, vocal music being the cheapest to make — and maximum effect/ minimum outlay still holds good today.*

> *"Christian church music, military bands, the patronising "plantation songs" of touring nigger minstrel shows, and the attention-grabbing antics of street corner medicine sellers, (whose increasingly eccentric dance steps were the basis of most we know now,) all combined in the late 19th century to produce the different strains of a new and specifically American black tradition."*

The article went on to trace the evolution of black music through the Delta Blues/ Jazz/ Big Band/ R&B/ Motown, Northern Soul, Funk and Disco eras, to where it had arrived at that particular point. It's difficult to accept that this level of knowledge had been accumulated merely as part of a job, or an allotted role. Far more likely is that these were the writings of a man genuinely passionate about the music and culture in which he had immersed himself.

On the other hand, by the 1980s, Hamilton's was such a strong influence on a clearly-defined segment of the music scene, that it becomes equally implausible that he had been *allowed* to gain this level of influence purely under his own steam — his obvious talents notwithstanding.

Such was the trust and faith that so many had in his writings that, by the mid-1980s when the first strains of House music coming out of Chicago, New York and Detroit had begun to emerge, DJs who had up to that point been Soul and Funk fans, allowed themselves to be led, trustingly, towards these new genres. Slightly later, when the Balearic Beat/ Acid House scene started to creep into British club culture, James enthusiastically endorsed this movement also.

Not all black music purists were quite as keen, however, many snubbing the House sound, dismissing it as a "fad" and clearly not realising the impact that this new culture was poised to have upon millions as it got exported around the world.

One young South East "Soul Mafia" DJ who embraced the new style with open arms, however, was **Pete Tong**, who had always enjoyed favourable press from Hamilton — as had many of the other names who moved away from more soulful styles to become early pioneers of the House style, among them **Danny Rampling**, **Paul Oakenfold**, **Carl Cox**, **Jay Strongman**, **Paul 'Trouble' Anderson** and **Graham Gold**. (The latter had been a personal friend of James, the pair sharing a long-running residency at Gullivers nightclub in Mayfair alongside a third DJ, **Graham 'Fatman' Canter**.)

It's difficult to imagine any of the above-named DJs becoming the prominent trailblazers they did — thus paving the way for the MDMA/ ecstasy-fuelled 90s club culture — without having attained enthusiastic promotion from Hamilton along the way. In a pre-internet era, radio and magazines were the only methods of building hype and fuelling trends.

It's been my observation that many Gatekeepers serve long periods as "sleepers," embedding themselves, *seemingly* organically into their respective scenes, by *appearing* to climb the ladder gradually through hard work and good luck alone. It can take many years for their true roles to become apparent.

I can only speculate, of course, but is it possible that Hamilton had been marked out early on as an asset by social engineers, with a far-reaching and long-term plan in mind? In this regard he shares characteristics with DJs **Tim Westwood** and **David Rodigan**, and Island label owner **Chris Blackwell**. All came from wealthy families and received public school education, only to eschew the kinds of careers that would be the more likely results of their upbringings to instead become flag-wavers for aspects of black music and associated culture.

Why do such prominent roles so rarely get taken up by black people who *actually come* from these cultures, rather than by white upper-class public schoolboys? It's an awkward question, but one which needs asking, and so rarely is.

Through two chapters in *'Musical Truth Volume 2'* I shared my grudging suspicions that the UK Acid House/ Rave scene, which had evolved out of the black music scene that had come before it, to a large extent constituted yet another culture-shaping psy-op, leading the way as it did for the clubbing culture of the 1990s and beyond, which has swept up untold millions of young people through the decades, re-shaping their attitudes, value systems and personal behaviours.

Nothing of this world-changing magnitude is *ever* allowed to evolve all by itself. And any such fad, trend, movement or scene has to have its genesis somewhere, and its trusted Pied Pipers to help them along their way.

There was one other aspect of James Hamilton's eccentric personality which marked him out as an original one-off. He was an affirmed foodie, and would often include mentions of newly-discovered gastronomic favourites in his columns.

As Pete Tong observed in tribute to James:

> *"As well as his expertise in music, James was a real foodie. I remember when we used to do the weekender circuit, he'd drag us all down these winding country lanes to some incredible restaurant that he'd know in the area. You'd get there, him bumping his head going into the room because he was so large, and the owners would always know him and the food would always be incredibly good. This would happen all over the country."*

Tragically, it would appear that his lifelong passion for food may have contributed to his early demise. James Hamilton passed away on 17th June 1996, aged 53, from cancer of the colon. His *'Record Mirror'* column having ended in 1991 when that publication folded, his more recent writings had been for the industry paper *'Music Week.'*

In one of his final contributions he warned his readers that, should they ever notice blood in their stools, they should get themselves checked out immediately, as he wished he had done before it had become too late. Only the previous year, **Bruce Springsteen** had personally requested that James be the DJ for his end-of-tour party in Norway.

Presumably, the plan would have been for James' career to have continued for many more years. Only a short while before his passing he had married for the first time. Prior to this he would have made for a most unsuitable husband.

For years he had lived in a small, one-bedroom flat in Harlesden surrounded by around a quarter of a million records. (James himself had written of meeting DJ Tim Westwood at his own Fulham home in the '80s, and had noted that he too lived in a small flat, ex-council, surrounded by records, and slept on a tubular frame suspended several feet from the floor. If these figures really are appointed Gatekeepers, they certainly go all-out in embodying the kind of lifestyle one might expect to see had they really achieved their climb to fame organically.)

Anecdotes persist of James not sleeping for days at a time in order to complete the huge number of record reviews to which he was committed. He had had a 12-inch wide slot specially carved into his front door so that, on the occasions that he did sleep, the postman could deliver his latest records securely without waking him.

His eventual marriage appeared to constitute him going back to his aristocratic roots, perhaps through a personal acceptance that his life was drawing to a close. He died in Blyth, North Nottinghamshire, close to his ancestral family home.

He left no children, but an estimated quarter of a million records.

Resources:

The complete archive of James Hamilton's columns and articles for *'Record Mirror'* magazine:

- https://jameshamiltonsdiscopage.com/

Record Mirror: James Hamilton letter to Blues & Soul magazine regarding his credentials:

- https://jameshamiltonsdiscopage.com/1982/05/18/autobiographical-letter-written-by-james-hamilton-to-blues-soul-magazine-356-may-18-31-1982/

Record Mirror: James Hamilton's reflections on black music evolution:

- https://jameshamiltonsdiscopage.com/1983/09/03/september-3-1983-now-seems-the-moment-to-put-recent-developments-into-their-historical-perspective/

DJ Magazine: Greg Wilson's Discotheque Archives:

- https://djmag.com/features/greg-wilsons-discotheque-archives-6
- https://en.wikipedia.org/wiki/James_Hamilton_(DJ_and_journalist)#cite_note-WRHObit-4

James Hamilton tribute page on Facebook:

- https://www.facebook.com/groups/jameshamilton

Matt Sergiou's Conspiro Media blog site:

- https://conspiromedia.wordpress.com/

AFTERWORD

I fully accept that many parts of what has preceded here will not have made for the happiest of reads, (despite my attempts to lessen the impact slightly with the odd injection of appropriate black humour!) No-one enjoys hearing that cultural heroes whom they have held in great regard were never who they appeared to be, implying as this does, that they have been duped.

We've all been there, and I'm no different. I've had countless heroes whom I've had to let go — some even from within the so-called "truth" movement. As I often remind the attendees of my public talks, however: There's no shame in admitting we were bamboozled. All of us are, from the earliest age. The dignity comes from acknowledging that it happened, and, now that we know the methods and tactics that were used, resolving to *never* be fooled in the same way again.

Maxims don't come about by accident, and there will be a reason for the well-worn favourite:

"*Fool me once, shame on you. Fool me twice, shame on <u>me</u>!*"

As I also remind my audiences, I, and the other researchers who expose all this stuff, *did not make things this way!* I dearly wish they *weren't* this way, and I would be happy to have never had to have written these books and put out the thousands of hours of broadcasts that I have on these subjects.

I *get* that these revelations make people mad, but that anger should not be directed towards those delivering the message, but at those who *created* these states-of-affair in the first place, *causing* us to *have* to deliver the message!

As will be clear, you have to go back a *long* way to get to the root of it all, as all-pervasive as this agenda has become. It can seem overwhelming, even impossible to undo the monumental damage that has been done by the real controllers of Organised Society. As many have surmised, the level of evil that would have been necessary to have *allowed* this destructive sickness to have thrived for so long, has to originate from somewhere beyond human minds. This is subject matter for another book, and I do intend to put one out giving my thoughts on these matters in due course.

In the meantime… just what are we to *do* with the deeply unsettling knowledge which many of us will now have gained?

Well, the first steps towards any of it *ever* coming to an end *has* to lie in the secrets and lies being exposed as far and wide as possible, and the spotlight of scrutiny being shone mercilessly into the darkness.

Evil agendas can never stop if they are not known about. All of us who consider our full humanity intact, therefore, (so psychopaths, sociopaths and narcissists excluded!) carry a personal responsibility to do all we can in this regard.

Not everyone is cut out to be an author, broadcaster, public speaker or film-maker, of course. I fully accept that. But *all* of us can do *something*. Personally, though I'm comfortable putting information out to large audiences, I'm poor at engaging in individual one-to-one conversations, (and it's been decades since I've had access to any workplace water-cooler!)

Others tell me that they've made great inroads in this regard, through conversations with family members, friends or colleagues. Seeds sown in this way can have a huge impact — particularly if every person who has had their mind opened were to tell just one other — then that person just one other, and so on. The exponential potential here is colossal.

I also have it easier than many other "conspiracy" researchers through talking about entertainment and popular culture. Those trying to engage attention towards politics, corporate corruption, financial scams, etc, have a tougher job, in that these are subjects that many find dusty and boring. But *everyone* loves music of *some* kind, so spark someone's curiosity through a conversation of this nature and you've got 'em! Even if they initially go into denial, as so many do when a favourite band's authenticity is questioned, they won't be forgetting the conversation in a hurry!

However things pan out — even if this realm *is* so far gone that it's *beyond* repair — one day we will all be exiting it, and I feel we will be in a far better position to encounter whatever lies beyond if we can say, hand-on-heart, that we did all we reasonably could to oppose evil, darkness and slavery, rather than go along with it all for an easy ride.

That, I hope, will be the lasting legacy of the words in these books.

Index

801 26

10CC 42, 127

A

Aaliyah 46, 200, 223

Aaron Carter 215

ABBA 199, 227

Above & Beyond 261

AC/DC 236

Adam & The Ants 123, 131, 183

Adam Ant 123, 221

Adele 168

Aerosmith 177

Afrika Bambaataa 237, 242, 274

Afrojack 274, 322

Alan Lancaster 220

Alan Merrill 220

Alanis Morissette 116, 130

Aldous Huxley 164, 240

Aleister Crowley 7, 11, 14, 20, 58–59, 126, 133, 148, 151, 169

Alex Napier 221

Alex P 290

Alice Cooper 123, 200, 204

Altiyan Childs 144, 157

Amanda Lear 138

Amy Winehouse 116, 182, 215, 222

Andrew Weatherall 221

Andy Gray 323

Andy Williams 329

Annabella Lwin 183

Annie Lennox 162, 167, 171, 233

Annie Nightingale 274, 276

Anton LaVey 134, 136

Anyma 121, 132

Arrows 220

Art of Noise 120

Astro 220

Avicii 219

B

Backstreet Boys 135, 215

Bad Company 220

Bananarama 272

Barbara Martin 221

Bar-Kays 223

Barry Manilow 148

Barry Ryan 220

341

Barry White 223

Basement Boys 16

Bassnectar 324

Bay City Rollers 221

Beach Boy 149, 168

Beach Boys 22

Beastie Boys 319

Beatles vi, 4, 8, 10, 12, 19–20, 22, 36–38, 40, 42, 51–55, 57–69, 73–77, 85, 91, 118, 123, 168, 182, 211, 225, 234, 300, 317, 328–329

Beats International 288

Beautiful South 287

Bernie Rhodes 99, 173

Bessie Banks 330

Betty Wright 220

Beyonce 13

Bez 2–3, 18, 325

Big Bopper 224

Bill Berry 24, 47

Bill Drummond 99

Bill Gates 108, 164, 278

Bill Haley 35

Bill Withers 220

Bill Wyman 200

Billie Eillish 142

Billie Holiday 222

Billy Davis 223

Billy Idol 177

Billy Jones 223

Billy Shears 56, 59, 66, 68, 77, 118

Black Eyed Peas 278

Black Sabbath 177

Blondie 32, 47–48

Bluey 16, 19

Blur 41, 168–169, 234, 237

Bob Dylan 149, 181

Bob Geldof 161, 196, 233

Bob Marley 9, 66, 319

Bobbi Kristina 219

Bobby Womack 206, 229, 319

Bonnie Pointer 220

Bono 161–162, 233, 276

Bow Wow Wow 183

Boyzone 137, 157

Brand Nubian 193

Brandon Block 290

Brian Eno 278–279, 283

Brian Harvey 138

Brian Howe 220

Brian Jones 9, 18, 207

Brian May 38, 198

Brian Travers 220

Britney Spears 7, 19, 115, 118, 130, 149, 320

Bruce Johnston 149

Bruce Springsteen 84, 161, 197, 336

Buddy Holly 224–225

Bunny Wailer 220

Burning Man 101–102, 111, 260–262, 266

Buzzcocks 2

Buzzy Meekins 223

C

Calvin Harris 322

Candace Owens 105

Captain and Tennille 149

Carl Cox viii, 102, 251, 255, 259, 261, 265–266, 272, 280, 282, 288, 297, 320, 322, 334

Caron Wheeler 150, 157–158

Cassie Gaines 223

Cassie Ventura 189

Cathy O'Brien 93, 113, 128, 211

Celine Dion 6

Chad Jackson 253

Chaka Khan 145, 157, 222

Charlie Daniels 220

Charlie Watts 160, 220

Chase 223, 297, 311

Chemical Brothers 314

Cher 168

Cheryl Cole 212

Chester Bennington 37, 66

Children In Need 196, 236

Chris "Merrick" Hughes 183

Chris Blackwell 335

Chris Cornell 37, 66

Chris de Burgh 7, 20

Chris Hill 270

Chris Stamp 42

Christopher Coe 264, 266

Christopher Cross 126

Church of Satan 12, 85, 134, 136

Clash 173, 182

Claudia Brucken 120

Cliff Richard 26, 66, 103, 111, 245, 251

Clive Davis 190, 222–223

Coolio 218–219, 227–228

Count Jean de Breteuil 206

Courtney Love 80

Craig Mack 193

Cranberries 299

Crass 99–100

Culture Club 182, 276

Cutmaster Swift 253

D

Damian Lazarus 261

Damon Dash 46

Danny Kirwan 29

Danny Rampling 253, 272–273, 277, 289, 308, 314

Dave Dave 210–211

Dave Grohl 145, 158, 231

Dave Pearce 271–272, 308

David Bowie 4, 11, 18, 66, 82, 127, 158, 167, 169, 200, 210, 276

David Cassidy 149

David Gilmour 28

David Grant 104

David Guetta 274, 322

David Rodigan 178, 262, 276, 292, 335

David Wilcock 179

Dead or Alive 125, 216

Deadmau5 275

Debbie Harry 32–33, 47–48

Deep Purple 269

Def Leppard 177

Denise Johnson 221

Dennis Thomas 221

Depeche Mode 42

Derek B 307

Derrick May 324

Destiny's Child 13

Diana Ross 179, 330

Diplo 102, 111, 261–262, 324

DJ Cash Money 253

DJ Cheese 253

DJ Jazzy Jeff & The Fresh Prince 318

DJ Karizma 16

DJ Spen 16

DJ Spoony 178

DMX 220

Doja Cat 146, 156

Dolly Parton 7, 19

Dolores O'Riordan 219, 299

Don McLean 224

Donald Trump 21, 179, 235, 242

Doors 8–9, 59, 123, 206, 208, 317

Dr. Richard Asher 71, 73, 77

Drake 191–192, 200, 203–204, 274

Duane "Keffe D" Davis 190

Duncan Campbell 220

Duran Duran 38, 126–127, 276, 320

Dusty Hill 220

E

Eagles 147–148, 157

Ean Evans 223

East 84, 138, 166, 195, 270, 334

Ed Sheeran 181

Eddie Gordon 273

Eddie Van Halen 220

Edward Bernays 15, 34

Ellie Goulding 121, 132

Elton John 66, 177

Elvis Costello 143

Elvis Presley 12, 35, 66, 93, 110, 200, 210, 225, 252, 333

Eminem 6, 227

Eric Clapton 223

Erick Morillo 220, 324

Eugene Robinson 24

F

Fabio 253, 273, 308

Fabio & Grooverider 273, 308

Fairport Convention 28

Falco 219

Faustian Bargain 135, 146

Fearne Cotton 196

Fergie 308

Flavor Flav 8, 19

Fleetwood Mac 29, 59, 220, 238, 330

Florence and the Machine 146

Florence Welch 146, 156

Foo Fighters 145, 231

Foreigner 182, 330

Frank O'Keefe 223

Frank Sinatra 95, 329

Frank Zappa 8, 18, 143

Frankfurt School 36

Frankie Beverley 319

Frankie Goes To Hollywood 120

Frankie Knuckles 272

Freak Power 288

Freddie Mercury 38, 122

Freddie Salem 223

Frightened Rabbit 217, 228

Froggy 270–271

Fruit Tree Foundation 217

Fugees 22, 47

G

Gary Glitter 196, 199

Gary Puckett 199

Gene Vincent 22

Genesis 10, 152, 236, 253, 335

George "Funky" Brown 221

George Harrison iv, 87, 91

George Martin 74, 300

George Michael 37, 66, 226–227

George Orwell 164, 167

Gerry Marsden 220

Gilles Peterson 253

Giorgio Moroder 239

Girls Aloud 212, 220

Glen Frey 148

Glenn Medeiros 194, 203

Glenn Miller 223

Gloria Jones 232

Goldie 178, 276, 314

Gordon Mac 178

Graeme Edge 220

Graham 'Fatman' Canter 334

Graham Gold 270, 272, 334

Grateful Dead 33–34, 48, 61

Greg Edwards 271

Guy Gerber 324

Gwen Stefani 168

GZA 8

H

Happy Mondays 2, 18, 320

Harley Pasternak 108, 112

Harry Nilsson 42

Hazell O'Connor 124

Herb Pino 223

High Numbers 42, 331

Housemartins 286, 288

Hughie Thomasson 223

I

Ian Brown 245

Ian Carey 220

Ian Copeland 24

Ian Dury 195, 204

Ian Mitchell, Kool & The Gang 221

Ian Watkins 195, 204

Ice Cube 45, 50

Idris Elba 277

Iggy Pop 128

Incognito 16–17, 19

INXS 215

J

Jack Steven 210

Jadakiss 107, 111

Jaguar Wright 105

James Baldwin 330

James Brown 329–330

Jane Asher 71, 73–74, 311

Janet Jackson 6, 19

Janis Joplin 66, 205–206, 229

Jasmine Dotiwala 178

Jay Strongman 334

Jazzie B 178, 276, 306–307

Jeff Howell 223

Jeff Young 270, 272–273

Jeffery Epstein 191

Jennifer Hudson 212, 227

Jeremy Spencer 238

Jerry Dammers 172, 185

Jim Croce 223

Jim Morrison 8–9, 18, 65, 205–207, 209, 219, 229

Jimi Hendrix 10, 29, 42, 66, 89, 97, 110, 330

Jimmy Cauty 99

Jimmy James & The Vagabonds 331

Jimmy Page 148, 200, 204

Jimmy Savile 10, 37, 73, 87, 103, 124, 189, 196, 233, 286, 328

Joe Biden 107

Joe Elliott 177

Joe Smooth 272

John Bon Jovi 177

John Bonham 145

John Coleman 36, 60, 62

John Denver 223

John Entwistle 41

John Hinckley Jr 82

John Lawton 221

John Lennon 42, 52, 55, 61–63, 66, 76, 80–81, 84–87, 89–91, 237, 317, 329

John Lydon 162, 185, 237

John Peel 30, 49, 200, 204, 276

John Todd (Collins) 10

Johnny Marr 151

Johnny Nash 220

Jon Carter 291

Joy Division 2, 320

Jules Buckley 275

K

Kaiser Chiefs 162

Kanye West 23, 105, 107, 112

Kate Bush 102, 125, 144, 171, 245

Kaya Jones 117, 130–131

Keith Green 223

Keith Moon 40, 42

Keith Richards 29, 160–161, 208

Kendrick Lamar 192, 203

Kenny Rogers 220

Kevin Godley 42

Kinks 168

Kirsty MacColl 96

Kiss 178, 198, 254, 268, 273, 282, 307–308, 315

Kit Lambert 42–43

Klaus Schwab 278, 283

KLF 99

Kurt Cobain 66

Kylie Minogue 125

L

LA. Mix 333

Lady Gaga 6, 128, 132, 239

Laura Branigan 93, 119–120, 131

Lee Burridge 261

Lee Kerslake 221

Leftfield 314

Lenny Fontana 314, 317, 326

Leonard Cohen 88, 92, 102–103, 159

Les Adams 333

Les McKeown 221

Liam Gallagher 161, 233

Liam Payne 212–213, 226

Lil' Louis 272

Lil' Nas X 142

Lil' Wayne 107

Little Simz 166

LL Cool J 193

Lord Jamar 193

Lori Maddox 200

Lostprophets 195, 204

Lou Reed 168

Louis Tomlinson 233

Luther Vandross 223, 333

Lynyrd Skynyrd 223

M

M.I.A. 105, 307

Madonna 6–7, 107, 113, 118, 126, 139, 141, 147, 156, 180, 201–202, 204, 304, 315, 320, 322

Malcolm McLaren 99, 183

Maluma 107

'Mama' Cass Elliott 42

Mamas & The Papas 42, 83

Mamonas Assassinas 223

Mandy Smith 200

Manic Street Preachers 217

Marc Bolan 167, 232, 242

Marco Pirroni 184

Margaret Eliot 74

Mariah Carey 140, 155, 221

Marianne Faithfull 208

Marilyn Manson 128

Marilyn Monroe 7, 19, 32, 48, 123, 181, 222

Mark Chapman vi, 79–80, 91

Mark E. Smith 1

Mark Ronson 68, 116, 181

Martin Duffy 221

Mary J Blige 150

Mary Wilson 221

Massive Attack 280, 283

Masters at Work 16

Matt Sergiou 10, 17, 20, 22, 73, 249, 328, 337

Maurice Chevalier 198

Max Martin 149

Maze 319

Michael Hutchence 215

Michael Jackson 37, 66, 210, 215, 219, 227, 320

Michael Stipe 24

Mick Fleetwood 59, 330

Mick Jagger 29, 66, 88, 103, 160–161, 177, 200, 208, 268, 291, 297, 311

Mick Jones 182

Midge Ure 126

Mighty Dub Katz 288

Mighty Mouse 221, 228

Mike & The Mechanics 236

Mike Love 168, 187

Mike McCartney 4

Mike Mills 24, 47

Miles Copeland 2, 18

Miley Cyrus 7, 19

Millie Bobby Brown 200, 204

Millie Small 220

Moby 21–22, 47, 320

Monkees 67

Moody Blues 220, 330

Morrissey 175–177, 185, 189, 222, 228

Mory Kante 220

Mumford & Sons 181

N

Neil Diamond 197

Neil Peart 220

Neil Sedaka 199

Nelons 223

New Order 320

New World Order 148, 161, 235, 238, 240, 242, 323

Niall Horan 213

Nick Carter 215

Nick Cave 96, 128, 132

Nick Kamen 220

Nick Rhodes 38

Nicky Holloway 254, 277, 314

Nirvana 145

Norman Jay 178, 253, 276, 306–307

Notorious B.I.G. 189

NSYNC 135

NWA 45

O

Oasis 233–234, 293

ODB 8

Offspring 3, 177

Ole Dammegard 87, 95, 110

Olivia Newton-John 25

One Direction 212–213, 226, 233

Otis Redding 223

Oxbow 24

P

P!nk 134, 154, 168

Pamela Courson 206

Passion Fruit 223

Pastor Bob Joyce 110, 210

Paul 'Trouble' Anderson 334

Paul Heaton 286–287

Paul McCartney 54–55, 60, 63–69, 73, 76–78, 80, 82, 106, 118, 124, 177, 317, 323

Paul Morley 120

Paul Nicholas 40

Paul Van Dyk 233, 274

Paula Yates 196

Peaches Geldof 196, 204

Pearl Jam 292

Pete Best 4, 52

Pete Burns 216

Pete Tong viii, 178, 253, 256, 262, 268, 271, 273, 276, 279–280, 282–283, 288, 292, 306, 308, 321, 334–335

Pete Townshend 38–39, 49, 240, 243–244

Peter Asher 300, 311

Peter Gabriel 152, 161, 233, 320

Peter Green 29, 220

Pharrell Williams 23, 50

Phil Collins 10, 20

Phil Manzanera 26, 48

Phil Spector 220, 317

Phoebe Bridgers 177, 185

Pink Floyd 28, 163, 165, 179, 186

Pizzaman 288

Pogues 37

Police 2, 21, 24, 28, 30–31, 41, 45, 54, 74, 80–81, 83–85, 87, 91, 196, 240, 257, 274, 277, 307

Pras Michel 22, 47

Predictive programming vii, 230, 234

Primal Scream 55, 221

Prince 66, 97–98, 110, 123, 131, 167, 181, 219, 237, 242, 262, 266, 275, 303, 318

Propaganda 62, 119–120, 131, 160, 162, 164, 177, 277, 285

Public Image Ltd 185, 237

Pussycat Dolls 117, 130–131

Q

Q-Anon 179

Quarrymen 52, 57

Quavo 147, 156

Queen 6, 10, 38, 121–122, 131, 148, 172, 177–178, 185, 198, 224, 239

Quiet Sun 26

Quincy Jones 276

R

R Kelly 200

R. Kelly 274

R.E.M 24, 47

Rachel Caruso 97, 110

Ralph McTell 30

Rammstein 127, 131

Ray Manzarek 9, 19

Red Hot Chili Peppers 152

Renegades 4

REO Speedwagon 127

Richard D. Hall 218

Richard Norris 319

Richard Thompson 28

Richard Wright 29

Richey Edwards 217

Richie Valens 224

Ringo Starr 4, 52, 61, 66, 177

Rise Above Live 20, 293

Robbie Vincent 270

Robby Krieger 9

Robert Johnson 145

Robert Plant 148

Rod Stewart 66, 175, 185

Roger Daltrey 38, 41

Roger Taylor 10

Roger Waters 163, 165, 185–186

Roisin Murphy 165

Rolf Harris 196, 199, 264

Rolling Stones 11, 22, 38, 85, 103, 160, 175, 207–208, 220, 234, 292, 297, 311, 320

Ronald Bell 221

Ronnie Van Zant 223

Rory Storm & the Hurricanes 52

Roxy Music 26, 28, 48

Run-D.M.C 319

Rush 220, 315

RZA 8

S

S.C.U.M 196

Sadhguru 278–279, 282–283

Salt 'N' Pepa 268, 272, 318

Sam Cooke 329–330

Sam Fender 1, 18

Sam Smith 146, 156, 167, 186

Sara Cox 291

Sarah Harding 220

Satoshie Tomiee 272

Saxon 177

Scott Hutchison 217, 228

Screamin' Jay Hawkins 152

Sean 'P Diddy' Combs. 200, 222

Sean French 270

Sean Lennon 15, 182

Sean McCabe 16

Seb Fontaine 308

Seona Dancing 4, 19

Sex Pistols 2

Shane Lynch 137, 157

Shane MacGowan 37

Shara Nelson 280

Sheep Farm 5, 14, 17, 20, 28, 162, 220, 311

Silver Beatles 52

Simon Le Bon 38

Sinead O'Connor 221–222, 228

Skrillex 261

Smiths 151, 175, 222

Soul II Soul 150, 158, 178, 306

Spandau Ballet 276

Specials 173–174, 185, 195

Spencer Davis 220

Status Quo 220

Sterling Void 272

Steve Aoki 322

Steve Gaines 223

Steve Lamacq 178

Steve Osborne 320

Steve Strange 126–127, 182

Steve Vai 143, 157

Stevie Ray Vaughan 223

Stevie Wonder 7, 19

Stewart Copeland 24, 83

Sting 41, 161, 168, 233

Stryper 177

Stuart Sutcliffe 53

Supremes 221

Syd Barrett 28–29, 165

T

Tavistock 17, 33–36, 38, 42, 60, 62, 76, 165, 167, 185, 244, 257

Taylor Hawkins 158, 231

Taylor Stratton Smith 10

Taylor Swift 12, 136–137, 157–158

Tenacious D 15

Terry Farley 253

Terry Hall 195

The Animals 330

The Blackwood Brothers 223

The Cheynes 330

The Crystal Method 261

The Fall 1–2, 18, 215

The Family International 238, 243

The Freehold 10

The Grid 319

The Knack 198

The Miracles 330

The Prodigy 314

The Second Summer of Love 37, 249, 254, 272, 307, 315

The Sound of Freedom 158

Thomas Cohen 196

Thunderclap Newman 42–43

Till Lindemann 128

Tim Westwood 172, 262, 270, 273–274, 276, 292, 306–307, 335–336

Timezone 238, 242

Todd Rundgren vi, 79, 89, 91

Tom Holland 270

Tom Jones 66

Tony Colston-Hayter 254

Tony Wilson 99, 320

Toyah Willcox 41, 152, 183

Tracy Chapman 7, 19

Travis Scott 292

Trevor Fung 253, 314, 319

Trevor Horn 120

Trevor Moore 138, 154

Trevor Nelson 178, 276

Tupac Shakur 190

U

U2 100–101, 110, 276, 322

UB40 220

Ultravox 125–126, 131

Uncle Ron 135–136, 155

Union Gap 199

Urge Overkill 197

Uriah Heap 221

V

Vince Clarke 42

Visage 126, 182

W

Waylon Jennings 224

Wayne Fontana 220

Whitney Houston 145, 215, 219, 222

Who 38, 41–43, 49–50, 69, 240, 243–244, 292, 331

will.i.am 274, 278, 323

William Shepherd 66

Winger 197

Winston Marshall 181

Wrecking Crew 317

Wu-Tang Clan 8, 19

Y

Yoko Ono 42, 63, 80, 87

Z

Zachary King 134, 154

Zoe Ball 6, 291

ZZ Top 220

www.ingramcontent.com/pod-product-compliance
Lightning Source LLC
Chambersburg PA
CBHW040240130526
44590CB00049B/4017